Space, Time and the Categories

Categories

Lectures on Metaphysics
1949-50

by

John Anderson

Challis Professor of Philosophy
University of Sydney 1927-1958

Introduction by D. M. Armstrong

Emeritus Professor of Philosophy
University of Sydney

Edited by Creagh Cole
Senior Research Fellow
University of Sydney

SYDNEY UNIVERSITY PRESS

SYDNEY UNIVERSITY PRESS
Print on Demand Service
SETIS at the University of Sydney Library
University of Sydney
www.sup.usyd.edu.au

Digitised from manuscripts held in the University of Sydney Archives of lectures
delivered at the University 1948-50.

Sydney University Press
Fisher Library
University of Sydney
NSW Australia 2006

E-mail: info@sup.usyd.edu.au

ISBN 978-1-920898-62-5

Designed and Printed in Australia at the University Publishing Service
University of Sydney

Table of Contents

Foreword to the John Anderson Series

In 2006 a senior academic advisory committee was established at the University of Sydney to oversee the publication of a series of books which would present the intellectual achievement and development of John Anderson, Challis Professor of Philosophy 1927–1958. In 2006-08 the committee members are Emeritus Professor David Armstrong, Emeritus Professor Paul Crittenden, and Professor Stephen Gaukroger. The committee is convened by the John Anderson Senior Research Fellow undertaking research into and publication of the papers of Professor Anderson.

To some extent a proper appreciation of Anderson's work requires an experience of his lecture room. From the notes in the University Archives we may be able to provide something of this experience. Many of these lecture notes have been transcribed and are available at the John Anderson Archive along with Anderson's previously published writings, allowing researchers and students to access the chief resources and to follow the course of his thinking over many years.

The published series to be selected from this material aims to provide scholarly editions of the most complete and significan lectures now available and will include works devoted to Anderson's metaphysics, logic, ethics, politics and aesthetics. The series will help younger students and scholars to understand why John Anderson was the most important, the most controversial and the most influentia philosopher ever to have worked in Australia.

Ongoing research into Professor Anderson's unpublished writings and the series of books drawn from this research has only been possible due to the generous bequest to the University of Sydney by his son, Alexander (Sandy) John Anderson (1923-1995).

Dr Creagh Cole
John Anderson Senior Research Fellow
University of Sydney 2007

Preface and Note on the Text

With the publication of the two-volume work *Space, Time and Deity* in 1920, Samuel Alexander (1859–1938) became for a time one of the most celebrated philosophers in Britain. His working life was spent almost entirely at the University of Manchester. He was, however, born in George Street, Sydney and educated in Melbourne before winning a scholarship as a young man to Balliol College, Oxford. Although he was never to return to Australia the story of his influenc on Australian philosophy was to take a surprising turn.

In the Gifford lectures of 1917–18 in Glasgow he presented the main themes of *Space, Time and Deity* for the firs time. One student who attended those lectures was the young Scottish philosopher, John Anderson, who was then completing his Masters thesis on the philosophy of William James (1917) at the University of Glasgow, and who was to have a powerful influenc on the direction of Australian philosophy following his appointment to the University of Sydney in 1927.

Anderson was to revisit Alexander's work on Space-Time and the Categories in a series of lectures delivered in the 1940s. These lectures renewed interest in Alexander at Sydney and became the means by which Anderson would elaborate his own systematic realism. His students were in no doubt concerning Alexander's importance and direct influenc on Anderson:

> Alexander profoundly stirred Anderson's philosophical imagination; those who heard his lectures on Alexander felt that they were being led into the very heart of Anderson's philosophy.[1]

He lectured directly on Alexander in 1941, 1944, 1947 and 1949. Among the students taking notes of these lectures in the fina series 1949–50 was the young David Armstrong who in the 1960s would take up Anderson's position of Challis Professor of Philosophy at the University of Sydney. Professor Armstrong's major writings since the 1970s on universals and scientifi realism, states of affairs and truthmakers have in turn inspired a new generation of philosophers in the questions of metaphysics.

Introduced by Professor Armstrong, this work brings together three of the major figure in the history of Australian philosophy. It

---

[1] John Passmore, "John Anderson and Twentieth Century Philosophy", introduction to *Studies in Empirical Philosophy* Sydney: Angus and Robertson 1962, pp. xii-xiii.

presents a unique record of personal influenc and inspiration over three generations and is a vitally important text in the history of the development of realist philosophy in Australian universities.

Acknowledgements

Many thanks to Eric Dowling for the high quality of his typescript lecture notes. Thanks are due most particularly to David Armstrong, not only for his own handwritten notes of the lectures and his personal recollections of Anderson, but also for his great enthusiasm for the project and his guiding hand and support throughout the editorial process. Thanks also to the University Archives for permission to reproduce primary materials from the Personal Papers of John Anderson.

Note on the Text

There are at least two versions of student notes of the 1949-50 Alexander lectures. The text followed here represents the notes by R. E. Dowling and David Armstrong. These notes consist of 176 pages of typescript (June to October 1949) by Dowling, and 50 pages of close handwritten notes by Armstrong (April to August 1950).

The second set of student notes, recently discovered in the University Archives, are those by Sandy Anderson. They are missing lectures 37, 41 and 42. Although the Dowling-Armstrong notes are a clearer presentation of the lectures, Sandy Alexander's notes contain extensive annotations by John Anderson added at a later date later (perhaps later than 1954). These additional notes have been included in Appendix 1 following the main lectures.

Full transcriptions of all versions of the lecture notes are available at the John Anderson Archive.[2]

There are 45 lectures in this lecture set and the original division of the lectures into six sections has been followed in the presentation:

Introductory Lectures (1-5)
Interrelations of Space and Time (6-12)
Transition to the Categories (13-16)
Categories I (Logical/Qualitative) (16-28)
Categories II (Mathematical/Quantitative) (28-32)
Categories III (Physical) (33-45)

[2] The John Anderson Archive at http://setis.library.usyd.edu.au/anderson/index.html

As explained in Professor Armstrong's Introduction the text includes prefatory remarks by Anderson which were not part of the dictated lectures. Although these appear in the body of the text, they have been indented from the left to mark them off from the formally dictated lectures. Professor Armstrong reveals that these remarks were not part of the dictated lectures and so were more difficul to transcribe. This is very clear in Lecture 1 where Anderson's preliminary remarks seem quite extensive. We have chosen to use Anderson's own more discursive notes in place of the student notes in this case (pp. 1-3 below).

Other Lecture Series on Alexander

The available lecture series on Alexander's *Space, Time and Deity*, include those of 1941, 1944, 1947 and 1949. The lectures of 1941 and 1947 are very short. The 1941 lectures (8 lectures) are available at the John Anderson Archive, and were introduced by the preceding course on Hegel. The 1947 lectures are a typescript copy of 7 lectures in the University Archives, Anderson Papers Box 32 Item 35 (2nd July 1947 to 13th August 1947). The major lecture series then are from 1944 and 1949. The 1944 course consists of 46 lectures and is similar in structure to the later 1949 course. The 1944 lecture notes are in Anderson's handwriting in the Personal Archives of John Anderson, Series 3, Item 25, University of Sydney Archives. It was transcribed at the University of Sydney Library in 1999, edited by George Molnar and Mark Weblin, and published by Sydney University Press in 2004 under the title *Space-Time and the Proposition*.

Appendices

Appendix 1 presents additional notes written by John Anderson and inserted into Sandy Anderson's notes of the lectures.

Appendix 2 presents two letters from the University Archives which demonstrate Anderson's relationship to Alexander at the time of the Gifford Lectures.

Appendix 3 is the abstract for Samuel Alexander's Gifford Lectures of 1917 to 1918, which were to be the basis for the book *Space, Time and Deity* of 1920.

Appendix 4 presents Anderson's notes for the Lectures on Logic for 1948, a series referred to repeatedly in the 1949-50 lectures on Alexander. The University Archives holds two versions of this logic series, one in Anderson's handwriting (P.A.J.A., Series 43, Box 102), the other consisting of student notes by Sandy Anderson and with annotations by Anderson himself (P.A.J.A., Series 5, Box 32). All of those annotations were incorporated into Anderson's handwritten notes which also include later addenda and references to articles published later than 1948. His handwritten notes then appear to be Anderson's fina version of the lectures. This is the version included here as Appendix 4.

Abbreviations

Several abbreviations have been used in the footnotes for regular citations.

A.J.P.P. — *Australasian Journal of Psychology and Philosophy* (later *Australasian Journal of Philosophy*).

[DMA] — D. M. Armstrong (responsibility statement for footnotes in the Lectures on Alexander 1949-50.

[JA] — John Anderson (responsibility statement for footnotes in the Logic Lectures of 1948.

J.A.A. — The John Anderson Archive at the University of Sydney at http://setis.library.usyd.edu.au/anderson/

P.A.J.A. — Personal Archives of John Anderson, University of Sydney Archives

STD — Samuel Alexander, *Space, Time and Deity; being the Gifford Lectures 1916-1918*. London: Macmillan, 1920. Two volumes.

Studies — John Anderson, *Studies in Empirical Philosophy*, Sydney: Angus and Robertson, 1962.

Introduction

by D. M. Armstrong

These lectures contain the most developed statement that we have of John Anderson's account of the general nature of being, what we may call his ontology or metaphysics.[1] They were given to Sydney University Honours philosophy students in their 3rd and 4th years, the first part during 1949, the second part in 1950. I am happy to declare an interest by saying that I attended those lectures, and that they inspired me with a passionate interest in the great questions of metaphysics.

The lectures were, as was usual with Anderson, presented as a commentary on another author, in this case that of Samuel Alexander's two-volume work *Space Time and Deity* (1920). This book was based on lectures given at Glasgow University 1916 to 1918, and Anderson, as a young student philosopher, attended these lectures. The historian Brian Kennedy says in his biography of Anderson[2]:

> During 1918 Professor Samuel Alexander, the Australian-born Jewish philosopher from Manchester, lived at the university for several months while he delivered the Gifford lectures. He frequently attended meetings of the [Philosophical] society and canvassed the realist arguments of 'Space, Time and Deity' in informal meetings with students and staff. The young man [Anderson] liked the affable and avuncular Alexander and had a number of discussions with him... (p.47).[3]

I have heard Anderson say that at that time he was looking for some figure on which to base his metaphysics on. He had considered but discarded Bertrand Russell. Alexander's empiricist scheme, a space-time world subject to categories, features that anything spatio-temporal exhibits, was just the sort of thing he was looking for.

This is not to say that Anderson was not very critical of the way that Alexander spelt out his argument. Some things, such as Alexander's 'emergent' Deity, he rejected without even discussing the view in these lectures. But as the reader will see, Alexander is continually criticized for all sorts of failure, in particular fallings away from 'realism' and 'empiricism' as well as numerous matters of detail. It has to be said, though, that Anderson was a fierce critic of any philosopher whom he discussed. There was just one who he seemed to admire, this was the

---

[1] Earlier lectures were given in 1944. These have been published as *Space-Time and the Proposition: The 1944 Lectures on Samuel Alexander's Space, Time and Deity*, by John Anderson. Edited and with an introduction by Mark Weblin. Sydney University Press, Sydney: 2004.

[2] *A Passion to Oppose: John Anderson, Philosopher*, Melbourne University Press, Melbourne: 1995.

[3] See also the extract from an interesting letter from Anderson to his future wife, Janet Baillie, in February 22nd 1917, in Appendix 2 to this volume.

Presocratic philosopher Heraclitus. I think he saw Heraclitus as giving a dark, poetic adumbration of his own position. Heraclitus said, in one wonderful fragment that we have:

> This world, which is the same for all, no one of gods or men has made; but it was ever, is now, and ever shall be an ever-living Fire, with measures of it kindling and measures going out.[4] (R.P. 355.)[5]

This could serve as a brief but pregnant summing up of Anderson's own world-view, reading 'fire' as metaphor for the doctrine Anderson upheld that everything was always 'in flux' (another phrase from Heraclitus); and the 'measures' as what Anderson called 'the ways of working' of things, what others might call 'the laws of nature'.

Following on an old tradition, which he presumably encountered in the Scottish universities, Anderson's lectures were dictated, using either his own notes for the lecture, or perhaps sometimes texts of earlier dictations. No guidance was given on punctuation, paragraphing, etc. except the tone in his own voice, something that should be borne in mind in the transcriptions of lectures that follow. The 1949 lectures are based on a typescript made by Dr. R. E. Dowling (Eric Dowling) who was another member of the class, and the 1950 lectures are based on my own hand-written notes, which were re-written shortly after each lecture. Discussion was not much encouraged, it was best if one had a query or difficult to approach him at the end of the lecture, though even that was not much done. What he wanted you to do was to master the material he had presented.

He did present some material informally at ordinary talking speed, often at the beginning of a lecture, perhaps some mention of the lesson of the previous lecture, but sometimes some illuminating extras. Some of us tried to take notes of this material also, but could do little better than a telegraphic rendering of what was said. In the present text of the lectures, these notes are marked by being indented on the left with the print size reduced.

We may now consider some of Anderson's philosophical pre-suppositions in these lectures, in particular ones that his students understood well enough, but which are likely to not be understood by present readers. But let us begin with Alexander's plan of attack.

---

[4] John Burnet, *Early Greek Philosophy*, 4th ed. 1930, p.134, Fragment 20. Among historians of philosophy, Anderson picked out only one of them to admire: the Scotsman John Burnet.
[5] R. P. is: *Historia Philosophiae Graecae*, H. Ritter et L. Preller Editio octava, quam curavit Eduardus Wellmann. Gotha, 1898.

What drew Anderson to Alexander's work in the firs place? He was greatly impressed by Alexander's central idea, which we may now consider. Alexander started from Kant. In Kant's metaphysics, space and time are argued to be mere forms of intuition under which we must experience the world, and categories such as causality and substance are mere forms of understanding under which we must understand the world. Things-in-themselves, what is objectively there, are not given to us, Kant argued, and so we could know nothing about them. With these doctrines Kant had moved significantl towards a philosophical Idealism. But Alexander suggested, and Anderson enthusiastically seconded the idea, that a Realist revolt be staged against Kantian Idealism. Space and Time are not forms of intuition, but are forms of being. Reality, that is, everything, is spatio-temporal. The categories are not forms of understanding but are categories of being, categories under which all being, which is spatio-temporal being, must fall.[6] Alexander's book, and Anderson's lectures both work this idea out, though with a great deal of difference in the detail.

We should now consider some of Anderson's philosophical pre-suppositions in these lectures, in particular ones that his students understood well enough, but which are likely to not be understood by present readers.

With regard to space and time Anderson took up a position that I think would be very difficul to take up today. He took space, with its three dimensions, and time with its one dimension, to be fundamental, to be ontological bed-rock. He took space-time to be infinite and to be continuous in the precise mathematical sense—governed by the 'real number' system. He also thought that its geometry was Euclidean, thus putting himself utterly at odds with modern cosmology. We are familiar now with the idea that space and time, or rather space-time, is a subject for empirical investigation and that its true nature is still to seek. Einstein's theory of General Relativity, contemporary quantum physics, and such further developments such as 'string theory', make this clear. What picture of ultimate physical reality they leave us with is very far from clear, but there is no going back to the old Newtonian account of space and time.

The American philosopher Wilfrid Sellars drew a famous distinction between the 'manifest image' of the world, the world as revealed to

---

[6] I record here that my BA. Honours thesis, which I should not care to re-read, was called "A Realist Reconstruction of Kant's Transcendental Anaytic".

ordinary perception, and the 'scientifi image' that fundamental physics and cosmology strives to present us with. He argued that the manifest image can hardly be maintained and must largely yield to the scientifi image.[7] It can fairly be said, I think, that Anderson takes the manifest image of space and time to be the ontological reality, and that this position is now very difficul to defend.

In the case of the categories Anderson is on what I judge to be more interesting ground. The categories of being dive so deep, that though quantum physics and other physics may have interesting things to say to philosophers—for instance, whether causation is in fact deterministic or not—the major issues involved are not susceptible of being resolved at the level of experimental science, yet seem to be real issues. Science may be able to cast light on whether causation is irreducibly statistical or not, but how can it decide what causation is in itself? Is it just a universal or statistical regularity? Or is it something deeper in the nature of things? What of the properties, numbers and quantities in which physical science inevitably traffics? Are they just concepts in our minds, or do they point us to features of physical objects that our concepts merely reflect? Alexander and Anderson give realist answers to such questions; and, furthermore, Anderson's answers are more sharply edged than Alexander's, and well repay examination.

One difficult that Anderson canvasses early in the lectures, but hardly resolves, is the question forced on him by the demand of his logic that his terms (and we shall see shortly how realistically he takes terms) should have real, existing, opposites. If A is term, then there must be non-A's. Applied to the categories this raises a problem, because the categories are, by definition properties or whatever we decide to call them, that everything must have, must fall under.

Anderson never embraced the new formal logic created by Bertrand Russell and A. N. Whitehead along with others. He was perhaps the last of the 'Aristotelian' logicians. He drafted a logic book[8] but it was never published. But there here exists in his handwriting an exposition of the central themes in his system of logic, marked as being lectures given in 1948. We think that they could be a useful companion to the Alexander lectures, and have reproduced them in Appendix 4.

---

[7] Wilfrid Sellars, "Philosophy and the Scientifi Image of Man", *Frontiers of Science and Philosophy*, edited by R.G. Colodny, 1962, reprinted as Ch. 1 in *Science, Perception and Reality*, Routledge & Kegan Paul, London: 1963.
[8] Manuscript and typescript copies of this book are in the Sydney University Archives, P.A.J.A. Series 2 (1914-1926).

But for those who do not wish to study the Logic lectures, or would like some preliminary guidance, I will call attention here to some of the main themes in his thinking on logic. He accepted the traditional doctrine of the subject/ predicate proposition, with its four Aristotelian forms:

All A's are B (the A proposition, in symbols AaB)

No A's are B (the E proposition, AeB)

Some A's are B (the I proposition, AiB)

Some A's are not B (the O proposition, AoB)

These terms are all supposed to have real opposites. There must be non-As and non-Bs, thus raising the problem about the categories, which by definitio have no opposites. One can see also that there may be problems about propositions that assert that a certain relation holds between two or more things, the propositions that contemporary logic symbolizes as e.g. R(a,b). How are such propositions to be rendered in one of the four forms? Anderson is aware of this problem and discusses that problem for his position in the lectures (See lecture 19, section 2, lecture 21, paragraph 3, see also lectures 22 and 24.) He suggests that relational properties (to be distinguished from relations) can be used, i.e., that 'having R to b' can be taken to be a term.

Notice that the singular propositions 'This A is a B' and 'This A is not B' are not included among the fundamental forms. This also created some difficult for Anderson. He tried to deal with it by treating e.g. 'Socrates is sitting' as a sort of I proposition, because Socrates is sometimes sitting and sometimes not sitting.

Anderson again follows the old logic in recognizing the copula, the 'are' in the four forms, or the 'is' in singular propositions ('Socrates is wise'). It is clearly not the 'are' or 'is' of identity, unlike 'The Morning star is the Evening star' which is an identity statement. Rather, it links particulars or a particular with their properties. Here it may be said of the old logic that it brings up-front what the new Russellian logic ignores. Or rather, the new logic hands over the problem to metaphysics, and contemporary metaphysicians well understand the pressure to postulate some 'fundamental tie' holding between an object and its properties, though not all of these metaphysicians actually accept such ties. Anderson, however, gives the copula ontological significance indeed identifie it with one of his categories, that of Existence. Furthermore, he also accepts a negative copula, needed, as he sees it, by the E and the O propositions, though I am not aware of any identificatio that he makes of this second copula with one of his categories.

Another important point to be noted in Anderson's logic is the doctrine of the 'convertibility of terms'. The term that in one proposition appears in the subject place can elsewhere appear in the predicate place. The argument for this is that, for example, in the syllogism 'All As are Bs, All Bs are Cs, therefore All As are Cs', the 'middle term' B must be identical in the two premises for the argument to be valid. The late George Molnar pointed out to me that this made the distinction between subject and predicate, particular and universal, a functional one for Anderson.

But the most unusual feature of Anderson's view of logic must now be introduced if much that he says in these lectures is to be understood. For him, logic is at the same time the science of the most general features of reality, and a true proposition is something in the world, there is no distance between the true proposition and reality. The world is propositional. (Notice also that in view of the negative forms E and O Anderson is committed to negativity in the world.)

This view does immediately raise the question 'What about false propositions, then?' and this was a problem that regularly exercised the minds of Anderson's students, and which we discussed among ourselves. But it can be pointed out that Russell had in his important lectures published in 1918 as *The Philosophy of Logical Atomism*[9] argued for a view of the world that it was constituted by what he called 'facts' (others have said 'states of affairs') which had a distinctly proposition-like structure, though the structure, such as it was, was given by his new, non-Aristotelian, logic. Anderson can be thought of as doing much the same thing, but retaining an Aristotelian logic. It is interesting to notice that Russell in his lectures accepted and argued for negative facts as ontological realities, which constitutes a further parallel to Anderson's E and O propositions.

A further problem that arises for Anderson is to determine just what categories should be recognized, and how they should be ordered. We fin him arguing both these points with Alexander. Anderson says that it is the proposition itself that answers this problem. If we consult its subject-predicate structure then, he thinks, with the subject indicating the place and time of something, and the predicate indicating what

[9] Russell's *Logical Atomism*, ed. David Pears, London, Fontana Collins, 1972.

sort of thing it is, we can get a systematic answer to these questions. Interestingly, Anderson was here following Kant's lead, but this time without a lead from Alexander. Kant had what Norman Kemp Smith, who made the classical English translation of Kant's *Critique of Pure Reason* called Kant's 'metaphysical deduction of the categories' (see the index to his translation), where Kant uses logical considerations to 'deduce' his list of categories. (See pp.106—119 in the Kemp Smith translation.)

It may whet the appetite of those philosophers who have metaphysical interests to give an immediate pre-view of his scheme of categories.

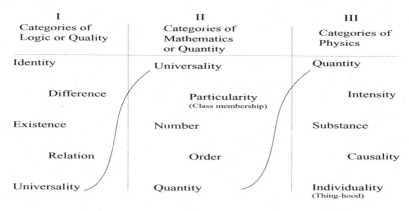

I Categories of Logic or Quality	II Categories of Mathematics or Quantity	III Categories of Physics
Identity	Universality	Quantity
Difference	Particularity (Class membership)	Intensity
Existence	Number	Substance
Relation	Order	Causality
Universality	Quantity	Individuality (Thing-hood)

Figure 1.

His set of categories of 13 categories (1 more than Kant's 12) is laid out in an almost Hegel-like 'succession' organized in three groups, with the categories of Universality and Quantity acting as 'link categories' in the two transitions between groups. 'Monadic' and 'dyadic' categories succeed to each other, so that Difference, Relation, Particularity, Order, Intensity and Causality are dyadic, the others monadic. Individuality, Anderson noted, brings us circling back to Identity again, though with a richer, more enhanced, notion of Identity.

With this scheme, John Anderson joins a very distinguished line of philosophers who have presented us with a set of categories. We have first Plato (the doctrine of Highest Kinds in his dialogue *The Sophist*), then Aristotle, Kant, Hegel, and Samuel Alexander.

Space, Time and the Categories

1
Introductory Lectures

Lecture 1   *(14th June 1949)*

Preliminary Remarks—Precursors: Kant and Hegel—Lack of Systematic
Derivation of the Categories by Alexander

The course is concerned with Alexander's "logic" (theory of reality)—with Space-Time and the categories; not with most of Volume 2 of *Space, Time and Deity*—which contains material on knowledge and "values". On this last question, Alexander hasn't really advanced from his position in *Moral Order and Progress* (published in the nineties), where his ethics, with a certain foundation in idealism (T. H. Green), is of an evolutionist character (*cf.* Herbert Spencer).[1] Some general remarks may be made on Alexander's evolutionism as it enters into his space-time theory. As regards his ethics, I take it to be incompatible with a thoroughgoing space-time view. His position may be compared with Plato's; in the later dialogues there is a definit advance on Socratism in logic, but in ethics and politics Plato substantially preserves the old position and this reacts on his logic so as to prevent a thorough working out of it—thus leading to a compromise between empiricism and rationalism. Thus rationalism appears in the doctrine of the "highest kinds", which is incompatible with a propositional logic. If this remnant of a hierarchical theory (coming over from his politics) were dropped, the logic of the *Sophist* would be of a thoroughly empiricist kind.

Alexander was influence by the later dialogues (particularly by John Burnet's presentation of them). It is with regard to this that he speaks of our having "two consummate guides" to the categories, "Plato and (with modifications Kant". From memory, it is I think, in the syllabus of the Gifford lectures.[2] He makes no reservations as far as Plato is concerned, and he is thinking especially of the *Sophist* but perhaps also of the *Timaeus* in which a theory of space and time is adumbrated. (Burnet's account is taken for granted.) In Kant's case also, we see a reactionary effect of his ethics on his theory of reality; it is particularly in his desire

---

[1] In all subsequent lectures, preliminary remarks will be left-indented as explained in DMA's introduction so as to mark them off from the formal lecture. Samuel Alexander, *Space, Time and Deity: the Gifford Lectures at Glasgow, 1916-1918*. London: Macmillan, 1920. Reprinted with new preface in 1927. This second impression was republished New York: Dover Publications, 1966, with a foreword by Dorothy Emmet. *Moral Order and Progress: an analysis of ethical conceptions* London: Trübner, 1889.
[2] See Appendix 2, Abstract to the Gifford Lectures, Course 1, Lecture 6.

to preserve an absolute morality (absolute right) that he adheres to the doctrine of things-in-themselves—though Adamson contends that this doctrine is also influence by the remnants of representationism in him, that "things-in-themselves" have something in common with Locke's "matter".[3] In this connection Alexander goes beyond Kant, wipes out representationism, and treats Kant's phenomena as things in themselves, as actual things and the only realities. Kant of course was influence by both Hume and Leibniz, and the latter is the source of most of Kant's rationalism (e.g., his rationalist ethics). If we get rid of absolute morality, then the main support of "things-in-themselves" disappears; the representationist division is easily seen to be otiose. Yet Alexander clings to one of the main bases of this division, the Cartesian *cogito*; this seriously confuses his psychology and in turn affects his logic in some ways. (Alexander's doctrine of "enjoyment" is Cartesian in origin; hence "perspectives", etc.) (*Cf.* my review article on Alexander—"The Non-Existence of Consciousness"[4]).

Alexander's other writings are not of much importance for his main position though some articles in the *Proceedings of the Aristotelian Society* give preliminary statements of it.[5] *Cf.* also Alexander's *Spinoza and Time*, in which he compares Spinoza's "attributes" of thought and extension with time and space in his own theory—he considers how Spinoza's position would have been affected if he had seen that thought is something empirical (a particular set of phenomena) and had realised the importance of time.[6] (There is an important firs statement of Alexander's psychological position in "Foundations and Sketch-Plan of a Conational Psychology".[7]

Alexander and the realist movement in Britain: began (about 1903) with Moore's "The Refutation of Idealism".[8] Alexander and Moore weren't very close in their views, but Alexander would have to be recognised as belonging to the realist movement—accepting the realist doctrine that the object is in no way constituted by being known. It is

[3] Robert Adamson, *The Development of Modern Philosophy*, Edinburgh: William Blackwood and Sons, 1930 New Impression; *On the Philosophy of Kant*, Edinburgh, David Douglas 1879.
[4] John Anderson, "The Non-Existence of Consciousness: *Space Time and Deity* by Samuel Alexander", *A.J.P.P.*, 7(1) March 1929: 68-73. Reprinted in *Studies*.
[5] Articles in *Proceedings of the Aristotelian Society* include "Freedom" (January 1914); "Self as Subject and as Person" (March 1910); "On Sensations and Images" (October 1909); "Mental Activity in Willing and in Ideas" (June 1908); Contribution to a symposium on "Mental Activity" with Ward, Read and Stout (June 1908); Contribution to a symposium "Has the Perception of Time an Origin in Thought?" with Dawes Hicks (February 1893).
[6] Samuel Alexander, *Spinoza and Time: being the 4th Arthur Davis Memorial Lecture delivered before the Jewish Historical Society at University College, May 1, 1921*, London: George Allen and Unwin, 1921. Reprinted in *Literary and Philosophical Pieces*, London: Macmillan, 1939.
[7] Samuel Alexander, "Foundations and Sketch-Plan of a Conational Psychology", *British Journal of Psychology* December 1911.
[8] G. E. Moore, "The Refutation of Idealism", *Mind* 12 (1903): 433-53. Reprinted in *Philosophical Studies*, London: Kegan, Paul, Trench, Trübner and Co., 1922.

important to remember that this "independence" of knower and known is not just a doctrine of knowledge (epistemology) but is part of a theory of reality (logic) (*cf.* my paper "The Knower and the Known"[9]). Moore and Russell didn't realise the full implications of the doctrine, they clung to rationalist assumptions, and got further and further from realism. *The New Realism* (especially the contributions by Marvin and Perry) is also important in the realist movement.[10] These thinkers were influence by William James, who upheld a partially realist position in *A Pluralistic Universe, Essays in Radical Empiricism* (including one entitled "The Non-Existence of Consciousness"), and the (earlier) *Principles of Psychology.*[11]

The Relation of Alexander to His Predecessors

Kant. First of all Alexander differs from Kant not only in taking the forms of our knowledge to be the forms of things but also in rejecting the view that they have two different sources as in Kant's distinction between forms of sense (space-time) and forms of the understanding (the categories).[12] Alexander maintains on the contrary that space and time are the sources of the categories—that it is as "determinations" of space and time, or as I would put it as features of things *qua* spatio-temporal that we know or can give an account of the categories—although as far as the doctrine of separate sources in Kant is concerned you have the theory of the Schematism of the categories which at least gives them as they appear in our thinking a temporal character, and it would be quite easy to argue in that connection that they must equally have a spatial character, e.g., in the Second Analogy it can, I think, quite easily be shown that causality which Kant there closely connects with time (i.e., our consciousness of causality is connected with our consciousness of time) also has to be connected with space to make the argument clear and convincing. (In dealing with Alexander's theory of causality we will also discuss Kant's and Hume's theories.)

> That is, the distinction between Kant and Alexander is not so definit as might appear. But Kant's position still differs from Alexander for whom space-time is the source of the categories: it is "as spatio-temporal, that things have categorical features".

---

[9] John Anderson, "The Knower and the Known", *Proceedings of the Aristotelian Society* 27(1926-27): 61-84. Reprinted in *Studies.*

[10] "The New Realism" was announced in the article "The Program and First Platform of Six Realists" by E. B. Holt, W. T. Marvin, W. P. Montague, R. B. Perry, W. B. Pitkin and E. G. Spaulding in 1910, followed by the collection *The New Realism: Cooperative Studies in Philosophy,* New York: Macmillan, 1912. Marvin's article was "The Emancipation of Metaphysics from Epistemology"; Perry's article was "A Realistic Theory of Independence".

[11] William James, *Essays in Radical Empiricism,* London; New York: Longmans, Green, 1912. *A Pluralistic Universe: Hibbert Lectures at Manchester College on the present situation in philosophy,* London; New York: Longmans, Green, 1909. *Principles of Psychology,* London: Macmillan, 1890.

[12] Immanuel Kant, *Critique of Pure Reason,* translated by Norman Kemp Smith. London: Macmillan, 1956.

Hegel. Now Hegel, on the other hand, (*cf.* brief note in "The Place of Hegel in the History of Philosophy",[13]) starts from the other side, from the side of the categories—of the various forms of the Absolute Idea—and the most that space and time could be would be such particular forms, that is, examples of categories—though in point of fact I don't think we can go even as far as that—for Hegel space and time are "general conceptions" but at a lower level with a less degree of generality than the main categories.

> They are operations of the understanding at a certain "level of the understanding" or "power of the idea", but can only be specifie as the *spatial* level.

> Kant refutes the view of space and time as "general conceptions" in the Aesthetic. The force of his argument not appreciated by Hegel.

> Hegel is unwarrantably ignored by Alexander in his explicit pronouncements on sources (consciousness of difference) but in fact he takes over Hegel's firs two categories: identity and difference.

Lack of Systematic Derivation of Categories in Alexander

But one point in which both Kant and Hegel are superior to Alexander is in connection with the classificatio and the order of the categories. After starting off with Hegel's identity and difference Alexander seems to take his categories quite at random—to decide under various influence that such-and-such conceptions *are* the categories but not to give any reasons why they should be or why there should be just so many categories and no more.

If we consider Kant we fin in the "Metaphysical Deduction"[14] that he enumerates his categories with reference to the forms of judgment or as we should say the forms of the proposition which is at least a definit method (whatever the arguments for or against it) and Hegel although he is not so explicit on this matter (though he speaks of successive forms of the idea from the most abstract to the most concrete) nevertheless does get his starting point from the proposition and really is working on the basis of what is involved in the proposition—in particular the firs categories of being and not-being can be regarded as the affirmat ve and negative copula respectively and it is, I would argue, in terms of the significanc of the copula (which means of the proposition in general) that the step is made from affirmatio to negation (being and not-being).

---

[13] John Anderson, "The Place of Hegel in the History of Philosophy", *A.J.P.P.*, 10(2)1932:81-91. Reprinted in *Studies*.
[14] Kant's *Critique of Pure Reason, op. cit.*, pp. 106-119: "The Clue to the Discovery of All Pure Concepts of the Understanding". Kemp Smith refers to this section in the index as "The Metaphysical Deduction of the Categories".

Hegel multiplies categories in an unjustifiabl way—there is no distinction between the categorial and the non-categorial:—but there is some semblance of method.

> Alexander uses the "empirical" method, the method of hypothesis. He throws a whole doctrine at you, there is no adequate test as he proceeds. We can connect this with his neglect of the proposition. Alexander thinks the whole doctrine of formal logic is unimportant—we can link this with his ethics.

Lecture 2   *(15th June 1949)*

"Alexander's Empiricism"—Logic as Theory of Reality—Logic of Events

The "empirical" method adopted by Alexander is really dogmatic. The whole theory is to be treated as a hypothesis—he doesn't show how it can be treated from point to point—the position is rather that given a space-time theory, with the various special theories that fall under it, we are asked if this theory makes sense or not—whether in a general way it seems plausible and coherent—which is clearly a very vague sort of test. If we were to choose between the theory that to be real is to be spatio-temporal and the theory that to be real is to be thought we couldn't very easily settle the matter in terms of general intelligibility or plausibility. On the other hand if we are to think seriously of the space-time theory as a hypothesis then we shall have to consider specifi consequences of it and then to consider directly whether these consequences are true or false which means that our empirical approach to the fiel is not a merely hypothetical one—means that we can know it otherwise than in hypothesis. In fact if that were not the case—if the conclusion as well as the other premises in any such testing had to be taken as hypotheses just as much as the premises we set out to test, then there wouldn't really be any test at all, i.e., the "empirical" method *can't* be identifie with the hypothetical method but includes the making of direct observations and assertions in the field whatever it may be, so that while Alexander might wish to have his theory fairly considered—not to have it set aside because of an initial unfamiliarity—still he would also have to say that we could directly fin some doctrine to be true—that the position in philosophy generally couldn't be that of waiting until a doctrine had been unfolded or worked out in a profusion of details before we could pass judgment on it.

> The *Phaedo*—Socrates used the hypothetical method to support Rationalism—but his procedure is inconsistent with his account of it.

It is also important to note that whatever character is assigned to this proposition, the hypothesis has to be combined in the other premises with empirical material and the question of the truth or falsity of the conclusion is again an empirical matter so that the procedure is at least partly empirical and of course, I argue, has to be wholly so—the hypothesis itself must be empirical if it is to be combined with and tested by empirical propositions in the manner indicated and failing all this—failing the procedure in terms of matters of fact and the bringing of the hypothesis itself into the realm of fact—there won't be any explanation.

Now in Logic there are special difficulties That is, in a theory that professes to deal with things in general as contrasted with a particular set of things—a point illustrated in the difficult concerning logical terms themselves, e.g., whether "*term*" and similarly "*proposition*" are terms, whether "sort of thing" is a sort of thing—a difficult which leads to the suggestion that the propositions of logic are not matters of fact—are other than empirical—a difficult apparently avoided but actually only evaded by Idealist views which take logic to be concerned with thought.[15] In the firs instance, we should have to say that even if there isn't a class "sorts of thing" there is a class "sorts of things contemplated by me" or, more broadly, "sorts of things contemplated by human beings" and, similarly, that even if there isn't a class "propositions" there is a class "things proposed or asserted by me or by anyone" so that the contention that a significan term must have a real opposite would not appear to provide an objection to logic conceived in the Idealist manner. However, the avoidance of the objection—the making of a distinction between things asserted or known and things not asserted or known—is something that would be possible on an empiricist view but not on an Idealist view to which *everything* is thought so that "being thought" has no real opposite.

Apart then from the plausibility of any particular theory in logic, all this indicates the difficult of *justifying* a logic and it could be suggested that a fairly loose criterion like intelligibility or making sense was the most we could hope for—that we fin we just have to say certain things even if we can't explain how we can say them—and the test of philosophic theory is whether in the long run it leaves us comfortable, leaves us feeling that the things we say are the things we have to say and enable us to proceed in our thinking without difficultie or at least with a minimum of difficulties But this is in fact the Idealist theory of

---

[15][DMA] This is the difficult mentioned in the introduction, that these terms don't have opposites—things that are not terms, or are non-propositional.

coherence or satisfactoriness without any testing of details, and in so far as Alexander puts to us a complete theory of reality and asks whether it fulfil our requirements of coherence and intelligibility he may be said to be proceeding in an Idealistic way. However, as mentioned above, there could be little philosophical discussion along these lines—we should require something rather more exact if we are to prefer Alexander to Hegel, or *vice-versa*—if we are to set up the doctrine that *to be is to be spatio-temporal* as against the doctrine that *to be real is to be thought*, or *vice-versa*.

Now I have argued that it is a firs description of logic—that it is the best approach to logic—to consider that it is connected with discourse—that its problems are presented by discourse, and are settled by reference to discourse—namely by what enables discourse to proceed or get over difficulties but allowing for this approach, it is still the case that the solution of problems that arise in discourse is independent of our discussions and inquiries—that we are dealing with a subject that doesn't depend for its existence on our existence or on our inquiries. We have, e.g., the problem of consistency, and this problem would be insoluble if we took it to be a mere question of our procedure, i.e., if inconsistency were merely something that some people avoided and other people didn't avoid but fell into. There would be no ground for supporting consistency, for saying there was something wrong with inconsistency—it is possible to maintain that position only by saying that thought is not something by itself, but is concerned with something else—that it is seeking to know reality, or, as the phrase goes, "to lay hold of what is". The point being that although what is thought or said can be inconsistent with what is thought or said, what *is* cannot be inconsistent with what *is*. Thus whatever kind of proof be given of a logical point and allowing that the point arises in discourse, it is only by reference to reality or what is, that there is any problem at all, and this applies incidentally to those who try to make philosophical problems into problems of language, i.e., it is only because to speak is to speak about reality that there are such problems—though once this general objectivity is recognized we can distinguish it from other problems—particular problems, problems about the special thing we call language or the use of language.

The position is then that the logical problems are problems of reality, but can be expressed and may have to be expressed, in the firs instance, in terms of discourse, i.e., we take our logical theories as showing what sort of statements and arguments have significance—wha sort of thing can be believed, contradicted, proved, understood, etc.—that is we can have a theory of significan discourse so long as we understand that what statements and arguments signify is reality or "what is the case".

Conceiving logic then as a theory of reality, we can say that Alexander's logic is a logic of events, i.e., for him, to be is be spatio-temporal, and this logic would be supported by showing that events are the subject of discourse—are what discourse is about—and that it is in terms of events or space-time terms that disputes and arguments can be settled. As against this it could be argued that some other logic, e.g., a logic of substance, cannot solve problems of thought and action—of what can be asserted and brought about—that the logic of substance leads us into the insoluble problem of the simple and the complex—the constant and the changing—which appear notably in Greek philosophy, though they recur in Modern philosophy—but Alexander at least doesn't work out any such contrast—doesn't show how a logic of events solves problems that a logic of substance can't solve—doesn't even present the logical basis of the hypothetical method to which he appeals—doesn't show that testing is only possible on a logic of events. At best we might fin and piece together from Alexander's work the sort of argument required, but it might rather be said that we have to supplement and correct it where he falls short of a logic of events or a philosophy of process. Now one way this criticism might be put (linked with the question of discourse) is to say that the sort of logic he requires is a propositional one—is to say he ignores the proposition—doesn't see that to treat things as spatio-temporal is the same as treating them as propositional—that the spatio-temporal theory is important precisely as clearing up the problem of the proposition and on the other hand the propositional theory is important as indicating what sort of problem it is of which the spatio-temporal theory is a solution.

Lecture 3   *(21st June 1949)*

"Vicious Intellectualism"—James and Bradley—Distinction and Connection

Alexander ignores, or takes insufficien account of the *proposition*. For him formal logic is "trivial", but in fact space-time theory requires a *rigorous* classificatio of forms. We must show that there are just so many forms of assertion, argument, etc. This is not given in "ordinary speech", which subserves other needs besides inquiry.

When the matter was thoroughly understood you would fin that a theory of things as spatio-temporal was the same as a theory of things as propositional. The space-time theory makes more precise some of the questions regarding propositions, and the relation to the proposition shows us what problems the space-time theory is trying to solve.

If you take William James you can say that he also neglects the proposition—that he treats questions as questions of *concepts*—which is natural enough for one who approached philosophy from the side of psychology though it should be noted that this sort of psychology had itself been determined by earlier idealist and representationalist philosophies. But nevertheless James attacks the problems, particularly in the *Pluralistic Universe*,[16] in a way that enables us to see clearly the importance of the proposition—the relevance of a propositional theory to their solution. What James calls "vicious intellectualism"—which is similar to what I call Rationalism—amounts to the separating off or isolating of some aspect or character of things, the assumption being that it excludes any character which could be distinguished from it. Which of course is closely connected with the principle on which Berkeley bases his rejection of abstraction, namely that it is impossible or at least wrong, (differing formulations fi different parts of his argument) to think separately what cannot exist separately—this being an example of Rationalism—of the principle that unless we are thinking of a thing in its essence or whole nature we are not thinking of *it*. Now this theory would make theory impossible—in particular would make propositions impossible, and it is from the side of the proposition—from the fact that rationalists have to use propositions which on their theory would be meaningless in order to present their theory and so "vicious intellectualism" would make theory impossible. In particular it would make propositions impossible, i.e., taking the outstanding example of Distinction and Connection then, as James shows, if being distinct excludes being connected, then there could be no account of distinction or connection of things. But, according to James, the only reason that can be given for believing in the exclusion is that saying that things are distinct is not the *same* as saying they are connected. Of course, that is not an adequate account of the matter—it is not on a mere basis of words or usages that rationalists have come to believe in what Hume calls "distinct existences", but it is still important to recognize that calling A and B distinct is not the same as calling A and B connected—it

---

[16]William James, *op. cit.*

doesn't lead to the conclusion that things can be connected without being distinct or they can be distinct without being connected, and in fact they cannot be. As we may put it in terms of the main contention of realism, a relation has two terms and those who attempt to uphold "distinct existences" are always found flounderin in the confusion of the notion of self-relation.[17] In the same way the fact that to say that X is a cause is not the same thing as saying X is an effect—that fact is not the slightest reason for saying that there are causes which aren't effects or effects which aren't causes and indeed the space-time theory, or, more broadly, logic, shows that these things are not the case.

> There is no particular problem of Distinction and Connection but *connection* confuses *being related* and *being the same*.

The point can be expressed best by reference to the term "unity"—the unity of A and B can be taken to mean that A and B which we thought were two things are actually one, or it can be taken to mean that A and B are joined or united in certain ways—which is quite a different matter. However in Idealist theory these two notions of being one and the same and being connected or joined are run together. And if we take Hume's problem, particularly his principle "that the mind never perceives any real connection among distinct existences" we can see that this depends on the treatment of connection as meaning "not distinct" or, more broadly, that Hume's difficulti s arise from the treatment on the one hand of "distinct" as meaning simply "different" and as meaning "isolated" or "unrelated" and the connected treatment of "connected" as meaning simply "related" or meaning "identified" "uniform" or "being one", so that while James himself doesn't seem to be quite clear on the point still he struggles with this problem.

Now in the controversy between James and Bradley (*cf.* "The Thing and Its Relations"[18]) in that controversy Bradley assumes that to have a different relation means to be a different thing. That is, he starts from a conception of what must be and takes this to override what we fin actually to be. The question of whether having a different relation makes a thing different is again a *confused* one, i.e., the question is on the one hand understood as meaning whether to merely say that a thing has a different relation means that it is a different thing and the question whether entering into a certain relation does in fact change the thing,

---

[17][DMA] Anderson held that things could not stand in any relation to themselves. For instance "a is identical with itself" fails to say anything.
[18] William James, "The Thing and Its Relations", *Essays in Radical Empiricism*, London; New York: Longmans, Green, 1912.

or at least is an occasion of its being changed, and it is acceptance in a certain measure of the latter possibility that often leads people to accept or at least be confused about the former.

Now it is a fact that some changes of relations are accompanied or followed by some change of character. On the other hand it is equally a fact that some changes of relations don't lead to changes of character in certain respects—that in particular some things are indifferent to certain environmental changes—which means that certain changes of relation make no difference to the things themselves and of course some characters of a thing are indifferent to the acquiring or the loss of certain other characters so that in terms of the former we can say that it is the same thing, while in terms of the latter we can say the thing has changed. If identity meant change in no respects then nothing would retain its identity over a period, and the thing with this supposed identity could enter into no situations, so that the question how it could be changed by having a new relation would simply never arise.

Now for Bradley to use such a concept of Identity is simply to dictate to experience—to impose on it a conception of what must be, whereas in actual experience what we call the same thing is a thing which retains *certain* characters over a period while changing in other characters and in its relations to other things. And while we think in that way of identity or sameness then we realise that there are some existences—some changes of environment—which would bring that identity to an end—would mean that there was no longer that kind of thing in that place—but that wouldn't in the least affect what we mean by its being the same thing or its being a particular thing of a certain kind while it lasted.

On the general point of the theory of Connection and Distinction, if we believed in *essential* distinction, i.e., in the possibility of things being distinct and nothing else, then we can't say of such things that they are connected, though equally we can't say they are not connected—and similarly if we believe in essential connection. But in point of fact such essences are not in the least what we mean by Distinction and Connection—are not exclusive of one another. Nevertheless it is in space-time or in propositional terms that we can see this fact—see the non-exclusiveness or non-opposition of Distinction and Connection—see that two different things can be in the same spatial situation, i.e., can be connected while remaining distinct, or see that two terms can be connected in the proposition without ceasing to be different terms.

Lecture 4   *(22nd June 1949)*

Alexander on "Distinction and Connection"—Neglects the Proposition—The
"Stuff" of Space-Time Theory

James' "Radical empiricism" is a clearing up of Hume's "Empiricism".

I made the point that the two terms of a proposition are both distinct and connected which, of course, is not exactly the same point as saying the two terms of a relation, say "beside" are both distinct and connected, but which illustrates the same sort of logic (situational logic) or what I call, in connection with Alexander, a logic of events (occurrences) and, referring back for a moment to James, we might suggest that even if it is true to argue that when saying a thing is X is *not* the same as saying it is Y, this doesn't imply that the same things can't be both X and Y—still there might be some point in saying that to call things connected is to call them distinct, or that being connected involves being distinct or again that being distinct involves being connected in some sense—involves being in the same situation. (If A is not B—if no A are B (AeB)—we call this a situation.[19]) However the position might be covered by saying that distinction and connection are bound up together or are *themselves* distinct and connected in all experience. Now that would mean that we could not ask in the Bradleian sense "How can things be at once distinct and connected?" That is, if there is taken to be any difficult about that situation—if it is suggested that there could be anything but experience (meaning the way we fin things, meaning the way in which we fin things are) to which we can appeal in order to settle the problem—all we can say is that in a situation or in a proposition things *are* distinct and connected and there is no manner in which they can be so, or in which we can show they can be so.

Now this takes us back to the point I made about Alexander that to treat things as spatio-temporal is the same as to treat them as propositional so that the question is not "how *can* things be distinct and connected?" but "how *are* they distinct and connected" and the answer is "in space-time" or "in the proposition" or in my phrase that covers the other two "in situations". This would link closely with Kant's solution of Hume's problem—Kant's overcoming of the difficultie of a doctrine of "distinct existences" even though it is overcome only for "phenomena" or things

---

[19][DMA] "We", that is, Anderson!

as they come under the conditions of our experience and *not* for things-in-themselves or things as they don't come under the conditions of our experience for which of course we have no evidence at all—anything we say about things-in-themselves being something that comes under the conditions of experience. However, ignoring that confusion, Kant's answer to Hume is that what we may call distinct things are connected in space and time and under the categories and that, as I suggested in Lecture 1, amounts to saying in space-time, and in propositions and if further in Alexander's manner we take the categories as implicit in space and time themselves then we have a single answer—though it may be variously expressed (spatio-temporally or propositionally)—to the question how are things distinct and connected.

But Alexander ignores the proposition, doesn't, like Kant, work out the categories in relation to the forms of propositions, and of course equally ignores it in connection with the general theory of space-time; and this gives an unnecessary arbitrariness to his account of the categories and to his theory in general—this is the main direction in which Alexander needs to be corrected. This is so in spite of the fact that in the section of the beginning of Volume 2 called "The Clue to Quality" he gives what is essentially a propositional explanation of the relation between mind and body—taking "mentality" or "being mental" as qualifying certain bodily processes but of course there are serious weaknesses in this part of the discussion, i.e., even when he maintains that the mental and the neural (a particular set of neural processes) are in the same place which we might take to mean they are the same processes, he *still* treats the mental as *higher* than the neural—more generally mentality as higher than vitality—so that he is coming back to a position in which what is supposed to be a predicate of a subject doesn't really inhere in that subject but somehow hovers over it, or, as we might say, is its spirit (*cf.* Moore's treatment of "good") and thus he creates insoluble problems and loses all the value of a propositional treatment in which while saying "some bodily are mental" (BiM) we also say "all mental are bodily" (MaB) so that the one is no more a subject than the other and the one is no more a predicate than the other.

We can link this doctrine of levels with Evolutionism.

Alexander's "Stuff" Theory of Space-Time

The clue to quality then is that mentality does characterize certain bodily processes—is one of their characters in the same sense of any other character they possess (so-called "physical" characters) and correspondingly that being bodily or physical is one of the characters of what is meant by mental processes—the point being that on a propositional theory there is no difference between the class of subjects and class of predicates and to say that there is a difference is to fall into what James calls "vicious intellectualism" and what I call Rationalism and of course an even more important and in fact quite central example of the same confusions in Alexander is his doctrine of space-time as "stuff" and that of which things are made—in other words as the ultimate subject of which everything else—every term of a less general character—is a predicate—a position which, in spite of Alexander's protestations, amounts to "substantialism"—a doctrine of a fundamental substance—and even further that space-time is the subject of which the various categories are predicates—that as space-time is the essential subject, so they are essential predicates—even if in fact they apply to everything so that once more we are confronted with terms that have no opposites—predicates that have no intelligible contradictory.

The doctrine of space-time as "stuff" is contrasted with space-time as "medium" or of space and time as media (an expression which Alexander also makes use of). That is, of things in general as being *in* space and time instead of *being* space and time and the difficult of that latter position—the difficult of taking space and time as in some sense things, and in some sense not things, is once more to be shown in terms of a situational or propositional logic. As a firs rough formulation: space and time are involved in any assertion whatever that we make.

Lecture 5   *(28th June 1949)*
Alexander's "Stuff" Theory of Space-Time continued—Objections

I had been pointing to an important departure of Alexander from a propositional or situational theory in the description of space-time as stuff—as that of which all things are made,—which, I said, amounts to substantialism—of the doctrine of a fundamental substance or subject of which anything else is a predicate (if we can talk about anything else!) as against the propositional doctrine of the convertibility of terms, i.e., the interchangeability of subjects and predicates. And I was suggesting here that the medium theory is preferable to the stuff theory, i.e., the view that things are *in* space-time as against the view that space and time are what things *are*. And while the "medium" formulation has its own difficulties at any rate it is preferable to the "stuff" formulation.

Objections to the "Stuff" Theory

1. In respect of *continuity* since to say that things are made of the same stuff is not to say they are continuous with each other even if we took it that this implied an original continuity of the material from which things were made or cut out, it doesn't imply that they are continuous now—doesn't in itself show any connection between them and if they still had a connection it is just because whatever is done to them they remain in a common medium—they still exist in the same situation—in the same space and the same time.

2. Again the doctrine of a common stuff or a common source doesn't imply that the relations between things are also made of that stuff or derived from that source whereas in thinking of things as spatio-temporal we also think of the relations between things as spatio-temporal (a point presented in a slightly confused way in James' *Principles of Psychology*, chapter on perception of space).[20]

3. In these ways, then, the stuff formulation lacks generality and doesn't meet the theoretical requirements—doesn't really amount to a situational logic. Now in other ways there are difficultie particularly whether on this theory we can account for differences at all—whether the substantialist starting point doesn't bring us back to Eleaticism—to what has been called in modern controversy a "block universe"—and Alexander's difficult about differences is seen in the doctrine of "levels" already commented on and the doctrine of degrees of complexity by which he endeavours to clarify it. Thus he calls mind higher than body on the ground that the mental is a species of the bodily or that mentality distinguishes some bodily processes from others and this could be supported logically by the consideration that the intension of the species *includes* that of the genus—the species has *all* the properties of the genus and others besides. But the confusion that emerges in this position is that if we are going to call one set of things higher than another then we are not comparing species with genus but species with the remainder of the genus—with *other* species which on the same theory would be higher than the genus and which we couldn't compare in the same manner with the given species. Thus if we say the Organic is a species of the Physical and is therefore higher than the physical we shall equally have to say that the Inorganic is a species of the physical and is therefore higher than the physical so that we

---

[20] William James, *Principles of Psychology, op. cit.*, Volume 2, Chapter 20.

won't get a general scale of complexity—which Alexander identifies of
course, with the evolutionary scale—won't fin in complexity a solution
of our problem, that is, of the problem of differences and we may also
say here that the treatment of differences as differences in complexity
is, in fact, a reduction of quality to quantity.

> We could also say of theory of levels that, even if the point about
> genus and species is ignored, the classificatio of levels will be *endlessly*
> complicated—between genus and species we could always fin intermediate
> classes. Alexander wants a number of *big* levels—the main or essential points
> of emergence—but the selection is made in a *conventional* manner by reference
> to the leading sciences. Even here there is difficu ty, especially to show that
> chemistry is "higher" than physics.

4.   The stuff theory makes it impossible to distinguish qualities
and it also introduces difficultie in regard to relations—difficultie
exemplifie in Alexander's description of the *knowing* relation as
"compresence" or "togetherness" which might be said to convey
that the things in question are related, but not *how* they are related
or, alternatively, could be said to imply that anything stands in
the knowledge relation to anything else—anything being together
with anything else in space-time.   In an attempt to get out of this
difficult Alexander further complicates and confuses his theory with
the doctrine of "perspectives" a doctrine in which a mental act is not
together with everything else in space-time or even with everything
else that we roughly say "is at the same time" but is only together
with *some* things—things which we can say are part of the same
motion or process.   Now this still doesn't get over the difficult
of reversibility—doesn't show why any one part of such a motion
shouldn't be said to know any other part, no matter which of them,
or even if neither of them, is mental.   *And*, of course, the whole
doctrine of perspectives or compresence in particular motions would
seem to cut across the major tenet of realism—namely that things may
be there—may be in our presence—even if we know nothing about
them and Alexander's confusion on this point is further seen in his
treatment of consciousness not as a relation but as a quality of what
knows or, it might be better to say, though he calls it a quality he is
really in this conception amalgamating quality and relation after the
style of Descartes.   However, this leads us to the important question
of the meaning of *relation* or of alternative senses of that expression
and (here to anticipate later discussion) the question whether what

we call a relation such as "knowing" may not be define in terms of qualities and of space-time relations such as "beside" and "after" so that we could say that the latter are relations in the strict sense while the former are relations in an extended sense—that is, the assertion of such relations conveys qualitative information as well as information about space-time relations. If you take the relation of sitting then in making the assertion "I sit in a chair" we imply certain qualities in the sitter as well as certain spatial relations of his parts—we don't say that anything other than a human being or, more broadly, anything other than an animal *sits*. Now the point is that to recognize this fact requires a distinction between the relations and the qualities involved and make it impossible to reduce the former to the latter and thus to describe knowing as mere "togetherness". We can say that "togetherness" or, more broadly, some space-time relation is necessary to the existence of any relation in the extended sense but is not sufficient At the same time we can say that Alexander's "stuff" theory prevents him from making this distinction—requires him to treat quality and relation alike as just space-time.

2
The Interrelations of Space and Time

Lecture 6   *(29th June 1949)*

Physical Space-Time—"Time is the Mind of Space"—Alexander's "Clue to Quality"

See especially Alexander Book I chapter I, "Physical Space-Time". Note the difficultie of taking space-time as a "medium" *cf.* especially Zeno's paradox on Space.

Coming back to the section on the "Clue to quality"[1] which Alexander discusses in terms of the mind-body problem, we fin him endeavouring to elucidate this point by means of the dictum "time is the mind of space", in other words, the relation of time to space within space-time is compared to the relation of mind to body within a person. It might in some ways be better—better convey Alexander's meaning—if for "time is the mind of space" the formula "mind is the time of body" were substituted. We have, of course, still to recognise the untenability of the theory of levels in terms of which Alexander would regard the comparison as limited, since time on his view is not higher than space—in other words there is nothing spatial that is not also temporal though there is something bodily that is not mental. However, as we have seen, even in the latter case—the case of the inclusion of the mental in the bodily—the two are equally subjects and equally predicates or qualities. Nevertheless, taking what Alexander thinks on this matter, we can come closer to an account of the proposition or of the connection between being spatio-temporal and being propositional.

As regards space and time themselves then, Alexander's formula is that time gives "structure" to space and space gives continuity to time which, on the mind-body side, would take the form: mind gives structure to body and body gives continuity to mind, i.e., it gives it a *place* of continued existence—a point of importance, of course, in connection with the view that mentality is *intermittent*—while mind gives body character or organization which it would not otherwise have. We are not to think of body without mind as completely unorganized but we are to think that body with mind has an articulation which body without mind doesn't have. Now this would bring us back to the difficult regarding complexity, and in any case there is still no question of mind

---

[1] *STD*, Volume 2, Book III, Chapter 1, "The Clue to Quality". The reference to "Time as the mind of space" occurs at the beginning of the following Chapter (Chapter 2, The Order of Empirical Qualities) on page 38.

being peculiarly a predicate or body peculiarly a subject, but at least it may cast light on the distinction *in any given case* between subject and predicate—in fact these formulae of Alexander's are the starting-point of my view that the subject is the region in which a certain occurrence is going on, or a certain situation existing, and that the predicate is the activity which is going on in that region, or the character of that situation (while the copula, of course, is just the fact of occurrence or taking place). And with reference to this formulation (region and activity) we would associate the subject especially with space and the predicate especially with time, or being a subject with being spatial, and being a predicate with being temporal. And, of course, if we accept the theory of things as spatio-temporal, then we are saying they are at once both subjects and predicates. Another formulation is that in thinking of a thing as spatial or as a subject we are thinking especially of its capacity for being acted upon and in thinking of it as temporal or as a predicate we are thinking especially of its capacity for acting—of its activity.

This material may be linked with discussion in Plato's *Sophist*.

The real clue to quality, on these lines, is the occurrences of qualities at places and, as I said, we can equally say that the mental qualities occur at certain bodily places and that the bodily or "physical" qualities occur at mental places, or, more broadly, that mental qualities, and equally bodily qualities, both place and are placed.

That, then, is a rough account of how in my view Alexander's position can be, and even needs to be, supplemented by, or developed into, a propositional theory. But if we limited ourselves to what he says about space and time themselves—to his treatment of this in abstraction from particular occurrences and situations—then we immediately encounter enormous difficulties If we are going to say literally that time gives structure to space and space gives continuity to time, then not only are we treating space and time as things and so requiring a more general logic which will apply to them as much as to other things—a logic perhaps of an Idealist sort in which the fundamental concept is "being thought", but also we are assuming an initial space without structure and time without continuity, which Alexander admits we never fin in experience—in other words we are back at a doctrine of things-in-themselves—in the form of "space-in-itself" and "time-in-itself" which are supposed to be the source of spatio-temporality as we know it, though again, as in Kant's case, the very expression "source" is intelligible only in spatio-temporal terms.

Now this problem can also be put in terms of connection and distinction or as I more usually put it, togetherness and distinctness, and Alexander's position quite definitel is that space is peculiarly the ground of togetherness while time is peculiarly the ground of distinctness—this being one reason why he thinks space and time have to be together, though also distinct, in order to give us the union of togetherness and distinctness or of connection and distinction that we fin in all experience. Space in itself then is pure undifferentiated bulk and time in itself is pure discreteness—is the separate and fleetin moment which only something else—only in fact space—can hold together and enable to exhibit succession and duration. It is time then that breaks up the undifferentiated bulk of space, it is space that holds together the fleetin moments of time and the consequence of these reciprocal operations between pure space and pure time is that empirical space and empirical time exhibit *both* characters—that we can have spatial distinction as well as togetherness, temporal togetherness as well as temporal distinction. But, as I say, not only does this involve a treatment of space and time as things, but it is an anti-empirical position, it is a rationalist theory of how things can be or what enables them to be what they are—it is opposed to what is admitted to be the empirical fact that we f nd togetherness and distinction in all experience and do not need a *source* for them—let alone separate sources for the two. As I said, instead of asking *how* things can be distinct and connected we should simply ask how *are* things distinct and connected and the answer would be spatio-temporally or propositionally (subject, predicate, copula) or "in situations" (covers both) and the theory of space and time may then be a development of this position as showing *in detail* how things are spatio-temporally distinguished and connected. But this could never be done if we took space as peculiarly the ground of togetherness and time as the ground of distinctness.

Lecture 7   *(5th July 1949)*

Physical Space-Time continued—Alexander's Use of "Space-Time"—Neglect of the Proposition

The association of the predicate with Time can be expressed in the identificatio of quality and activity, i.e., "X is red" might be better expressed: redding, as going on in the red way. *Cf.* article by Mace and Wisdom.[2] Note some difficult

---

[2] John Wisdom, "Logical Constructions II", *Mind* 40(160): October 1931, credits C. A. Mace for his use of "redding".

for what might be called *situations* as opposed to *occurrences*. For example, "A is inside B". We could not say that B is going on in the inside manner. But while this is a different conception, yet it can be covered by the space-time theory.

The suggestion of Alexander is that space is the basis or ground of togetherness and that time is the ground of distinctness and thus that the togetherness and distinctness of things in experience (meaning of course in actuality) is accounted for by the togetherness and distinctness of space and time in space-time. Now, as I said, to say that space and time have certain functions in relation to one another—that they do things to one another—that space makes time x and time makes space y (whatever x and y may be) is to speak as if space and time were things, and thus is speaking metaphorically. And even if in speaking of space and time as constituting a *medium* of things we also seem to be regarding them as things, i.e., as having a relation of containing or embracing—which we are empirically acquainted with as a relation *between* things—then of course we have the dilemma: either space and time are not things and hence can't be media of the existence of things or else space and time are in space-time which seems unintelligible. Now while Alexander by no means solves all the difficultie of the position—while he largely ignores them—at least he suggests one possible line of solution in the *dual* nature of his medium—the possibility of saying space is in time and time is in space so that taking space and time we should be able to give some description of space as well as other things and similarly with the other case. And thus Alexander's account of the relation between space and time is particularly important and whatever difficultie may remain in all this we at least see that there is a *concreteness* about space-time that there is not about the Hegelian Absolute Idea which must be regarded as a quite empty notion of "that which is experienced or manifested in everything", i.e., as "something we know not what" which has to fulfi a certain function, or in other words as a statement rather than a solution of a problem. At the same time, as far as a solution is suggested—namely that the Absolute is *mental* or spiritual—we may observe that Hegel is treating as Absolute something that Alexander presents as one particular thing, just as space and time in Hegel's theory (space in particular) become one empirical thing or empirical mode.

While admitting the difficultie of Alexander's view we may still learn something from his treatment of the interrelation of space and time by way of justifying among other things the expression "space-time". First of all he tries to show that neither space nor time can stand by itself as the stuff or medium of things, secondly that space and time can be taken together as the stuff or medium of things—can give connection between distinct specification (*coordinates*, as we may put it) of things and thirdly, that space and time must be taken together, that they are, as we may put it, bound up with one another—we have not succeeded in grasping space unless we take it with time, or time unless we take it with space. I have already suggested that Alexander throws his position at people without adequate examination from point to point, but *here* in this chapter he seems to be committing the opposite error—namely of trying to prove what cannot be proved—what can only be found—because the required premises would not, on the theory itself, be intelligible. But perhaps the two points are not really opposed—perhaps they could be united in the statement that Alexander does not know what sort of *test* can be applied to logical theories, and thus when he supports them he does it in the wrong way.

When Alexander says that space alone cannot be the stuff of things but needs supplementation—when he says that space by itself is pure bulk without differentiation he is, as I said, appealing to something that is not an object of experience and the question is if we cannot experience space by itself how can we say that space by itself is without differentiation—similarly time by itself without connection. Even if it is argued, in what I think is a better way, that things cannot be spatial without being temporal or temporal without being spatial (this is quite an important point because many philosophers have conceived *mind* to be temporal without being spatial)—even if we take that line, it would still be necessary to reject a supposition which actually would be impossible for us to make—the criticism of the Idealist view of mind being particularly of that character, that they cannot think of mind as non-spatial, that even when they say that they are so treating it they are actually treating it as spatial.

If then it is unintelligible to say "suppose things were spatial and not temporal" then we would not be able to say that supposition has false consequences and therefore must be rejected. Nor if we amended the formula and said that motion cannot be spatial without being temporal or temporal without being spatial—then this formula could be defended but only as descriptive—only as saying motions are spatial and temporal. And if Alexander thinks that we are begging the question in identifying things with motions or occurrences the answer is that that is the sort of thing that has to be *found*—that can be proved in a special sense, that is, can be *exhibited*—only by consideration of the proposition but that can't be made to follow from something that would not embody exactly the same problems. And thus we might say that it is Alexander who is begging the question because not only is his discussion of the relations of space and time really a discussion of the spatiality and temporality of things, but also even if we could demonstrate that space and time, or spatiality and temporality, are bound up together that would not show that space-time was *the* medium or *the* stuff of things—won't show that spatio-temporality was an account of being as such—that it was not just one particular form of being. To show that we are talking about "conditions of all existence" we should have to do something more than merely to show the close connections of one to the other.

Coming back to the firs point in Alexander's argument that things can't be in space alone, I should argue that all he can say is that things *aren't* in space alone and that he could never justify his contention that if they were considered in space alone they would have to be considered as lacking differentiation or as he puts it in objective terms if space were without time then it would be pure undifferentiated bulk. Alexander, I say, is not able to talk about pure space and what it would be without time any more than we can talk about pure subjects and what they would be without predicates. If there is any way of distinguishing the contributions or functions of space and time it can only be in terms of the proposition—it can only be as we distinguish functions of subject and predicate—but even so we can't literally speak of space giving something to time when space and time are not *things*.

Lecture 8   *(6th July 1949)*

Physical Space-Time continued—The Role of Repetition—Successiveness, Irreversibility and Transitiveness

Alexander is guilty of "abstraction". He doesn't use tests where he could use them. He also attempts impossible feat of strict proof—we could never get out of non-spatial non-temporal premises that things must be spatio-temporal. One can only give supporting arguments: anyone who denies the position cannot help implying it; also, space and time are linked together involved in the form of the proposition.

The second part of Alexander's argument is, as said, intended to show that space and time can be taken together as constituting a medium in which there will be both connection and distinction and Alexander expresses this position as one of the possibility of *repetition*—as he puts it that space can be repeated in time and time can be repeated in space or, as we could put it, that things could be in different places at the same time and things can be in the same place at different times so that the spaces and times or places and dates of things vary *independently* and together defin a situation, i.e., you could not infer from a thing's place what its time is or from a thing's time what its place is—the space and time co-ordinates are independent and they may be taken as formally specifying a situation, i.e., apart from the qualitative or material peculiarities—then you might roughly specify a situation as Here-Now X (X is a particular quality, say "humanity", the formal and material designations together specifying the whole situation.

> The formal and material designations are independent (*cf.* Hegel's phrase, the "indifference of space"). We would have to carry argument further to get to the proposition. We also have the complication that we specify places by qualities and qualities by spaces.

This independent variation and repetition does give what Alexander wants—the possibility of taking space and time together but, as previously indicated, that doesn't *prove* that space-time is a universal medium or is involved in being and on that side Alexander's argument is defective just because he doesn't take a propositional view, or conduct his argument in connection with the propositional form.

Now the third part of his initial argument is intended to show that space not merely can but *must* be bound up together and *must* be thought of in relation to one another, and, as suggested previously, it is by the togetherness and distinctness of space and time that we can fin empirically togetherness and distinctness in each of them, especially that we can fin spatial distinction and temporal connection, though abstractly considered space is pure togetherness and time is pure distinctness. Thus the argument is that the characters we attribute to empirical time can be understood only by taking space along with time, and similarly the characters we attribute to empirical space require for their understanding the taking of time along with space, and yet the two sets of characters are quite different from one another, space having three dimensions and time having three fundamental characters which cannot be described as dimensions, namely successiveness, irreversibility and transitiveness. Alexander wants to show not just in general that time requires space and space requires time but that there is an *essential* connection between the three dimensions of space and the three characters of time. He wants to establish a connection of mutual implication between *1*. the successiveness of time and one dimension of space; *2*. the irreversibility of time and two dimensions of space; *3*. the transitiveness of time and three dimensions of Space.

Now if we can say that successiveness is necessary and sufficien for one dimension, irreversibility for two, transitiveness for three, this would seem to imply that time also is 3-dimensional and space also has the three fundamental characters. In other words it would do away with the distinction between space and time and Alexander, I think, does not get over this difficult (if "mutual *implication*" is taken literally). Also some of his special arguments are not cogent—he gets the correlation of dimensions and characters wrong though it is still possible to get a correlation and to see in particular that irreversibility should be correlated with 3 dimensions.

> The exact extent of this correlation is very difficul to express. Has space 3 characters to be correlated with characters of time? Or is there only an *analogical* connection?

To say in general that it is only in space-time that space and time can have the characters we experience them as having would seem, as before, to be treating space and time as particular subjects or things and even if we say that it is only because things are at once in space and in time that we can distinguish dimensions and recognize successiveness, irreversibility and transitiveness *still* this must be said to be unintelligible on the ground that we asked to make the impossible supposition of these conditions *not* being fulfilled—o a situation that didn't exhibit 3 dimensions or successiveness, irreversibility and transitiveness.

> Space is in time, time is in space—does this get over the diffic lties? But the *dual* nature of medium is important.

Assuming for the sake of argument that Alexander's reasoning can be made intelligible, we may take the firs contention to be that there cannot be successiveness in time unless there is a distinct dimension, a possible direction in space, and similarly that there cannot be a direction in space unless there is successiveness in time or, putting it in terms of thinking, that in thinking of succession we are bound to think of 1 dimension and *vice-versa*. Here of course we have to remember that time is something spoken of as a dimension though we would still have to avoid identifying the time dimension with a spatial dimension and so it might be better to avoid the use of the term "dimension" for time and say that the sort of relation we fin among the terms in a temporal series is the sort of relation we fin among terms arranged in a single spatial dimension. But if we maintain the distinction between temporality and spatiality then all we have here is an analogy or resemblance between a temporal and a spatial arrangement of things and this would be no reason for saying that time is necessary for space or space for time—nor for arguing, let us say, that there couldn't be spatial irreversibility unless there were temporal irreversibility and vice-versa—a proceeding which would require us to think, as before, of the non-temporal and discover it to be non-spatial as well and similarly in the other direction, which it is assumed we cannot do. It would seem then that Alexander should say that merely as a matter of fact and without any question of necessity things exist in a medium—are at once spatial and temporal—though he might still be able to say that it is because of its spatiality that we can *describe* its temporality and vice-versa since clearly such descriptions could be absent even if the connections themselves could not be.

> *Cf.* questions about the categories, e.g., "nothing can exist without a cause".
> But could we *think* of it as being without a cause? Could this be done?

As I said, to say that the 3 dimensions of space and the 3 characters of time are necessary and sufficien for one another would imply that space is time and time is space, and what has to be said *instead* is that although time has the three characters, it has not 3 dimensions but one dimension, and further that while we distinguish spatial character and arrangements of things from temporal characters and arrangements of things the one casts light on the other, and that if things are events or motions then any set of things we like to take will exhibit both kinds of arrangement: the spatial and the temporal.

Considering then not separate units of space and time but motions, we can take Alexander as saying that the *recognition* of the successiveness characteristic of a motion is necessary and sufficien for the *recognition* of the motion as one dimensional—in other words that experience of time is necessary for the recognition of spatial direction and experience of space for the recognition of temporal duration. This can be connected with the problem of the definitio of a straight line—Russell criticizes the current definitio of it as "the shortest distance between two points" on the grounds that it is question begging[3]—that it has not been shown that there is *one* distance between two points that is shorter than all the other distances between them, and Alexander might be said to be

---

[3] Bertrand Russell, *Problems of Philosophy*, Chapter 3. London: Oxford University Press, 1912.

particularly trying to bring out that our assumption of the *uniqueness* of that relation—of a unique straightness or a unique distance between any two given points, is bound up with the assumption of the uniqueness of time—that time is so to speak the model of straightness that we recognize in spatial situations, or that there is some correlation between the shortest distance and the shortest temporal interval.

Lecture 9   *(12th July 1949)*

Physical Space-Time continued—Successiveness, Irreversibility and Transitiveness continued—Alexander and Point-Instants

There is at most *analogy* between temporal and spatial successiveness. There is no mutual *implication*. Is it only a matter of the *recognition* of succession being bound up with the recognition of a dimension of space? It may have to come back to this. Note that Kant represents time as the prototype of the straight line or direction. We could not recognize a motion without recognizing space and time, so to say that one can see that a straight motion requires time may not be very informative.
Russell's problem of the straight line. We definitely do have knowledge of *direction*—knowledge that Motion involves *uniqueness*—whatever we might take to be the connection between that uniqueness, and the uniqueness of time. In popular thinking there is a link between the shortest distance and shortest time in moving from one point to another.

The appeal to direct experience, to what we simply *fin* , is opposed to the attempt to base geometry or knowledge of space on logic (*cf.* my article "Empiricism"[4]). Take the case of the axiom of parallels—Euclid's 5th postulate—you fin   that it is asked how we can *prove* that two intersecting straight lines cannot both be parallel to a third straight line and it is contended that if this cannot be proved then we can have alternative geometries—the Euclidean in which the postulate is accepted, and other non-Euclidean ones in which it is not. But the essential point here is that we are dealing with a question of fact not with an arbitrary manipulation of symbols which would not be theory at all; and if we were asked how we know which of two contradictories is the fact it is quite possible to answer that we see it—we see that two intersecting straight lines cannot be parallel to a third straight line and to deny that we could see such a thing is to deny that we could be empirically aware of an E proposition (No As are Bs) and finall of a universal proposition. And without calling it proof, we can say that our recognition of the fact (i.e., the truth of Euclid's 5th Postulate) is bound up with the recognition of direction and difference of direction—that

---

[4]"Empiricism", *A.J.P.P.*, 5(4) December 1927: 241-54. Reprinted in *Studies*.

is, in knowing that a line has a certain direction we also know that other lines have the *same* direction and others again have a different direction, i.e., we recognize intersection and we recognize being parallel and so we can see that to deny the postulate is to say that two directions are at once the same and different and whether this is proof or not, at least it is empirical and anything at all that can be called proof must be empirical—that is it must start from premises which we simply fin to be the case.

So in regard to spatial and temporal successiveness it can be said that we *fin* them together, in other words we see that they are together and this empirical procedure is opposed to starting with Absolute space and Absolute time—the point being that even in professing to think of pure space (space without time) we should already be thinking of it as within the space-time system or in terms of a logic of events. And thus when we bring back Alexander to an empirical procedure—to what on his own view must be an empirical procedure—what "must be" must be what we find—the we have to reject his method of abstraction as rationalist. Now it would be in similar terms—in terms of a logic of events, in terms of what is involved in the being and the knowing of motion—or simply in terms of what we fin in motions—that any connection there may be between the other characters of time and a 2nd and 3rd dimension of time can be upheld and here, as I said, there is a correlation but not the way that Alexander puts it.

Alexander:

Time	*Space*
successiveness	1st dimension
irreversibility	2nd dimension
transitiveness	3rd dimension

Anderson:

Time	*Space*
successiveness	1st dimension
transitiveness	2nd dimension
irreversibility	3rd dimension

Alexander, then, fails to establish the other connections and in particular he fails to argue to a three-dimensional space, for he has to show not merely that an additional dimension is introduced when we recognize a succession as irreversible and that this is also done when we recognize a succession as transitive *but* that these additional dimensions are distinct from one another, i.e., not that each adds a dimension to a firs dimension, but that one does so and the other adds a dimension to a two dimensional system. This latter procedure is not adopted by Alexander—his only argument to show that the dimensions implied by transitiveness and irreversibility respectively are independent of one another is that irreversibility and transitiveness ("betweenness" as he sometimes calls it) have been proved to be distinct and therefore the dimensions they imply must be distinct. But first his argument to prove that the two characters as he define them are distinct is not a sound one, and second, even if it had been sound, he should treat one of them as adding a dimension to 2 dimensions and this he does not do.

One source of difficult in his own argument is that it proceeds in terms of what he calls point-instants and we can object to this, first that the use of the hyphenated term implies that intimate relationship between space and time which it is the object of the argument to establish; and, second, that it involves the assumption of *units*—of the point as the ultimate constituent of an extension and the instant as the ultimate constituent of a duration—as against the view that all constituents of an extension are extensions and of a duration durations, and that there is no such elementary unit as the point, the instant or the point-instant—though this is not saying that there are not points or instants.

Now the conception of point-instants is useful to Alexander because it enables him to treat the units or elements of motion sometimes as spatial and sometimes as temporal and by ambiguity to reach results which don't really follow from his data. Thus in his argument regarding "betweenness"[5] he uses the illustration of *pendular* motion to show that transitiveness and irreversibility are independent. He takes pendular motion to exemplify irreversibility without transitiveness but the series he is describing as irreversible but not transitive cannot be the series of instants in the motion in question (i.e., cannot be the temporal series) since there would then be no point in the pendular illustration and on his own showing this series would be irreversible and transitive characters of time. Then it is either the series of points in the path of the pendulum, or the series of point-instants, i.e., each point that the motion goes through in conjunction with the time which it goes through it—something having

---

[5] *STD*, Volume 1, pp.54–55.

both spatial and temporal coordinates. Now if we take the points alone then transitiveness as Alexander understands it does *not* hold but equally irreversibility does not hold. The fact is that Alexander has define transitiveness so as to *include* irreversibility—the formula being not merely "if A is before B, and B is before C, then A is before C" but also that this C is *not* before A which brings in irreversibility. And the reason why the series of points does *not* exhibit transitiveness in *this* sense is simply that it does not exhibit irreversibility, and so Alexander has not got an illustration of irreversibility without transitiveness.

But his procedure is, having proved the absence of *his* transitiveness (irreversible transitiveness) by reference to the points, to shift his ground and prove the presence of irreversibility by reference to the instants, i.e., to the *temporal* character of the point-instants, when in fact if we do introduce the temporal co-ordinate we have a series which is not merely irreversible but also transitive, even in Alexander's sense.

Summing up, then, Alexander relies on the instances to assert the irreversibility of the series and he relies on the points—on the fact that pendular motion passes through the same points many times—to deny the transitiveness of the series in the special sense of asymmetrical or irreversible (same thing: reversible equals symmetrical) transitiveness which really amounts to denying the irreversibility of the series. And it is just by confusedly including irreversibility in transitiveness that Alexander makes transitiveness appear the more advanced or complicated character whereas if we take transitiveness in the natural way meaning merely that "if A has r to B, and B has r to C, then A has r to C" without any indication whether C has it to A or not than pendular motion with respect to the point, which recurs, gives us an illustration not of a series which is irreversible without being transitive but of a series which is transitive without being irreversible, and of course, with respect to the instants, or to the point-instants with reference to their time component, it gives a series which is both irreversible and transitive though here it is time that is relevant and the reference to the pendulum is irrelevant.

Lecture 10   *(13th July 1949)*
Physical Space-Time continued—The Example of Pendular Motion

In pendular motion as far as the points are concerned, we have transitiveness without irreversibility. A is before B and B before C, ∴

A is before C. But that doesn't hinder C being before A (on the back swing).[6]

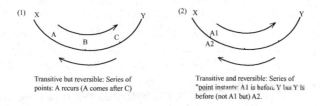

(1) Transitive but reversible: Series of points: A recurs (A comes after C)

(2) Transitive and reversible: Series of "point instants: A1 is before Y but Y is before (not A1 but) A2.

Figure 2.

The series of points is transitive but not irreversible. The only way of denying transitiveness in this sense, as Alexander does, is to introduce irreversibility into the conception of transitiveness so that what we are really denying on the side of points is irreversibility and not transitiveness in the ordinary sense.

Equality: Transitiveness and reversibility

Ancestor of: Transitiveness and irreversibility

If we take the temporal co-ordinate into account so that there is no question of recurrence, i.e., if points in the swing of the pendulum one way are distinguished from points of the swing the other way because they are passed through at different times, then we get a relation no longer transitive and reversible but transitive and irreversible—the irreversibility of time itself. When A_1 is before Y, Y is not before A_1 but is before A_2—a different member of the series. The relation in both cases you could call "coming earlier in the series than" and then you have transitiveness but not irreversibility of the series of *points* in question, and transitivity and irreversibility if it is the series of *instants* or *point-instants* so that Alexander has failed to exhibit a series which is irreversible but not transitive.

Coming then to the argument as he should have presented it—to the sort of correspondence we *can* get—to what we may call, as in the case of temporal successiveness and spatial direction, the connected characters of any motion, we fin as I said:

---

[6]This diagram was adapted from Anderson's own notes along with the explanatory note differs from the student notes.

First, transitiveness connected with two dimensions, because transitiveness involves a difference of relation which can be connected with a difference of direction, i.e., if ArB and BrC then we are distinguishing two directions of relation from B, namely, having something to which it is r and having something which is r to it,—having in Russell's terms a relation and a converse of that relation (BrA), so that B has two distinct types of relation, or has two directions of relation, in a series in which each term has the relation r to the next term, and that is quite irrespective of whether the relation is irreversible or not, because even if r were reversible so that when ArB also BrA then these are still two different facts, in other words it is one thing to speak of what B has the relation r to and another to speak of what has the relation r to B, even if these two classes coincide, or, in Russell's terms, even if the domain and the converse domain of the relation are co-extensive. (*cf. my article* "The Problem of Causality".[7]) Then in recognizing that B is before certain things, and has certain things before it, we are recognizing a difference of direction from B, even if "before" should be a reversible relation (though, of course, it isn't).

Now what corresponds to this on the spatial side—what we mean spatially by a difference of direction is an *angle* and an angle is the mark of a 2-dimensional system, or is necessary and sufficien for two spatial dimensions, and thus the notion of difference of direction is fundamental alike to the transitiveness of time and to what might be called the two-dimensionality of space. Here again we might have to say that just as to be able to *know* successiveness is to be able to know one dimension so to be able to know transitiveness is to be able to know two dimensions, or just as because a motion has temporal succession so it can be found to have direction, so because it has temporal transitiveness it can be found to have difference of direction. (Of course all the relations could be reversed—it is a question of necessity and sufficien y.)

But I am not quite satisfie with the formulation in terms of knowledge.

Note that recognition of difference of direction doesn't imply departure from the strait or straightness on the part of the motion or series we are considering, otherwise it would be difficul or impossible to assign a meaning to temporal difference of direction. But if we take the two sets of relation possessed by a point B in a straight line, then:

---

[7]"The Problem of Causality", *A.J.P.P.*, 16(2) August 1938: 127-42. Reprinted in *Studies*.

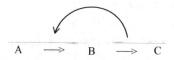

$$A \longrightarrow B \longrightarrow C$$

Figure 3.

in order to know that the relation of B to A differs from the relation of B to C and similarly with any pair of points, that, as we put it, are in opposite directions from B, we have to bring in the notion of angle or turning even if it is in the form of a straight angle, or angle of 180°, and since there is no actual turning in time, this might be held to support Alexander's view that in order to understand difference of direction in time—the difference between having predecessors and having successors—we have to be acquainted with space in which actual turning is possible. That is motion can actually diverge or deviate in space while it can't do so in time, and it might also be said on the side of space that we can't grasp the meaning of a strait angle if we didn't have acquaintance with angles or turnings of less than 180°—with crossings or with simple divergences.

Second, now as against Alexander's procedure of arguing in each case from one dimension to show that irreversibility and transitiveness respectively add another dimension, we have to argue from the two-dimensional system we have arrived at—from the situation determined by an angle or turning which we have correlated with transitiveness. And irreversibility comes in the notion not simply of a difference of direction or turning but of an *absolute* difference of direction—an unambiguous or fi ed difference of direction—the sort of difference we recognize in time between before and after. The position would had been logically the same if we have used the illustration: if A is after B and B after C, then A is after C, instead of using the relation *before*. But of course in our theory of time we can't always substitute one of these relations for the other,—we have to recognize that in whatever way *before* resembles *after*, there is still an absolute difference between them—that the statement A is after B and A is before B are not merely distinct but incompatible, and this absolute direction of time is connected with an absolute direction of turning—with what we may call by analogy *spatial irreversibility* which is the mark of a three-dimensional system.

Lecture 11   *(19th July 1949)*

Physical Space-Time continued—The Example of the Screw

In recognizing the absolute difference of temporal direction we are brought to consider an absolute difference in direction of turning—an absolute difference between a positive and a negative turning and speaking geometrically or spatially we fin this difference to be necessary and sufficien for three dimensions. As we may put it "after" is the negative of before in the same way that counter-clockwise is the negative of clockwise but to make the distinction between those two directions of turning we require three dimensions.

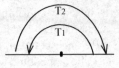

Figure 4.

T_1 can be contrasted with a turning in the opposite direction T_2, T_2 being clockwise and T_1 counter-clockwise, but in order to say that, we can't take this by itself but as regarded or looked at from this side because if looked at from the other side it would be T_1 clockwise and T_2 counter-clockwise, in other words in considering an absolute difference in turning we are considering the situation in three dimensions—we are considering a three dimensional relation—a relation which is referred to by some mathematicians as a "screw" because it is illustrated in the use of a screw, the point being that there is an absolute difference between a right-handed and a left-handed screw such that if we turn the firs to the right (clock-wise) the point goes in, and if to the left (anti-clockwise) the point comes out and the opposite is the case with a left-handed screw. This difference between two types of screw corresponds to the absolute difference of direction in turning and is something that can be grasped only three-dimensionally and, of course, in its irreversibility it corresponds to the absolute difference between before and in measuring of movement—resolution along three axes if given the positive directions of two axes (X,Y) then if you fi upon say Z1 as the positive direction then by no sort of manipulation could you get these three directions to coincide with the three directions constituted by the same positive directions of X and Y as before and the inward

Figure 5.

direction of the Z axis as positive (Z_1). Taking then a relationship of that kind that relation between the three positive directions is again called a screw, and is absolutely different from and couldn't be translated into the other relationship (XYZ_2)

You get the same sort of relationship in the human body, i.e., it would be only arbitrarily that we could decide which were the three positive directions but we get three absolute differences of direction as between left and right, head and feet, front and back respectively, and if (say) we take right, top and front positive, you were to change one of them (translate the body so that one of them becomes different from what it was before, e.g., stood upon head) you would change one other, i.e., we could have a change in two while one remained constant, but couldn't have a change in all three, e.g., if you have the reversal of head and feet while front and back remain the same then right and left would also have been altered. There again we have a type of interrelation which permits of certain alterations or translations but not of others, and the same sort of point is made by Kant (in one of his early works[8]) in relation to the two human hands, namely that by no sort of translation, movement through space, can the left hand come to occupy the precise spot that has been occupied by the right hand, or come to occupy what we might call the space occupied by the mirror image of the left hand. You could, assuming the two hands to be otherwise similar and neglecting any roughnesses, unevenness etc.—get a left-hand glove to fit to occupy space previously occupied by a right hand glove merely by turning it inside out, but that is something you cannot do when the question is one not merely of surfaces but of solids as in the case of the hands.

Cf. H. G. Wells' "Plattner",[9] where a man's organs are reversed. This is taken to mean he has been beyond three dimensions—impossible in three dimensions. But the account (as always) proceeds in three dimensional terms only.

[8] Immanuel Kant, "On the First Ground of the Distinction of Regions in Space", 1768.
[9] H. G. Wells, *The Plattner Story and Others*, London: Ernest Benn, 1927, pp. 5-28.

This spatial irreversibility which is similar to temporal irreversibility can be expressed by saying that you cannot transpose two solids with a different screw, though you could transpose two surfaces—i.e., two similar triangles turned in opposite ways—then you could assume one of them turned round and imposed on the other, namely, because there is a third dimension, because there is space of the plane in which the turning round could be considered to take place and that is why we don't have irreversibility in two dimensions or correlated with two dimensions.

But incidentally, this argument, this assertion of a connection between irreversibility and three dimensions is an argument against recognition of more than three dimensions of space, i.e., just because if there were more than three dimensions then the screws wouldn't be irreversible, there would be the same possibility of reversal as there is in two dimensions of space because of the third, so that there is no question of a fourth dimension or any higher number.

> There are recent mathematical doctrines of more than three dimensions, where time and space are taken to be reversible. I don't mean to say that multi-dimensional theories don't mean anything at all. We can have functions of two variables in two dimensions—three variables in three dimensions—function of four, f ve, variables etc. are taken to rest on four, f ve dimensions, but we are no longer talking about space—the spatial propositions with which we began are mere illustrations.

As I said, if the argument showed that a succession implied and is implied by one dimension, transitive succession by two dimensions and irreversible transitive succession by three dimension then it would be abolishing the distinction between space and time—obscuring the point that Alexander also made that they vary independently ("Repetition") and the argument, that is the correlation argument might be taken to show that the spatial and temporal characters respectively can only be grasped together, i.e., that in grasping the temporal character of a motion—particularly the three Alexander specifies—w are also grasping its spatial characters—those that have been correlated with the temporal characters—direction, difference of direction, and absolute difference of direction or difference of direction of turning.

We should still have to try to avoid the method of abstraction—avoid saying, e.g., that something is enabled by its temporal successiveness to have some other character since this would require us to consider things which didn't have temporal successiveness and that, it is assumed, we are unable to do.

Nb. This leaves the problem in an unsatisfactory state. There is a real similarity between the three characters—is there anything more? It is not clear what further correlation there is.

We can raise the question whether to speak of spatial irreversibility isn't equivalent to speaking of spatial and temporal quality, using quality in the broad sense of being of such and such a character or kind—that is, whether spatial irreversibility doesn't just mean spatiality, mean what is peculiar about space or being spatial, and similarly with time. The position may be compared to Kemp Smith's reference to the "intractability" of qualities (*Prolegomena to an Idealist Theory of Knowledge*[10]) particularly what he refers to as "secondary" qualities. This intractability meaning simply that they can't be reduced to anything else, cannot be translated into one another, cannot be shown to be built up or constituted in such and such a way, in other words, cannot be "rationalized"; and the important point about spatial irreversibility in turn is just the "intractability"—is just the limit of the translations things *qua* spatial can undergo (similarly with time) which is a position which is opposed to Cartesianism as Smith also presents it—opposed to the recognition of the rationality or "transparency" which Descartes attributes to space, and to the spatial or primary qualities—in other words supports an empirical as against a rationalist view of Space and Time.

Lecture 12   *(20th July 1949)*

Physical Space-Time continued—Three Dimensions of Space and Time—Alexander's Departure from Empiricism

The relations of the 3 characters of time and the 3 dimensions of space. Do they help us to know the correlated characters? Or do they help us to know the correlated characters? Or help us to give a precise account of the correlated character? It is not a question of implication, but there is implication among spatial propositions (just as in geometrical propositions generally); *cf.* angle and two dimensions.

This discussion can be connected with Kant's argument in the Second Analogy in which he connects temporal irreversibility with what we may call material irreversibility or intractability—connects, i.e., the knowledge of one with the knowledge of the other, namely knowledge of a certain order (an irreversible order) in the phases of a process with knowledge of temporal order as such, though Kant puts the point in the opposite way to what we might expect and particularly what we

---

[10]Norman Kemp Smith, *Prolegomena to an Idealist Theory of Knowledge*, London: Macmillan, 1924.

might associate with Alexander's position, namely that recognition of material irreversibility is a condition of the recognition of temporal irreversibility—that to have the notion of "before" we have to recognize that A must come before B or that in recognizing such a necessary order of succession of phenomena (as Kant would put it) that is for him in recognizing causality—that we recognize temporal order at all.

Of course even if we did accept Kant's position here we would have to amplify it because there is no necessary order between an abstractly considered phenomenon A and an abstractly considered phenomenon B because anything that could be earlier than another thing could also be later than it if we simply consider any time and any plane; and what Kant should say is that we recognize that a phase A must come before a phase B in a particular process of the kind C.

> *Cf.* Kant's example of the boat floatin down stream. There is no absolute necessity connecting this with later time (the boat could be propelled upstream etc.) and further distance—only as an aspect of whole phenomenon of "floatin downstream" is there any necessity.[11]

In other words, the recognition of irreversibility is dependent on, or has to be taken in connection with, the recognition of a certain kind or quality that is of what we were calling qualitative intractability. It could be argued at the same time that as part of the recognition of any qualitative intractability or irreducibility we have to recognize temporal irreversibility—we have to observe that to be a certain kind of motion or process is to be unable to do certain kinds of things or to have certain states in a particular order—to be unable to be in the state A before being in the state B so that anything that was A before being B or did A before doing B would not be C (be processes of a general kind C), e.g., that a screw which did certain things in a certain order cannot be a right-handed screw.

Referring then back to the general position, I would say we do fin an essential connection between certain spatial characteristics, as I said, between the absolute direction of turning and three dimensions; we cannot fin the same connections between spatial irreversibility and temporal irreversibility, but we fin that the recognition of the one facilitates recognition of the other, and in the same way recognition of temporal irreversibility is linked with the recognition of intractability or qualitative distinctness—this point being connected with the general

---

[11] Kant, *Critique of Pure Reason, op. cit.*. "Second Analogy: Principle of Succession in Time, in accordance with the Law of Causality" pp. 218-33.

treatment of qualities as activities—if we say that to have a certain quality is to be going on in a certain way, then that will include going on in certain temporal orders or having specifi phases—and I would say there was the same sort of linking with spatial irreversibility—that there would be certain definit spatial orders or arrangements involved in the possession of a specifi quality that, e.g., taking the distinction in the human body between right and left we fin that distinction to be involved in the recognition of certain types of human activity (*cf.* playing the piano).

These considerations—these suggested connections between qualities and space and time indicate again the importance of an empirical treatment of space and time—as said before, space in particular is not rational or transparent, i.e., isn't something in which we could see simultaneously all the characters including all the reasons for these characters, but it is something in which we have to accept certain characters and certain conjunctions of characters as brute fact.

But, allowing the irreducibility of space to simple or self-explanatory notions we must also allow the irreducibility of qualities to space or to space-time—to spatio-temporal characters, and this again emphasises emphasizes the departure from empiricism in Alexander's treatment of space and time as the stuff of which things are made—that being a reductive doctrine opposed to intractability and irreversibility. One of the major forms of reduction in modern philosophy and science is the reduction or qualities to the so-called primary qualities—the contention that when we really speak of colour, for example all that confronts us is vibration at such and such a rate—that such vibration is the reality of colour and the empirical theory—the doctrine of intractability—involves a rejection of such a quantitative treatment of things—a treatment which implies universal transformability or exchangeability of equal quantities. It is, of course to be remembered here that even in space—even in the so-called primary qualities—we still don't fin any universal transformability (*cf.* the screw) but certainly the reduction of everything to the primary qualities would involve allowing of more transformability than there actually is. Regarding the reductive view then, we have to assert that in whatever way red is connected with a certain rate of vibration (obvious connection: red is vibrating at a certain rate) the connection doesn't *reduce* red to the primary character, the quality red remains in all its peculiarity.

Alexander, as a realist, would of course want to say that the so-called secondary qualities are objectively independent but he has confused his position, he has left open the way to the reductionists by his doctrine of space-time as "stuff". (Similarly his concessions to Cartesianism on the side of knowledge have confused his empirical and realist position hence as I have indicated in "The Non-existence of Consciousness"[12] confused his account of mind and knowledge.)

Rejecting then a theory of rationality or reduction—recognizing the irreducible diversity of qualities—we also recognize the irreducible distinction between space and time, so that when we set spatial irreversibility along side temporal irreversibility we are really bringing out the difference rather than the similarity between space and time—that is, seeing that each has its own intractability or peculiar character, and though we might say that knowledge of the one could facilitate knowledge of the other (not forgetting the difficult of saying this if all knowledge is of space and time) we certainly cannot say that knowledge of the one *gives* knowledge of the other, that we can in any manner deduce space from time, and time from space—deduce what is peculiar to time from what is peculiar to space, or, as Alexander seems to have been attempting in the argument we have been considering, deduce what is peculiar to space from what is peculiar to time. This position might again be called a reductive one,—we might object to it on the same grounds as we should object to the attempt to deduce qualities (say red) from space and time, so that here again we could say that Alexander's procedure confuses what is empirical in his position—namely the absolute distinction between space and time, a distinction we have to recognize even if, or all the more, because we take spatial and temporal conditions (coordinates) together in giving any account of motions or of states of affairs.

---

[12]"The Non-Existence of Consciousness: *Space Time and Deity* by Samuel Alexander", *A.J.P.P.*, 7(1) March 1929: 68-73. Reprinted in *Studies*.

3
Transition to the Categories

Lecture 13   (26th July 1949)
Mathematical Space-Time—Relations in Space-Time

Alexander's doctrine of mental space-time is unimportant, it is a departure from his original position ("enjoyment" etc.). He should only be concerned to argue that *the mental is spatial.*

How would this be demonstrated? It involves interesting material. The general line of argument would be that the mental would have to be propositional, and therefore spatio-temporal.

The correlation of dimensions and the characters of space and time:

1.   One dimension—successiveness, i.e., any relation suggests interval and connection;

2.   Two dimensions—transitiveness, i.e., to get the correlation a temporal relation must hold between any 2 terms of the series (*cf.* turning) (hence time can be treated as a dimension);

3.   Three dimensions—irreversibility—no question of implication (then time would be 3 dimensional) but it is suggested that by reference to time alone one couldn't recognise temporal irreversibility.

In chapters V and VI of Book I, Alexander is dealing with mathematical space-time and with relations in space-time and while he makes a number of sound points in these discussions he also seems to me to show some of the weaknesses of his position—once more. There is his failure to take a propositional view—what we might call his realism in the sense of an emphasis on "*res*" or things. My argument has been that a theory of space-time and the categories must be a theory of the *form* of the proposition, of what is involved in a proposition (allowing some difficult   about the word "involve") and not of the material or term, of a proposition—in other words we must take the line that the proposition is prior to the term, and not the term to the proposition—it must be a situational theory, a theory that there is nothing less than a situation and, we might say, nothing more than a situation, which would involve us in saying that in recognizing a situation at all, we are recognizing space-time and the categories, though we are able to make our theory of them more precise as we proceed. From this point of view, while we can say that terms or things are in situations we have also to recognize that they are situations and this does away with the difficult   of how terms can enter into situations, a difficult   that would be insoluble if we started with non-situational terms, with "natures" or essences as we may put it, and then tried to fin how they could enter into situations. That is the sort of position characteristic of rationalism or Idealism and it is in these terms that Bradley has his difficultie or is able to say that thought must fall into contradictions when it tries to give an account of relations. Bradley's treatment of space and time in particular, namely that they must and cannot be relations between terms, depends on his not recognizing that the things themselves are spatial and temporal to begin with.

If we start, then, with essences or what I have sometimes called internality, we can give no account of externality. But the point is that there is already externality—there is a distinction among parts and tendencies in any possible term we might propose to begin with—which means that Bradley's problem, granted that it would be a problem, is not a real one.

I have pointed out some of the substantialist features in Alexander's theory—some of the ways he takes space and time as substances, or space-time as the substance of things, and while we may think him right in attacking the view that space and time are relations—that is, fall between things that are not themselves spatio-temporal—while we can agree with him that spatio-temporality in some way characterizes things and the relations between them (a point on which he is influence by James in his *Principles of Psychology*[1]) we can equally say that space and time are not to be characterized as things, neither as material from which other things are made, nor as containers within which other things fall, because then we should not only have the problem of what space and time themselves were contained in or, failing that, of the division of reality into containers and contained, but also the problem of the relation between these universal containers or original materials and the things they contained or the things that were made from them. And, as I said, we don't have a logic, we don't have a coherent philosophical position, unless it applies equally to everything—things, qualities, relations, whatever we may call them, which we can recognize.

In fact, then, we must reject equally the view of space and time as relations and the view of them as things and instead of taking them as constituting a universal container or a whole of which all other things are parts (as when Alexander speaks of "portions of space-time") we

---

[1] William James, *Principles of Psychology*, London: Macmillan, 1890.

must take space and time and particularly their infinit as implying that there is no universal container, no totality, no thing which embraces all other things. Now I have argued in connection with Heraclitus and also with Zeno that the two concepts of infinit divisibility and infinit extensibility go together;[2] as I put it, all things are systems of constituents and constituents of wider systems and it is no more true that there are ultimate constituents than there is an all-embracing system, and it is interesting here to notice that Alexander does accept ultimate constituents of space and time namely points and instants—that is, he is looking for the "*res*" of which space and time are composed and he gets into very serious confusions in his account of these things (confusions which he shares with people like Russell and Whitehead but they of course do not take a spatio-temporal view of things in general, they are quite openly rationalistic).

Now the notion of a point as an ideal limit of division (or alternatively of the shrinking of a solid) is untenable because to think about division and even to think about solids *we have already to recognize points*.

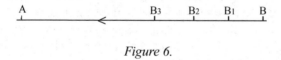

Figure 6.

Cf. The doctrine of the point as a "shrinking line".

The limit of the series of lengths is supposed to be a point. The absurdity of the position appears when we see that in order to have a line, whether it shrinks or not, we must have terminal points, and if we didn't take so simple example—if we started from a solid we would have to admit that the conception of a solid includes the conception of the surface—the region of contact or division between solids and this, even if it doesn't include, at least easily leads on to the conception of the line (the intersection of surfaces) and so to the intersection of line (the point). Or, taking it in on more Alexandrian lines in terms of motion we can see that in the conception of the motion of a solid there is the concept of the direction of motion, i.e., a line and of points in the solid, e.g., the case of the centre of gravity moving along that line, so that we neither can nor need to arrive at the point or instant as a limit of shrinkage or

---

[2] The most extensive discussions of Heraclitus and Zeno in the publicly available lecture notes appear in the 1927 and 1928 lectures on Greek Philosophy, the lectures on Zeno (n.d.) and the 1929 Lectures on Greek Philosophy typed by Frank Fowler (all available at the John Anderson web site http://setis.library.usyd.edu.au/anderson/).

division—it is part of what we recognize when we recognize solids and their relations—in recognising concrete processes in the firs instance.[3]

These are some of the arguments by which we can reject these forms (or manifestations) of his substantialism and the same, of course, will apply to the categories. As I said before, Alexander, from his substantialist point of view, treats the categories as predicates, in other words, treats them as belonging not to the form but to the material of the proposition, which would mean that they weren't part of logic (of its subject matter) but the subject of some particular enquiry and of course in that case we can't treat them as pervasive—to use Alexander's expression, they would have real opposites, there would be places from which they were absent as well as places where they were present. Now it might seem a more promising line to treat the categories as relations instead of predicates, e.g., causality (recognized as a category by Kant and Alexander) does seem to be a relation. But there is the same general objection to the treatment of the categories as relations as to the treatment of space and time as relations, which is that it depends on a doctrine of "*res*"—of ultimate things between which they, as relations, hold; whereas the categories must be of things just as much as between them—we can't treat them consistently as between things—that is, we have, to treat the terms as propositional and not just in propositions—as themselves situations, and not just in situations—and the same will apply to space-time and the categories.

Lecture 14   *(27th July 1949)*

Mind as Spatial—Categories Viewed as Predicates

If the categories are relations then they hold between units which are not subject to the categories (therefore the relations wouldn't be categorical). *Cf.* the terms of the proposition.

The view of modern philosophy that mind is not spatial goes with a doctrine of internality—that is of the internality of all its characters and relations to mind, so that mind is the supreme *unit*—it is that to which the notion of individuality is above all attached (*cf.* Leibniz especially). And then you get various forced solutions of the problem of externality of the fact that there are, e.g., many minds—and here you get mystical theories of identificatio of minds as members of one another—a position which Russell says would have been the consistent one for Berkeley to adopt

---

[3] [DMA] Thus, Anderson recognises points along with line and surfaces (and would reject the view that these lines and surfaces are *made up* of points). Notice that because Anderson accepts the mathematical continuity of space and time there could be no *next* points.

and which is certainly the Hegelian doctrine (more exactly, that what we call an individual is a manifestation of the Absolute, so that in some manner minds are manifestations of one another) and of course the doctrine of the Absolute is that for which internality is the supreme principle.

Alexander refers to space-time as an infinit given whole, though he goes back on that formulation in Chapter X, denying that any of the categories (of which he takes whole and part to be one) apply to space and time as such; but in spite of this retraction it is impossible for him with his substantialism to adopt anything other than a totalistic line—a belief in space-time as the totality or whole which, as I said, is really opposed to the recognition of this infinity— recognition which could be roughly put in the form "All wholes are parts".

Now I have argued that to say that things exist in space and time is to say that they exist in propositional form—an assertion which requires the distinction between the functions of a subject and predicate which is overlooked or denied by idealists like Bosanquet for whom symmetry is the mark of the ultimately real, and for whom therefore the solution of a problem makes the original statement of it meaningless (*cf.* my review of "Scepticism and Construction", and my article "'Universals' and Occurrences"[4]) and also by the Cambridge thinkers who follow Keynes (or follow one of the suggestions of Keynes) in taking the proposition to be an assertion of existence or non-existence.[5]

I have put the function of the subject particularly in spatial terms, suggesting that the subject locates the predicate—that without reference to space we couldn't distinguish subject and predicate—and that would apply to mind of course—that any statement of a mental process would be unintelligible unless it asserted that something was going on somewhere; and though we seem to be involved in paradoxes when we say that whatever locates is located and *vice versa*—in other words no term gives an absolute location, the position is that since in any proposition we distinguish something that locates from something that is located and thus location or spatiality is an ingredient in whatever we take to be the case and it is this and not the ability to fi a place once and for all that we mean by referring to the absoluteness of space and we could have a similar argument about time, and again about

---

[4] John Anderson, "Scepticism and Construction, by Charles A. Campbell", *A.J.P.P.* 13(2) June 1935: 151-156; "'Universals' and Occurrences", *A.J.P.P.* 7(2) June 1929: 138-145. Reprinted in *Studies*.
[5] J. N. Keynes, *Studies and Exercises in Formal Logic*, London: Macmillan, 1894. Keynes offers for discussion "various suppositions concerning the existential import of categorical propositions", suppositions "not intended to be exhaustive", page 186.

the categories—which, as I said, could be called pervasive (though not pervasive predicates) only if they are involved in being propositional, apart from the peculiarities—the material—of any given proposition. Alexander's confusion, again, is connected with his substantialism—that is, with his belief that the materials—the empirical qualities—are made of space and time—a view which would be opposed to any distinction between the categorical and the empirical because there could be no special features of special situations.

> On Alexander's view qualities hover above, or stand above, things like Plato's forms, or G. E. Moore's good.[6]

On a substantialist view of space and time the categories come to be regarded as predicates, but this involves us in difficultie that can't be got over. This is the same weakness as in the *Sophist*—the doctrine of the higher kinds being a treatment of the categories as pervasive characters and indicates the incompleteness of Plato's emancipation from the theory of forms—emancipation from belief in the unhistorical with consequent insoluble problems of relating it to the historical.

Considering what is meant by historical here (not in the social sense, but in more general logical sense) we can see that in order to treat things historically we have to have some view of what history itself is and that this is something that doesn't itself have a history, a point indicated in the reference of Heraclitus to the *eternity* of his word or doctrine, even though it is a doctrine of universal flux It has to be possible to make exactly the same type of question about any material at any period. And it is here we get the distinction between Logic and Science—you have scientists or people interested in science maintaining, e.g., that our enquiry into the question of causality is on the same footing as our enquiries into any particular fact or connection among things. That is to say, we get verification of it—that we get various examples of it which bear out the hypothesis of universal causality and after a period of such verification we then come to accept it or at least to accept it as a tentative hypothesis, to conduct our further enquiries in terms of it—the success of such enquiries further strengthening our belief. Now the point is that what belongs to experience as such is not something specificall supported by particular experiences—unless there is a causal principle—a principle to the effect that things occur when and only when certain conditions exist—the conjunctions that occur in particular

---

[6]G. E. Moore, *Principia Ethica*, Cambridge: Cambridge University Press, 1903.

experience are no evidence at all. And only if there is a causal principle will the presence of Y when X occurs be of any evidential value—that is it could confir the suggestion that X is the cause of Y (if we know that Y *has* a cause) it could not confir the suggestion that Y has a cause if *that* were under examination. As far as causality can be argued for, it has to be argued for in this way—as involved in the possibility of existence, and the so-called experimental evidence of science is quite beside the point, or, more particularly, the so-called evidence assumes, is meaningless without what it is supposed to support.

Lecture 15   *(2nd August 1949)*

Can There Be a Theory of Categories?—Universals and Particulars—Kant and Aristotle on Categories and the Proposition

Logic—gives us nature of a fact; Science—gives us particular facts.

To profess to prove in the ordinary (scientific way that (say) universal causality holds is to beg the question, to advance arguments which: (i) are of a forced character; (ii) are unintelligible without prior acceptance of a causal principle.

This doesn't imply a clearly separated and distinguished recognition of causality, but only that there will be some recognition of causality in any recognition at all.

If we distinguish logical questions from scientifi questions, questions of categories, e.g., from questions of predicates, we are faced with the problem how there can be a theory of categories—how there can be an issue concerning this or that category, particularly whether or not it is a category—which would mean whether or not any question concerning it belonged to logic or science.

We could maintain that Alexander's view that categories are peculiarly predicates and are not subjects indicates a position similar to that which Moore adopts regarding "good", a position which I argue in "The Meaning of Good",[7] depends on an ambiguity, because if good were quite unambiguously a predicate—a quality of things—then it could be a subject just like any other term. The confusion need not in Alexander's case be between a qualitative or ordinary predicate and a relation, but at least we might say that the bringing out of a certain relational character in the categories helps towards clearing up the difficulties Firstly, if "X is a cause" were an issue in the ordinary way, we would firstl have to be able to contrast X with other things that are not causes (which, of course, would be to deny that causality is a category) and secondly we would have to be able to say "a cause is of the kind X" or "some

---

[7]"The Meaning of Good", *A.J.P.P.* 20(2) September 1942: 111-140. Reprinted in *Studies*.

causes are X" which would suggest that we could locate something by means of the term "cause" and then go to it and see whether it is an X or not, and similarly if we took particularity as a category, we should have to say that there is a class of particulars—that there are various thing that we recognize by the category particularity and that going to such a thing we could fin it had further characters, A, B and C. Now, on Alexander's own showing, "X is a cause" or "X is a particular" isn't an issue, but "X is a cause of Y" or "X is a particular Z" (is an example of Z) is an issue so that the categories might then signify the distinct types of issues that can be raised (which, I think, is the Aristotelian position—the doctrine of the categories as *predicaments*). At any rate, we can certainly have a real issue of the form "Is X a cause of Y?" or "Is X a particular of Z?" but we are still faced with the fact that some people deny that anything whatever has a cause (namely the doctrine of epiphenomenalism)—who postulate things supposed to be mere effects without any power of causality, of having further effects—and on such a view "being a cause" would mean having some positive or distinctive character (as Berkeley, for example, holds that all causes are minds) and again there are those who hold that not all things are caused, that certain things are free or spontaneous in the sense that they are not led up to or conditioned by anything distinct from themselves, so that on this view there would be something peculiar on the one hand in what can be called an effect, and on the other, in what cannot be an effect. Then again, you certainly have doctrines which deny that particularity is a category and equally that universality is a category—the theory of forms, e.g., for which universals are one class, and particulars are a quite different class, so that "X is a particular" would raise a definit issue which might be settled one way or the other.

Now, we have seen the confusions of this position—especially the fact that Socrates cannot deny particularity to his so-called universals or universality to his so-called particulars, and we could say in general that this sort of position that here confronts us is one of "vicious intellectualism"—the assumption that something has one and only one function or office that if we recognize universality in any sense we have to recognize something whose business it is to be universal and nothing else, similarly in the other case, something whose business it is to cause or something whose sole function is to be an effect. But if we are going to criticize such theory it can only, as I have argued, be by reference to the *form* of the *proposition*—to the sort of thing that can be asserted or can be an issue—which will be distinguished from any concrete propositional issue like the issue whether "the chalk is white". We may still however see how the theory in question, the categorical issues in question, could have been raised. If, e.g., we fin that X is not caused by Y and is not caused by Z and is not caused by any other of a group of factors in which we thought its cause could be found or which are the only ones whose operations we observe at the time, then we might go on to form the notion of not being caused at all; that is, we should have an actual basis for that notion in the recognition of not being caused by Y and not being caused by any of the other factors which were considered.

It might be questioned at the same time whether this is adequate or rather, while this might give the formal explanation of the notion of the uncaused, it wouldn't show how anyone in a particular case came to form that notion, and here we should observe the duality or ambiguity which such doctrines ordinarily exhibit—namely in the case of causality, the treatment of a thing is in some manner or measure free, and in some manner or measure determined, which doesn't mean that a thing has a free part and a determined part, because these parts would be different things, but rather that the same thing is from a certain point of view free and from another point of view not free, and this amounts to knowing the definit conditions of a thing (up to a point at least) but at particular times ignoring them, pretending they do not exist, in that when we like we can treat X as caused by Y, and when we like we can treat it as not caused by Y, and this means not caused at all, just because Y really is the cause.

Coming back to the question of the categories and the proposition, we fin Kant associating the categories with the various forms of proposition—somewhat in the Aristotelian manner—so that you would have one category associated with or derived from propositions, say of the affirmat ve quality another with propositions of the negative quality, and similarly with the different quantities.[8]

Now it might be contended that this wouldn't give the generality required, that is to say that if a category is to stand for a type of question that can always be raised, or, alternatively, for something that is in the proposition as such, then it cannot be specially associated with one form of proposition and not another—that is to say if identity and difference

---

[8] [DMA] Different "quantities". Anderson is here distinguishing A and E propositions from I and O propositions, using the term used by the old formal logic.

(taking these for the sake of argument as the categories associated with affirmat ve and negative propositions) are to be categories then they must be found in any material whatsoever,—in any proposition whether we call it affirmat ve or negative, and similarly to take universality and particularity as categories we would have to fin them in *any* proposition whether we call it universal or particular.

It is possible then that the position could be met in this way, that the different types of propositions emphasise particular features of the proposition as such, and thus we get a distinction between the A and the E proposition, and yet in fact any proposition both affirm and denies. Taking the E for brevity, a negative proposition affirm the fact of exclusion and similarly an affirmat ve proposition denies the fact of exclusion. Again it might be argued that there is universality (even if we have to say only implicitly) in the particular proposition, as would appear if we took both terms and general terms or kinds, but further that AiB, for example, does convey to us a general truth even if we are not able to definitel formulate it, because it raised the question *what* A are B and suggests the answer All A that are X are B, even if we don't happen to know what X is. Similarly XaY might be taken to convey particularity in the fact that it has a subaltern, or putting it in terms of the location formula "where X is, Y is", to suggest possible syllogisms, i.e., AaX suggests places A in which X is found and therefore in which Y is found, to suggest the conjunction of X and Y which is the subaltern XiY.

XaY (All X are Y)

AaX (All A are X)

∴ AaY (All A are Y)

∴ XiY (Some X are Y)

Lecture 16   *(3rd August 1949)*

Empiricism and the Categories

It may be said that in distinguishing forms of propositions we are emphasising bringing out more distinctly particular categories, but our previous line of argument commits us to holding that every category is involved in every proposition whatever its form.

That is, (i) The affirmat ve proposition denies—(It has a negative character? but it is not just this, rather it is a matter of a relation between propositions.) Likewise, negative propositions assert; (ii) The particular proposition (AiB) involves the universal proposition(AXaB), even if X is unknown.

Nb. For Bosanquet: the latter statement, where X is known, is nearer to definit knowledge. For him AiB (Some As are B) and AoB (Some A are not B) are not real knowledge and require to be reformulated as A and E propositions (All As are...) and (All As are not...). But incomplete knowledge is not inexact, knowing more doesn't alter what we know before—there is no need to eliminate it, to put it in a different form. For Bosanquet only when we have symmetrical relations (necessity and sufficien y) is it real knowledge. For him, things are a system, therefore to know them we need systematic knowledge.

One general objection to this sort of procedure is, as I have said, that the solution makes the problem unintelligible—if the solution is knowledge, the statement of the problem isn't knowledge, whereas from an empiricist point of view, even if we arrive at these universal propositions, the particular propositions we started with would be as true as ever, or taking the solution in the form above, unless you still grasped the particular proposition Some A are X, and so on, you wouldn't know what that solution meant. In fact it is impossible to have a body of knowledge embracing nothing but symmetrical relations, and if we have in any case to accept the non-symmetrical or asymmetrical then admit it to begin with and deny that there is anything defective in having knowledge which isn't a statement of necessity and sufficien y, and the only effect of the dogma that knowledge had to be necessary and sufficien would be to make up, to bring such relations into the facts, even where they are not there. (In the appendix to Bosanquet's *Logic* he has a discussion on the question of disjunction with G. R. T. Ross—for Bosanquet the alternatives should be exclusive—and it is clear that the effect of Bosanquet's position will either be to falsify the facts or to make us abandon certain forms of statement or argument which we do regularly use and which even Bosanquet can't get rid of.[9])

Cf. my review of "Scepticism and Construction".[10] The point made there is that the relation between the system and the parts of features of the system cannot be itself a symmetrical one and that the perfection of knowledge on the understanding that it was completely systematic and symmetrical would be the perfection of emptiness—a point indicated in Bradley's theory of the Absolute and his attack on relational thinking—in other words that the Absolute is something about which we can say nothing at all, and think nothing at all, but it is as I put it, "unspeakable".

---

[9]Bernard Bosanquet, *Logic: or the Morphology of Knowledge*. Oxford: Clarendon Press, 1911. 2 Volumes. Appendix to Chapter VIII, On Some Recent Discussions of Disjunction, Volume 1, pp. 355-362.
[10]"Scepticism and Construction, by Charles A. Campbell", *op. cit.*

A philosophy of identity, then, one that holds that the only true reality—the only true relation—is identity, is refuted whenever the philosopher says anything at all.

4

The Categories I: The "Logical" Categories
Categories of Quality

Lecture 16   *(3rd August 1949) continued*
The Category of Identity—Identity as Co-extension

The Category of Identity

Coming onto the discussion of identity which for Alexander is the firs of the categories, corresponding of course to being in the Hegelian and also the Platonic system, we may firs of all consider whether identity can be called a relation (link this with general discussion of categories as relations or having a relational element). On the realist view that a relation has two terms, or holds between two different things and we couldn't call one a relation, that is we couldn't say a thing has the relation of identity with itself but, popularly, we speak of identifying one thing with another so that while as before "is X identical or not?" isn't a real issue "is X identical with Y or not?" is a real issue. For instance, if we were considering the identity of the author or authors of Ern Malley poems, and we say that they were identifiabl with McAuley and Stewart, we do seem to be saying that a relation of identity exists between the author of the poems and these two persons.[1] Now it might be suggested that logically the form of this situation is just co-extension—that we identify X and Y or fin X and Y to be identical when we fin XaY and YaX, but when we say X and Y are co-extensive terms we would still hold that they are different terms, they are not the same or the identical term. (We should certainly not say that X is co-extensive with X any more than we should say A is A—we have taken the description of that as an identity to amount to denying that it is a proposition which requires two terms, not only one term.)

Now this would seem to suggest that there are two senses of identity or identifying—a sense in which we can identify different things and sense in which we cannot identify different things, in which to say *different* is to say not identical.

Identity as Co-extension

Now even if we took the broader sense—the sense of co-extension—we should have to consider the difficult involved in

---

[1] "Ern Malley" is the name of a fictitiou poet created by James McAuley and Harold Stewart in a famous literary hoax of the 1940s.

this notion if we take it to mean that the two terms have exactly the same subjects, or same extension, because, as has just been indicated while we say that X is part of the extension of Y(meaning just that Y is predicable of X) we don't say that X is part of the extension of X, or that X is predicable of X, and similarly, Y belongs to the extension of X but not to the extension of Y. Now we might say that while the two terms are said to have a common extension, when it is said any term, of which X is predicable, is a term of which Y is predicable, what is really meant is terms other than X or Y—that is that any third term, A, of which X was predicable would also be a term of which Y was predicable, and vice-versa, and that amounts to saying that co-extension means simply two propositions of the form XaY and YaX, and that any other description is a loose or inexact one.

What would keep the ordinary logician from recognizing the difficult and its solution is that he takes the extension of a term to be the individuals to which the term as a description applies, so that here he would be saying that individuals described as X are also the individuals described as Y; but we have seen some of the difficultie of that view and this way of putting the matter is not possible to a logic that rejects the distinction between the purely particular and the purely general.

And the rejection of the individualist view would also lead us to call in question the contention that when two terms are said to be co-extensive what we really mean is two words with the same meaning—different words and not different terms—as in Moore's case of the word "good" and the words by which it is translated into other languages. If on the contrary we take the doctrine of the infinit complexity of things—the view that a predicate carries with it any number of other predicates—then we don't fin it at all difficul to believe that two predicates X and Y always belong to the same subjects—that two different qualities always appear in the same places.

There might of course be a difficult as how we could distinguish two such qualities, but again we realize that when two qualities belong to the same thing, and are even, so we say, connected, it is still possible to be aware of one and not the other. The case is simpler when it is a matter of definition—o a complex term MN, let us say, being co-extensive with a term because there is a possibility of findin the terms M and N separately in other places.

I would say then that it is possible for two terms to be co-extensive—for X to be different from Y and yet to be in the broad sense the same thing but this still leaves us to consider whether anything further can be said about identity in the narrower sense.

This suggests (1) occurrence of co-extensive terms—categorial, i.e., all terms have, co-extensive terms; (2) no limit to the number of terms co-extensive with a given term.[2]

Lecture 17   (6th September 1949)

*"Deduction" of the Categories of Quality—Identity
continued—Difference—Existence—Relation—Universality*

The firs set of categories are the categories of "quality" (as against the quantitative categories.) They are the categories of "logic" (as against the mathematical and physical categories).

> Identity
> > Difference
> > Existence
> > > Relation
> Universality

Figure 7.

Difference and relation are "dyadic" categories—in the sense that they involve two terms, hold between two things, have something of a relational character. *Cf.* Plato's *Philebus*—generation of number by one and the "indeterminate dyad". In my scheme the dyadic categories are in a sense indeterminate. "A is different from B"—the respect in which they differ could be anything at all (though these categories are definit enough in own way, they are still saying something).

The Category of Identity *continued*

The question we have been considering was whether we could distinguish identity in a narrow sense from identity in a broad sense in which it could be taken as a relation—namely the relation of co-extension which, as I was arguing, could be taken to hold between different terms but is such that when it does hold we could say, in a sense, these two are the same thing. (Just as we might say "triangles and 3-sided rectilinear figures were the same thing or "equiangular triangles" and "equilateral triangles" are the same thing though we also recognise them as different things when we take as significan the

---

[2] [DMA] Conversation with Anderson.

assertion all equiangular triangles are equilateral triangles, and of course *vice versa*.

Now when we are said to identify something, when we identify let us say the perpetrator of a certain offence, it might still be said we have co-extension, but the point is that we have started with a certain predicate or description and we want to see what that description applies to or what is its extension and, of course, we can easily substitute for findin its extension findin its location or places of occurrence, findin its subjects. Thus having identity is treated on this view as having a subject or subjects, having place or places so that on this view identity might be referred to as being a subject, or exercising the function of a subject—that is locating. Now of course, I have argued that any subject can be a predicate and any predicate a subject but similarly have stressed the importance of distinguishing the two functions and what enables us to make this distinction—to distinguish the localising from the describing, the *where* from the *what*, is just the distinction between place and what occupies place—that is, even if we can never specify a place except in terms of what occurs in it or surrounds it, the very notion of occurring and surrounding require this notion of place—of absolute place if we care to put it so—and it is that which I am suggesting that is the notion of identity, which is involved in every situation. Well, then, it is so far in accordance with the doctrine that the categories are inherent in the form of the proposition if we take identity to be equivalent to, or to be brought out in, the notion of being a subject.

The Category of Difference

Now we might be tempted, having taken this step to go on to identify difference with being a predicate and this at least would be in accordance with the view that we know qualities as differences, as distinguishing marks between one thing and another, as solutions of problems, or as it might be put in more psychological terms that we learn or come to know certain things (that is, kinds of things) by the want of them and, of course, by the satisfaction of the want. However this might be considered to be using difference in a technical sense and the notion of difference might arise not so much from the distinction between subject and predicate as simply between the subject and the rest of the proposition—from the fact that a subject is not a whole proposition or a whole situation—that distinction is required even for the subject to be a subject, or for location to locate, and this might lead us, in the Hegelian manner, to say that identity embodies difference, that to have identity is to have distinction, that the later categories are somehow involved in the firs category of identity. At least, we can say, that a subject or thing is not a thing-in-itself—is not a self-subsistent or simple entity but is actually propositional or situational—that situations are not made up by taking things and adding relations to them—that, as I put it, the thing is not prior to the proposition. But, allowing for possible development along these lines, the main point is that the subject as such is not a proposition—that it so to speak calls for propositional completion and it is recognition of the subject's incompleteness—its pointing beyond itself—that would lead us to say that in recognising identity we are at the same time recognising difference.

The Category of Existence

Well now the point here, as I said, is to distinguish the subject from the rest of the proposition and the next definit element in the proposition that we recognise is of course the copula, and this I take to give the category of existence.[3] Now here we have to consider the position of those who reject the subject-attribute, or as it might be called the "predicated" view of the proposition—that is, those who deny the copula is necessarily a feature of all propositions—who think that we can have various relations other than predication between A and B, and that it is artificia to force the assertion of such relations into predicated form—to introduce in every case the copula "is" or "are" (*Cf.* the 1948 Logic course—I will not traverse the same ground.[4]) Here, though, I would just say that even such theorists must admit that any assertion requires a verb, and that where the verb is not the verb to be, it actually has two functions—namely a material one and a formal one—that is, something that is part of what is being asserted and something that merely indicates that an assertion is being made—or, putting it objectively, that something is the case or is taking place—and that it is necessary in order to see just what the issue is to detach the formal from the material feature—to separate mere occurrence from what specificall is occurring and the formal feature is something that is invariable in all propositions and just as we can equate the category of identity with the function of the subject

---

[3] [DMA] Anderson's use of the word "existence" for this category is rather puzzling. He wants to link this category with the copula of the old formal logic, but it is not clear why the copula has a special link with existence. All the categories exist. What he is trying to bring out is the propositional nature of reality, and he may think that the copula is of especial importance when insisting on this propositional nature. It is true, though, that it not easy to suggest another name. Perhaps his second suggestion, "Occurrence", would be the best that can be done.

[4] Anderson refers repeatedly in these lectures to the 1948 lectures on logic. A transcription of handwritten lecture notes for 1948 are included in Appendix 3 below.

so we can equate the category of existence (or occurrence) with the function of the copula—with the fact that the proposition has a copula.

Now this would hardly justify us in taking Hegel's line, that in speaking of the 3rd Category which in his scheme is called definit being, as the union of the firs two categories—the union of being and not-being, or of identity and difference. That way of speaking obscures the reference of the argument to the form of the proposition for though we might obscurely speak of the copula as the union of subject and with the rest of the proposition, yet we need the distinct features of the proposition to indicate what we are doing, to show the sort of distinction we are laying down.

The Category of Relation

Well now we take the expression "existence" for this third category to have as alternatives actuality and occurrence and since, of course, I identify truth with "existence" and here it might be said that in raising the question of truth you also raise the question of falsity or alternatively that in raising the question of the copula you also raise the question of the negative copula, in other words, the question of different ways of coupling or relating the subject and the copula to the rest of the proposition—namely the predicate—a point that can be put by saying that just as the subject isn't the proposition—isn't by itself, isn't a thing-in-itself, so the subject with the copula isn't by itself but requires completion or coupling, and I suggest that this possibility of these alternative couplings introduces the category of relation.

The Category of Universality

Then, of course, the proposition is completed by the predicate, that is by the consideration not of occurrences or of non-occurrence at a place, but of what occurs or doesn't occur at a place and that brings us to the description—to a category that may be referred to as that of quality or universality or Kind—what is spoken of by Alexander as generic identity as contrasted with numerical identity. But it is perhaps better not to use the expression "identity" in these two cases because it would have different meanings and because the use of the same expression might lead us to confuse the function of subject and predicate which is still a mistake even if every term has both functions.

"X is"—difference (passage to rest of proposition)

"is Y"—relation (passage from copula to predicate)

Identity	Existence	Universality/Kind
X	is (is not)	Y
Difference	Relation	

Figure 8.

Lecture 18   *(7th September 1949)*
The Category of Relation—The Status of Predication

The Status of Predication

It might be said that identity is always a limited identity and so leads on into difference or involves the notion of the different or other and similarly that existence is always limited and leads you to think of other existences and in that way involves the notion of relations between existences.

Now in speaking about relations I had connected it with the copula—talked about "coupling" as a relation involved—which seems to imply that the relation we are concerned with is the relation between the terms subject and predicate. But that treatment involves difficulties—i leads at any rate to the question whether predication is a relation or whether we should distinguish predication from relations. Now in attacking relativism, in insisting on the distinction between qualities and relations, I have emphasised the fact that a relation holds between two things, whereas a quality belongs to a single thing—that when we are speaking of a thing's qualities we don't have to go beyond the thing itself—we don't fin its relations *in it* but fin them between it and other things, or, putting it otherwise that there is nothing in a thing itself to tell us what its relations are and, of course, we could also say, nothing in a thing's relations to tell us what its qualities are unless we are using "relation" in the loose sense in which a relation can include qualities, as for instance we talk about the relation of being a husband and we imply certain qualities in the thing so related, or again that having the relation of sitting implies certain qualities in the sitter (though it conveys more strikingly certain interrelations of the parts of the sitter) but at least it implies something that is found within the sitter himself—something not between the sitter and something else.

More dubiously, I would say relations of *knowing* include certain qualitative material and if it does it would be a relation in the loose sense—but I would argue, relation in the strict sense is a spatio-temporal relation like "on" or "after" and that relations in the loose sense, or what we can call the loose sense, are certain combinations of qualities and relations in the strict sense—(spatio-temporal relation) where, of course, we could still sharply distinguish the qualitative from the spatio-temporal relations and argue that no inference would be possible in either direction between them.

Well now, predication has at least something in common with relations even in the strict sense—namely that it involves two terms and we could raise the same sort of questions regarding it as we raised concerning relations—whether it is transitive or intransitive, symmetrical or unsymmetrical—we can, I'd say, raise that sort of question about different forms of proposition, e.g., we see that the E and I propositions [No X… and Some X…] are symmetrical while A and O propositions [All X… and Some X are not…] are non-symmetrical.

Now the question isn't quite accurately put as whether or not the two terms are external to one another because in other than affirmat ve predication and especially in the E proposition we would at least have to say that the two terms are external to one another or whether we precisely identify the relation of exclusion with the E proposition we would at least have to say that exclusion and thus externality were bound up with the E proposition—they are always found together.

On the other hand we have to admit some sort of internality in relations in the strict sense—we say that A contains B is a relation where B certainly falls within the region indicated by A and yet the relation is certainly one we would call external in the sense that there can be no general argument from the quality of the one thing to the quality of the other—speaking roughly, or taking the thing just spatially, any sort of thing could be inside any other sort of thing—and taking again the slightly different conception of whole and part—the distinction between my hand containing the chalk and my hand containing my little finge in the sense that my little finge is *part* of the hand—in the new case we have to distinguish having a part from having a predicate and we have to say that there is no general argument from the character of a part to the character of the whole that transcends it or *vice versa*—that you have to distinguish between a predicate which belongs to a given whole but not to all parts of the whole and perhaps not to any, a predicate of a part of a whole and perhaps to all parts of it which yet is not a predicate of them all and thirdly a predicate of the whole and any part of it. (For example, we say that Socrates is a man but don't say that any part of Socrates is a man, on the other hand we say Socrates is organic and we do say that any part of Socrates is organic.) These are reasons for not identifying or confusing predication with containing or being contained.

Now this requires a modificatio or at least a certain caution in the use of the location formula because if we say simply that the subject is a region within which the predicate occurs then we are reducing predication to containing and overlooking the distinction I have just been making—the implication being that what we have considered the function of the subject (locating) is not to be taken as a full account of it or as more than an approximate description for if we took the given account of the function of the term quite literally that would be as good as saying that something else could be substituted for the proposition—that we can explain the proposition in other than propositional terms. Here then we may refer back to the description or the function of the predicate as an activity—of the predicate as a way in which the subject is going on, on which view the subject does not merely locate—is not merely where the activity is but is what has this activity. In this connection I said that we could substitute "X is red" "X is redding" or "is going on in the red way", the point being that it is only an accident of language that some terms cannot take the form of the verb (have not what I would call an "operational" form) just as it is only an accident of language that some terms have not an adjectival form and other terms not a substantive form, though in fact any term can be a subject and *vice versa*, anything can be a quality or be qualifie and in the same way anything can operate even if the verb form is missing from the language. Logically there is no distinction between the adjectival, the substantive and operational—they are just different ways (in which perhaps are involved different categories) in which we can consider any material whatever. The main point is that more is meant by saying that red is an activity of a certain thing than that it goes on inside a certain region—we do not call a thing "red" because it has something red inside it. For example, we don't call a man red because he has a certain amount of red blood and here we may note the difficultie of Alexander's theory of substance which takes any quality to occur only in a part of a substance—which holds that qualities never interpenetrate, because this would mean strictly that a thing cannot have two qualities.

I am arguing as against this that we do require the notion of a quality or activity of a whole subject with no question of marking off inside the subject the special location of that activity though of course we do have a temporal marking off—we have a distinction between occasional or intermittent activities of a person, e.g., and his persistent qualities—between qualities he always has and qualities he has only sometimes, though he has them fully for a certain period. My view is then that predication is not a relation though there are relations connected with it like class relations—better to say that when X is going on in the manner Y that there isn't a relation between X and "going on in the manner Y"—better to keep relation for something holding between different things with different locations while still admitting that there are relations between, and also within, the situations that predication specifies In fact, I think it is possible to suggest that in some sense predication is prior to relation—qualitative assertions to relational assertions—and it might be said that the treatment of the proposition as a relation is connected with false views of the proposition, for instance, the class view, here the two terms stand for two sets of individuals and the question is to what extent the sets of individuals are identical or different, or again the doctrine of the ambiguity of the copula with distinctions between say the "is" of identity, "is" of inclusion, "is" of membership of a class—along these lines predication could be a relation but these views I consider false.

Now, if we take predication as not a relation, the introduction of the category of relation at the place indicated would be connected not with the coupling of the subject and predicate but with the distinction between the affirmat ve and negative copula—between being and not being such and such. That is, it could be a question of a relation of contradiction, or again a relation of change where something passes from being to not being of such and such a kind and thus a question of phases, and the passage in the list of categories from existence to relation would amount to the relation of the interrelated phases of anything that exists.

Lecture 19   (13th September 1949)
The Category of Relation continued——Relational Assertions—Relational Arguments

A note on error: I suggested that *change* was one of the matters to be considered in the association of relation with the difference between the affirmat ve and the negative copula because we don't of course actually fin two contradictory situations, but change might be regarded as the empirical equivalent of contradiction or as that which suggests contradiction in so far as at one time X is Y and at another time X is not Y. And since there is no way of absolutely determining times (that is apart from the things that happen at those times) we can treat them as an opposition between situations or, more generally, we can treat the phases of a developing situation as giving the distinction between the affirmat ve and the negative copula and of course as related to one another temporally and other ways. Thus we could introduce the relation of contradiction, or something very like it, without specificall referring to error.

Relational Assertions

Now there is one point to be considered here before we go on to detailed account of relational arguments and arguments involving relations, the point that the relational assertion ArB is subsequent to the qualitative assertion A is C. The position, as before, is best considered in terms of contradiction and implication—you could symbolise the contradictory of ArB simply by drawing a line through the r but if you are going to consider what that *means* then, as I have argued (see the logic lectures, 1948) you have to come back to the unambiguous copula—to the question whether or not A is to the right of B—and that could be expressed by saying that the question is whether A is or is not a *thing to the right of B*. At any rate it appears that "to the right of" falls within one of the terms and not between the terms of the assertion, and the point comes out if we consider implication in the form of conversion. If we convert ArB into rBiA then that could not be interpreted as meaning that "being to the right of B is sometimes being A"—having a certain relation is sometimes having a certain quality. It would have to be interpreted as "some things to the right of B are A" and this supports the view that terms are primarily qualitative—that even if as in the sort of assertion we are now considering "all A are things to the right of B" or "some things to the right of B are A" we don't specify qualities or a quality of one of the terms it is only by understanding that term also as qualitative or as having qualities that we can understand the assertion and carry through ordinary logical operations on it.

Relational Arguments

Coming to the general question of relational arguments we fin that support of a special logic of such arguments is connected with opposition to syllogism, or at any rate with the attempt to reduce the importance of syllogism, since syllogistic argument is clearly in line with a qualitative or predicative logic in so far as in the characteristic figur (the "firs figure" the same term—namely the middle term—functions now as subject now as predicate. Now in our logic we have recognised certain non-syllogistic arguments which nevertheless are still in line with a qualitative logic, namely conjunctive and disjunctive arguments.

a. Conjunctive and Disjunctive Arguments:

AaX	AaX
AaY	BaX
∴ AaXY	∴ (A or B)aX
One form of conjunctive argument	One form of disjunctive argument

Now these arguments include two relations that we can call conjunction and disjunction though we have started simply from qualitative assertions. In presenting identity as *being a subject* I argued that a subject is not itself a proposition and so we have to go from identity to difference, and yet that a subject is in some sense propositional, that it has to be understood as not simple but complex—as involving a relation of constituents that could be made explicit and it would be in terms of some such view that we could say (if we could say it at all) that all the other categories are involved in the firs one: identity. Conjunctions and disjunctions then might be taken as the sort of thing we could mean by this complexity—the conjunctive term indicating the possibility of a propositional extension of a given term as in the notion of a definin proposition (the class of men being define by "some animals are rational" where animal and rational are interrelated qualities of the proposition, but note this is rough, a definitio is properly a *group* of propositions) and the disjunctive term bringing out rather the fact that the subject has distinct parts, giving us the notion of spatial extension or things being alongside one another and both types of combination (of qualities and of parts) are involved in what we mean by the complexity or spatio-temporality of a thing or a term.

In general then it is not going beyond the subject-predicate logic to recognise that the same subject has many predicates and the same predicate many subjects, and recognition of these facts leads us straight into the theory of relations. The disjunctive term, in particular, gives some indication of how in terms of a predicative logic we can take account of extent or quantity.

b. Quantitative Arguments.

Further in this connection there is the sort of thing that is called a quantitative argument which is held to be a peculiar type of argument characteristic especially of mathematics and concerned with relations of equality and to some extent of inequality. Now I should argue, contrary to what is generally supposed, that this reasoning is syllogistic or can, at least, be taken as syllogistic—we can get a syllogistic expression for it, this being done quite easily if we take quality and inequality of classes as characteristic of equality and inequality in general. We are, of course, under a limitation in comparing quantities in that the only class relations in question are co-extension and inclusion there being no sense in talking about equality and inequality in the cases of intersection and exclusion. However, that only means that the scope of such arguments is limited—it doesn't mean that they are not syllogistic. Now without going into the matter too closely we can see that whenever two quantities are equal anything that is measurable by the one is measurable by the other and so there are two co-extensive classes covered. For brevity then I shall present the quantities as themselves classes—take the assertion that A is equal to B as the assertion that the class A and the class B are co-extensive and the assertion that A is greater than B as the assertion that class A includes B. On that understanding:

the assertion A=B would be represented by AaB, BaA

Similarly B=C would be represented by BaC, CaB

From this we get the syllogistic conclusion AaC, CaA which will be represented as before by A=C.

Thus this sort of argument can be presented syllogistically and the so-called axiom "things which are equal to the same thing are equal to one another" is not an axiom at all but just an example of syllogistic reasoning. The assumption has only been that when two qualities are equal there are two classes of things which are co-extensive and similarly when one quantity is greater than another there is one class that includes another. Expressing the correspondence then in this rough way I would say we can give similar syllogistic justificatio for the rule that when A is greater than B and B is greater than C then A is greater than C or, as it might be also put, that "greater than" is a transitive relation.

That is,

A>B becomes BaA (all B are A) and AoB (some As are not Bs); B>C becomes CaB (all C are B) and BoC (some Bs are not Cs)

BaA (from A>B)

CaB (from B>C)

∴ CaA

though here, while the A conclusion follows from the two A premises, but the O conclusion (AoC, that is, some As are not Cs) follows not from the two Os but from one of the As and one of the Os, for example.

BaA

BoC

∴ AoC — which is A>C

though here while the A conclusion follows from the two A premises the O conclusion follows not from the two O premises but from one of the O's and one of the A's.

For example, BaA and BoC $\longrightarrow$ AoC

and also AoB and CaB $\longrightarrow$ AoC

So that while for the conclusion A is greater than C we need both the A premises, we only need one of the O premises—either of them would have enabled us to draw the conclusion, e.g., from the three premises BaA, CaB and BoC we can draw the conclusion that A is greater than C and this, of course, is in accord with the axiom in mathematical theory that when A is greater than B (or A is greater than or equal to B) or when A is not less than B, and B is greater than C then A is greater than C and we could equally argue that if A is greater than B, B is greater than or equal to C then A is greater than C and further we could argue that when A is greater than or equal to B and B is greater than or equal to C then A is greater than or equal to C which, on this understanding on which we have been conducting these arguments, would amount to the Barbara syllogism.

Lecture 20   *(14th September 1949)*

The Category of Relations continued—Relational Arguments continued

Note that we only have co-extension, inclusion in quantitative arguments. Where different ranges are in question (say, size, weight) is intersection and exclusion possible? But unless we have the same range quantitative comparison is not strictly possible.

This is an indication of the way in which arguments which are taken to involve a breakdown of the syllogistic logic or at least an alternative to the syllogistic logic can actually be expressed syllogistically and the vital point in criticism of the alternative view—namely that here in the case of quantities we have a quite unique type of assertion and a quite original type of argument involving such assertion—is the one I emphasised in the logic lectures of 1948, that no provision is made for contradiction, that the denial of an equation is not itself an equation just as the denial of a class relation is not itself a class relation so that it is only by coming back to the *predicated* form of the assertion that we can make the issue perfectly clear.

One special point regarding axioms or governing principles, namely that one way we cannot turn such apparently non-syllogistic arguments into syllogistic form is by setting up a general principle as major principle—this is no more successful than a similar procedure in syllogism itself of taking a certain dictum as a firs premise in each case, i.e., taking as a rough form of the dictum "whatever is true of a class is true of every member of that class" then that is not really an original major premise on which the Barbara syllogism can be based—a premise from which the validity of the Barbara syllogism can be inferred—it is the form of that syllogism itself and yet we could see the soundness of a concrete Barbara syllogism just as easily as you could see the correctness of the dictum—the point being that it is the syllogistic premises that prove the conclusion, not anything outside the syllogism that proves the whole syllogism. The same way "things that are equal to the same thing are equal to one another" is not a general major premise for all equational arguments but is merely a statement of the form of such arguments and we can directly see the validity of any concrete relation argument just as easily as we can see the soundness of the so-called axiom.

Now then, in syllogistic argument we recognise formal validity and if we can reduce any given relation argument to syllogistic then again we have a formal test of its validity—a test that we shouldn't have if we simply took relations without any examination or consideration of what they formally involve, we have to know in some way whether a given relation, for example, is transitive or not—we couldn't tell just by looking at ArB, BrC, therefore ArC that the argument is therefore valid as we can tell by just looking at the syllogism AaB, BaC, therefore AaC that it is valid—we have to have some particular knowledge of the relation in question since clearly there are relations which wouldn't permit us to argue in this manner—for instance "next to" and "father of"—thus in the argument "A is the father of B, B is the father of C, therefore A is the father of C" the conclusion would always be false if the premises were true and in the case of the argument "A is to the right of B, B is to the right of C, therefore A is to the right of C" if the premises were true the conclusion would be false in every series but one, namely where you had three things arranged in a ring, that is, when any pair of these terms in the group we have chosen were next to one another.

Figure 9.

The question then is whether when we look closely at any transitive relation we cannot express arguments involving it in syllogistic form, not by setting up a principle as an invariable major premise but by giving a certain interpretation to each assertion of the relation in question—an interpretation which as before would be an assumption of either inclusion or co-extension according as the relation was reversible (symmetrical) or not. Now this is the case, particularly, with the relation "to the right of" which has been held up as definitel giving us a type of non-syllogistic reasoning—arguments involving such assertions can be expressed in precisely the same way as arguments involving greater and less and equal quantities because this sort of argument (A is to the right of B, B is to the right of C, therefore A is to the right of C) is an argument involving quantities—that is, the notion "to the right of" is relative to a certain point of view and a certain direction of view and a point "to the right" can be taken as indicating a greater range than a point to the left—a greater swing or turning from a postulated extreme length and of course a lesser turning from a postulated extreme right.

Well, then even if we didn't have it exactly we could have a suggested base with an observer and you would have, let us say, a swing to the right. Then, ArB, BrC, ArC so that A is to the right of B when and only when there is a greater swing from L to A than from L to B and so this can be expressed once more in terms of the relation of inclusion, remembering that we could always express the inclusion in the opposite

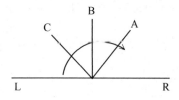

Figure 10.

way if we took the swing to the left and that therefore we have to stick to one form of correspondence (say, right means >, left means <) as far as any given argument is concerned.

Not bothering for the moment about the precise form of the terms, we can see that the argument could be syllogistic in exactly the same way as arguments involving quantity and we could have the same modificatio of the arguments. Corresponding to "greater than or equal to", we could have "to the right of or level with", or putting in its other form, corresponding to "not less than", we would have "not to the left of" and then we would have the valid argument "when A is to the right of B and B is not to the left of C"—the assumption being of course that all these terms—all these positions—fall within the same range and once more we should have a type of argument corresponding simply to Barbara namely "A is not to the left of B, B is not to the left of C, therefore A is not to the left of C". There you have a treatment of arguments involving "to the right of" as quantitative arguments which in turn have already treated as syllogistic arguments and, as I said, it will be in this manner that we can get a syllogistic exposition such arguments without having a general principle or dictum as our major in every case.

The argument doesn't require us to fin a precise right or left point—we only require to recognise left and right simply—in the question of the fiel of view we never have an exact fi ed point, yet we talk intelligibly about further to the left or further to the right of—there are more positions to the left of A than there are to the left of B because all positions to the left of B are to the left of A but some positions to the left of A are not to the left of B (e.g., B itself). Or, more simply, eliminating reference to "left", A is to the right of B when and only when all things to the right of A are to the right of B and some things to the right of B are not to the right of A, that is, where you have a relation of inclusion and now if we say "C is not to the right B" then we have

All things to the right of B are to the right of C and taking this with both the previous premises:

R_a a R_b	R_b o R_a
R_b a R_c	R_b a R_c
$\therefore R_a$ a R_c	$\therefore R_c$ o R_a

and from these two conclusions we get ArC.

So we have the argument "A is to the right of B, C is not to the right of B, $\therefore$ A is the right of C" represented by two syllogisms remembering that it is understood at the outset that A, B, and C are all positions, or all points, within a common point of view.

Lecture 21   *(20th September 1949)*
The Category of Relation continued—Relational Arguments continued

In putting these arguments into syllogistic form I have equated "A is to the right of B" with R_aaR_b and R_boR_a. Now it could be contended that in making that identificatio and particularly in asserting the firs of these two propositions as involved in "A is to the right of B" we are begging the question—that is we are assuming not demonstrating the transitiveness of "to the right of" and the argument to which we go on to is therefore pointless. A similar point might be made in regard to inclusion as a relation of "greater than": that is to say, when we equate A is greater than B with a relation between two classes (things measured by A and things measured by B) we have actually to interpret "measured by" as "greater than" so that we are equating "A is greater than B" with "All things greater than A are greater than B and some things greater than B are not greater than A" and thus begging the question.

> *Nb.* "measured by" here is a rough expression—it can cover both relation of greater to less, and less to greater
> A———B
> A———B_1———B_2
> That is, either line in the diagram could be used to measure the other line, therefore we should strictly talk about "greater than".

Now one point to be made here is that this transformation (let us say "A is to the right of B" is the proposition mentioned) is not intended as a definitio of "to the right of". The question is just whether we can say that we can formally exhibit by means of such propositions as what follows from "A is to the right of B" the assumption having been made that we were able to carry out the transformation, to understand it and recognise its truth in the firs instance.

You might notice this transformation wouldn't apply if A happened to be the extreme right point—nothing to the right of A—but this means that in a fiel of vision we never have determinate extreme points—always something indeterminate about the edges of such a field—w could alternatively say that we limit application to points not the extreme right or left—we simply have rightward or leftward extremes—something assumed in the very formulation of the problem and not requiring to be explicitly stated.

Now as to the question how we are aware of this truth the point is that we are aware of it in being aware of a fiel of vision—in seeing what is meant by moving round from the left or moving round from the right in that particular field We can see, that is, that in moving from the left in order to go through A we should pass through B but that in order to go through B we don't have to pass through A and whether or not these are said to be part of what we mean by "to the right of" they are certainly things that can be grasped along with our grasping the relation of "to the right of". A similar position would arise in syllogism itself where it could be said that unless we can observe in one situation the whole syllogistic principle it would seem that we couldn't justify that principle—that we would have to have got our belief in the validity of, e.g., Barbara, by something other than observation with all the difficulties—indee the impossibility—of applying that to observation. We could roughly say that the argument BaC, AaB, therefore AaC *assumes* and doesn't demonstrate the transitivity of the relation "a"—that what it demonstrates in fact is the conclusion "All A are C". And similarly, what I will call for brevity the angular argument doesn't by being put into syllogistic form demonstrate the transitivity of "to the right of" but shows more clearly how the conclusion of a given argument is demonstrated. Unless we had some way of simply seeing the validity of the whole process the argument would be simply arbitrary—we should have no reason for saying that it held for a given relation and nor for some other relation, for instance, "being f ve miles distant from" which of course isn't transitive, if we couldn't see the whole situation and see the difference between one sort of relation and another.

It is no objection, then, to a particular way of setting out the argument that it implies that we can see transitiveness since if we couldn't we couldn't get out the argument at all. I would suggest, then, that is every case of a transitive and irreversible relation the argument is transformable into one involving relations of inclusion and similarly in every case of transitive and reversible relation the argument is expressed in terms of co-extension—as in the example of equal quantities. The only point is that we must have direct recognition of what we may call the interrelation of relations—of the structure of a certain fiel so as to be able to say, e.g., that when and only when P is an ancestor of Q then and only then A_p a A_q, and A_q o A_p (for instance P itself) and this is something that we at least can know at the same time as we know the given proposition—that is, ancestor implies a series of generations, and a direction of descent, just as "to the right of" implies a fiel of view and a direction of turning through it. In the same way we have the similar case of before and after when for "A is before B" you could substitute "Some events before B are not before A and all events before A are before B." And where once more you can know the truth of the A proposition merely by seeing A is not after B—that is A is either before or simultaneous with B.

Now there are more complicated relations which it might be difficul or at any rate cumbrous to put into syllogistic form—for instance A is an uncle of B, C is a child of A, therefore B and C are cousins and I have already pointed out that conjunctive and disjunctive arguments which are taken to be valid are not syllogistic but would still suggest that the same sort of priority that belong to the predicative form of the proposition—the attribution of a quality to a thing belongs to the syllogistic form of argument in which when A qualifie B and B qualifie C, A is said to qualify C, and just as we fin it possible to put into logical form statements that don't initially appear to be covered by the four forms,[5] so we fin it possible to put into syllogistic form arguments that don't initially appear to be syllogistic, and that have even been used in attacks on syllogistic logic.

We saw also that if contradictions and implications are to have application to a relational assertion then it has to be treated in a predicative way even if we can say that in one of the terms, at least, the qualitative character is only implied and not stated—that we are referring

---

[5] [DMA] It was, as I remember, common for students to discuss examples of statements that were difficul to put into one of the four forms.

to the sort of things, whatever they may be, that have the relation R to X and thus instead of treating a relation as an alternative form of copula we have to treat it as part of the material of the proposition and not part of the form—as falling inside the terms or one of the terms.

Now the initial position in regard to arguments that we can tell from the form of a syllogism whether the argument is valid or not even if we know nothing about the form whatever except that they are terms—if we have no acquaintance with A, B, C themselves but know that there is a sort of thing called A and a sort of thing called B and a 3rd called C then we can see that the syllogism AaB, BaC, therefore AaC is valid but we can't without special knowledge tell whether ArB, BrC therefore ArC is valid and the point might be put in this way—that we haven't got logical form—we haven't arrived at what the assertion really is—until we can tell from its form alone whether it is valid or not and on that view the syllogistic form will be the strict logical form of the relational arguments we have dealt with involving *greater than* and so forth.

Lecture 22   *(21st September 1949)*
The Category of Relation continued—Relations as Situations—"Sense" or "Direction"

One result of this treatment of relations, of taking the predicative form as the logical form even of relational assertions is, as I said, that we have to take a relation as falling within a propositional term and this is connected with my view of the subject as emphasizing the quantitative or extensive character of things—indicating that it has parts between which, of course, there would be relations and not merely that it has qualities—whereas a term in its use as a predicate is thought of particularly from the qualitative or intensive side—a point which is reinforced in conjunctive and disjunctive arguments where we have the contrast between intensional combination—combination of predicates—in a term of the form XY and internal combination or combination of subjects in a term of the form (A or B).

> This sort of position is opposed to Leibniz's notion of an intensive unity. For him there are various qualities but no parts. I would support Leibniz's objection to ultimate parts but it is no solution to reject parts altogether.

Relations as Situations
Now this line of argument, or this treatment of relations, is in accordance with the point made by Alexander and others that when we speak of a relation we shouldn't simply think of "r"—the bare relation

by itself—but of a whole situation ArB though, we should, of course, have to have a way of distinguishing Ar_1B from Ar_2B with A and B being the same in both cases, e.g., let us say A is larger than B from A is later than B and we do seem naturally to make the distinction by saying that "larger than" is a different relation from "later than" even though we never have "larger than" except in a situation of the type "A is larger than B" and even though it may be convenient to refer to the whole situation as a certain relation.

And referring back to the account given of relational assertions it would seem to be necessary to distinguish between ArB and a single term (that position is implied in calling it a situation)—what we might express as (rB), as a single term—to distinguish, that is, between "A's having the relation r to B" and "having the relation R to B" or "a thing which has the relation r to B" which is what we could predicate of A, i.e., we could have two quite different forms involved: "A is rB"—A is related in the r manner to B—and "(ArB) is X".

"Sense" or "Direction" Of Relation

Well now we can go from this discussion to a question that involves Alexander in some difficulty—namel the sense or direction of a relation—the distinction between a relation and the converse relation—the converse of a relation being the relation that must hold between B and A whenever and only when the given relation holds between A and B. For instance, B is after A when and only when B is before A so that "after" is the converse of the relation "before". The difficult then is to take the assertion of the relation and the assertion of the converse relation as two different assertions ArB and BrA—to take them as not simply different forms of the same fact—not really different assertions, even if the matter can be presented in two different sets of words.

Thus we fin Alexander saying things like this: "The proposition "A is a mother of B" and "(the same) B is a child born of A" describe precisely the same fact but they describe it in the light of the general relations of maternity or "filial relation" (p. 243).

However we can equally say that the two general relations that is the maternal and filia relation describe precisely the same facts so that he has not made it clear what are the different lights that would be cast on the situation by the two different ways of speaking. Then again, referring to the relation of "preceding" and in particular the distinction between A preceding B and A succeeding B Alexander says "The quality of the situation is the same but its direction is reversed" (p. 243). If this not a mistake on Alexander's part (should it not be B succeeding A?) the distinction here is between two entirely different and, in fact, incomparable situations and at any rate in other cases that he takes, we do simply have a distinction between a relation and a converse relation, e.g., "Edinburgh is north of London and London is south of Edinburgh". In this case Alexander says "the difference is not indeed a merely verbal one-though perilously near to it but a difference of aspect or description, what Aristotle expressed by saying that the two things are the same but not in their being" (p. 243).

We should here have difficult in understanding what is meant by being perilously near to a merely verbal difference without being actually there, and, more importantly, we might fin it difficul or, rather, impossible to say that two things are the same but not in their being—that seems to imply their being the same and not being the same—and the essential point, I think, is that on the relational view the distinction cannot be made whereas on the predicated view it is perfectly obvious, that is, in the one case we are talking about Edinburgh and applying a certain description to it—a relational description no doubt—in terms of which we can class it with either things north of London whereas in the other case we are talking about London and similarly making it possible to class it with other things south of Edinburgh and in raising the question of the two different classes, or similarly of the two different descriptions, we are raising two quite different questions even though if either of the two statements is true the other must be true.

Now here we have a case of what we may call a many-many relation—there are many places north of London and many places which Edinburgh is to the north of, on the other hand the mother and child case is complicated by being a many-one relation since only one being can be mother of a given child while many beings can be children of a given mother (no doubt what Alexander has in mind in his parenthesis "the same") and this fact alone makes it clear the two assertions "A is the mother of B" and "B is a child of A" are not identical. But, finall , even if the relation were what Russell calls one-one this is something that can be known only as a matter of empirical fact and not as a matter of logical form and on the predicative view we can still see the difference between the two statements of the relation and the converse relation—namely that we have two propositions with different terms.

But then again if we go back to the question of equivalent propositions with the same terms, say AeB and BeA [No As are B and No Bs are A], we could still, as I have argued, say that these are two different assertions—since the two have different subjects—since, as we put it, one of them is about A and the other is about B—since, in other words the point of agreement or the point of reference is different in both uses. And, that brings me back to the general point that in order to see how relational statements can be denied or what the distinction is about when they are disputed, we have to put them in the ordinary predicative form.

Lecture 23   *(27th September 1949)*
The Category of Universality

One major point that we have to consider is whether it is in any sense proper to speak of universals—that is whether we can speak of a certain entity called a universal, and another entity called a particular and if not how we avoid the difficult   in speaking of universality and particularity. Now Alexander says that "Strictly speaking there is no such thing as a particular or a universal" (p. 208) but at the same time he doesn't carry on his argument in terms of the proposition by reference to which, I have suggested, we can speak of the same thing having both particularity and universality and can reject the view that there are such entities as particulars and universals, and consequently a good deal of the force of his contention is lost. In fact much that he says seems to imply that there are universals. For example, he says:

> "All things are individuals. But every individual possesses particularity which
> separates it from others of the same kind or under the same universal; and it
> possesses universality which converts its bare particularity into individuality.
> Universality is thus a categorical character of all things." (*STD*, Volume 1, p.
> 208)

This seems far from convincing and it strongly suggests a doctrine of Natural kinds, but, more generally, on the view of categories as predicates—"pervasive characters of things"—we couldn't very well distinguish possessing particularity from being a particular, or possessing universality from being a universal (*cf.* possessing humanity and being human) so that we should be driven back to a belief in particulars and universals whereas if we take a propositional view and uphold in that connection the convertibility of terms then we can distinguish the two functions of the term—we can distinguish its characterising from its being characterised and its universality from its particularity.

Now the denial that there are universals as a separate set of entities—for example that they are subsistents as contrasted with existents—commonly goes with the assertion that there are particulars—that in fact there are only particulars. It is suggested, in other words, that you could point to something and say "That is a particular" while you couldn't point to something and say "that is a universal". The criticism of this view is that the general notion of a particular has no meaning—that we can point to or speak about a particular man—we can recognise X's manhood but there is no question of recognising X's particularity either as a separate character of his or its or as the totality or sum of characters.

Now, G. F. Stout attributes to me the view that a thing is identical with the sum of its qualities or predicates.[6] Actually I do not believe in any such sum, I would say we could know X as a man and as having various other properties at the same time but that we don't have the notion of a totality of his properties—not, merely, that we are not acquainted with an actual totality of this kind but that even to speak of such totality is to speak loosely. The point is that in speaking of a particular or a thing at all we are speaking of it as a thing, of some sort—as a particular instance of some kind and that any issue is concerned with things of some sort. Now in dealing with a thing of the sort man there are various characters of his that we know and various others we can fin out by further inquiry but there is never any question of *all* his characters. The very expression "particular" of course is related to the expression "partaking of", that is, as we might say "being an instance of", and "being an instance of" would appear to be just predication. "Socrates is an instance of humanity" is the same as "Socrates is a man". We might indeed think of Socrates without thinking of him as a man but we must think of him as a something, as of some kind, if we are to think of him at all.

I would say that the notion of a totality of characters belongs to the logic of totality or system—the Hegelian logic—and although Stout, for example, has many apparent differences from Hegel and does all he can

---

[6] *Cf.* G. F. Stout, "Things, Predicates and Relations" *A.J.P.P.* September 1940.

to emphasise the differences, the same Idealist strain can be traced in him and in others who deny a Hegelian affiliation

Here again you get a close connection between Kant and Hegel—the notion of system or unity as a regulative idea had much in common with the Hegelian notion of system as an active governing principle. Kant no doubt dodges some of the difficultie by maintaining that systematization is a way in which we have to think rather than the way things have to be—similarly James dodges difficultie when he maintains, despite his avowed Pluralism, that things are gradually becoming united.

In general we can say about optimistic thinkers like James and the so-called personal Idealists (including Stout) that they are merely less consistent than Hegel and that when the matter is thought out everything has to be taken as governed or embraced by or as a manifestation of a central principle like Hegel's Absolute Idea. We might note in connection with Optimism—with the notion of all things working together for good—Burnet's description of the Platonic dialectic as a sort of "teleological algebra". The point is that if to fin out the character of anything is to fin out its reason or principal purpose then to be consistent we have to take it that there is not only a purpose of the thing A and a purpose of the thing B but there is a purpose of the difference between A and B and a purpose of any relation between A and B and so on indefinitel . Burnet's suggestion is that as we proceed in the understanding of things we get more and more complicated equations but the real point is that we couldn't get an equation at all—that we could never on this line know the future of anything until we knew the future of everything so that the notion of purpose would be of no use to us in any special inquiry. Similarly, in regard to Hegel, it can be said that we couldn't know the character of anything unless we knew the character of everything—in other words, if the totalistic logic were correct we could never get started in our inquiries.

Well then, the notion of system and totality is the same as the notion of the concrete universal whereby everything is under a single governing principle or is a manifestation of the same central idea and in particular all characters of a thing are expressions of its total character and all members of a class are expressions of the general or class character. It would be maintained, of course, that ultimately that which is expressed and that which expresses it are identical but there is at least an initial distinction, in fact there is a distinction all the way even if it is a distinction in an identity and so the concrete universal is some sort of distinct entity—that is, the theory would require us to speak of a universal or the universal.

On the other hand we have the doctrine of the abstract universal, the doctrine of the "universalia post res"—of a universal as something derived from particulars—separated or abstracted from them by a mental operation and thus a separate object of contemplation even if it is taken to be inferior or subordinate to the things from which it is derived. The sort of logic that is of an openly instrumentalist kind best illustrates this position with the notion of the universal or concept as something that we form and something that we employ in the arranging of our material. In this view we do the ordering by means of concepts and other instruments of thought, on the other view it is the universals that do the ordering or that are the governing principle.

Lecture 24   *(28th September 1949)*
Addendum on Relation—The Category of Universality continued

X is a particular and X is a thing—one objection to that formula is that the converse clearly has no meaning. If we say "Some things are X" then we are not being referred to any place where you can settle the question. It seems to me in that connection that the account I have given of relational assertions and their converses (that is of terms which were implicitly, but not explicitly, qualitative) might be open to similar objections. For example, if we take the case of "X is to the right of Y" then the converse will be "Some things to the right of Y are X" and the question is what sort of location this is. We have that is a certain direction—we are told in a broad way where to look—though that wouldn't be the case if we had taken the example of "knowing" (some things which know Y are X) and even in the other case it might be argued that there has to be some suggestion of a quality if we are to know where to look to test the assertion. In other words, when we said X is to the right of Y we were saying roughly "Among the Zs X is to the right of Y" or "X is a Z to the right of Y", which would give the converse "some Zs to the right of Y are X" so that the suggestion is that we had some quality in mind when we are making the relational assertion—some "field as we might put it—for instance, it might be a row or simply a collection of men and when we say "X is to the right of Y" it would be maintained that it was the position of me in this collection that we are discussing. We have already noted that "to the right of" is relative to a fiel of view; it might be taken also to be relative to some particular interest.

Is there a real problem or difficult here? I am unsure whether it would be necessary to hold that there was an explicit quality involved in the assertion.

The Category of Universality *continued*

Coming back to the argument about types or theories of universals we can say that the theory of forms has often been taken as a theory of the abstract type—the form being the pattern to which the thing can conform to a greater or less extent—but the doctrine of the form of the good certainly comes very close to that of the concrete universal since it is essentially an organising principle which establishes the proper order among things and the forms generally, and not just the Form of the Good, are governing principles—that is, they are taken to make things what they are and not just enabling us to judge what they are—so that while the theory of forms has something in common with instrumental or conceptual accounts, it has perhaps more in common with the doctrine of the concrete universal.

Now in recent theories—theories of the Moore-Russell type—you get as near as possible to straight dualism—to just having on the one hand, things, and on the hand, universals without any suggestion that either is governed by or subordinated to the other but of course such a dualism leaves many questions unsettled which Absolute idealism and Instrumentalism are at least trying to tackle, and this might indicate why Moore and Russell have formed much less of a school than the Idealists and the Pragmatists.

> It is true that there is a school which has been considerably influence by Russell, but its success seems due to the element of instrumentalism in it.

Broadly, then, doctrines of universals are concerned with the notion of ordering or arranging things whether on what we might call the lower level of using a thing for our purposes or on the higher level of the operation of independent governing principles and we can see a connection between doctrines of universals and mentalism, that is, the doctrine of the primacy or at least the special importance of mind in reality, in so far as it is from our experience of the mind distinguishing and arranging things that we get our general notion of disposing and arranging. And here we might be able to say that not only is there a kinship between doctrines of universals and doctrines of mind-dependence of things but the former are derived from the latter or at any rate from the general notion of the human disposal of things—that the real content of governing principles may be the correlations of different forms of human activity.

> I have always argued along Burnet's line in saying that the forms are not mind-dependent in the *Phaedo*. (*Cf.* also the *Parmenides*.) Still, in the *Phaedo*, Socrates refers to the doctrine of Anaxagoras that "Mind is the disposer of all things",[7] and doesn't seem to see any incompatibility between this and view that the forms dispose of all things. The theory of forms is not of a simple subjectivist character, but there is something of a "mentalist" character in it. *Cf.* also the sympathetic attitude of Absolute Idealists to the these dialogues. (Bosanquet says that the Form of the Good is a Concrete Universal.) *Cf.* Book I of the *Republic*. On my interpretation, Socrates here puts forward a teleological account of forms—it is more "mentalist" than appears at firs sight.

Cornford, of course, simply treats the theory of forms as having a social character, that is, he takes it to be the prototype of the notion of the participation in religious groups and this is connected with the general point that Cornford over-emphasises the religious content of philosophy and underestimates its scientifi character, since whatever may be the source of belief in particular theories, Socrates in the *Phaedo* is definitel wrestling with logical questions.[8]

Cornford also, of course, takes an over-individualistic line in that he makes it a question of participation in groups—that is, a question of individuals—rather than in types of social activities, departments of social life—in many of which a given person might participate at different times. At the same time, if it is with reference to departments of social life (social provinces) that we have the firs classificatio of natural phenomena in general then we can see how the notion of governing principles could be carried over from the social to the natural or to the logical sphere.

Of course, even if we fin a certain social content still you have certain distinct and independent logical issues. Social content may account for distortions, but shouldn't blind us to the logical questions themselves

"Empirical Equivalent"

I have used this phrase loosely for the discovery of the natural stimulus to a metaphysical notion, but when the phrase was coined

---

[7] *Phaedo* 97b5, Jowett translation. *The Dialogues of Plato translated into English by B. Jowett.* 5 Volumes. Oxford: Clarendon Press, 1892. Volume 2, p. 243.

[8] Francis M. Cornford, *From Religion to Philosophy: a Study in the Origins of Western Speculation*, London: E. Arnold, 1912.

I meant "equivalence" strictly. The contention was that by means of certain Rationalistic conceptions the metaphysician is able to pass from certain empirical data to certain empirical conclusions or results and the "empirical equivalent" of his conception would be such additional empirical data as would actually enable the passage to be made. Of course, if we got that explicitly formulated we would see that a good deal of this additional material required was actually false, consisted of false propositions, but at any rate, the point to notice is that there might not always be an "empirical equivalent"—that there might be no additional information which would enable the passage to be validly made and that when we refer to the "empirical content" of such a theory or to the material as we may put it "lying behind it" then we may still have to make allowance for invalid argument—for thorough mental confusion—for the mixing of social and logical questions and so on, though even here it might be contended that there must be an "empirical equivalent" of the fallacies and confusions in the sense of alternative relations among the terms (including the identificatio of the social and the logical) which would enable the transition validly to be made.

Lecture 25   *(4th October 1949)*

The Category of Universality continued—Alexander on Universals

Here, as elsewhere, Alexander somewhat confuses his position by notions of point-instants, and space-time as "stuff".

In Chapter III of Book II entitled "Universal, Particular, and Individual" Alexander is especially concerned with the question of universality. His main point is that a universal is a "plan" and that it is a spatio-temporal plan—that universals, in his phrase are "habits" of space-time just as a man's qualities can be identifie with his habits or ways of behaving. Now we may adopt the latter view but it is a different thing to speak of space-time itself as behaving in a certain way and here we may notice the confusion of the "stuff" theory because there is no way in which space-time behaves everywhere and anywhere and there is nothing in space-time itself to show why a particular habit—a given universal—should crop up at one place or time rather than another. We have here the same weakness as in Anaximander who takes the determinate to arise out of the indeterminate but could give no account or no explanation of the occurrence of this separation at one place and time and not at another—couldn't do so, in fact, unless there was already a qualitative distinction between the two places.

There are two general points that I might mention here.

1. Alexander's treatment seems to imply that everything has a plan but that is to say, not that a thing is a universal, but that it is a particular. To treat universality as all-pervasive he would have to say that everything is a plan—that is, he would have to be referring to the peculiarity of things and not just to their spatio-temporality or, in my previous terms, he would have to be referring to the thing as characterising and not as being characterised.

2. Such peculiarities may be of a strictly spatio-temporal character. That is they may have the sort of thing that is called a "primary quality"—size, shape and so forth and here it might he said that there is no place at which a given shape couldn't occur though there might be a difficult in saying there was no place at which a given size couldn't occur but, of course, even Alexander doesn't treat these primary qualities as categories (they might be what he calls "determinations" of categories) but the point is that when we talk about a certain size or shape occurring somewhere—when we think of it as a "habit" of something—it is always of something that has a concrete quality—the sort of thing that is loosely called a secondary quality—which again indicates that it is not habits of space-time itself that we are concerned with.

Whatever qualities or universals are habits of, then, they are not habits of space-time. Alexander says that empirical universals like "dog" or "tree" or "justice" are possible because space-time is uniform and behaves therefore on plans which are undistorted by differences of place and time. Now clearly space-time is not uniform in respect of these universals, it does not always and everywhere behave doggishly or arboreally or justly—it is not space-time that explains why these forms of activity take place when and where they do.

We might say vaguely that concrete uniformity is possible because of the uniformity of space-time, that is, we might speak in terms of what Bosanquet calls the indifference of space (in the "Philosophical Theory of the State"—the phrase originates in Hegel) that is, as far as space is concerned (and similarly time) anything might take place anywhere though we might still not recognize as significan the hypothesis that space and time are not uniform. It is this very indifference of space and time that shows that universals are not habits of space-time—the point being the same as in the assertion of the synthetic character of the proposition—that is we have to learn from experience that a certain predicate has certain subjects, that a particular character occurs in some places and not in others. There is nothing in a description by itself to tell us where it is to be located—nothing in a quality to tell us what will be its particulars—that is, what will be the peculiarities of its subject apart from this having this common quality—nothing in a genus to tell us what its species are, that, of course, being what is denied in the doctrine of Concrete universal—though if we take matter concretely, if we talk about things and not about pure space-time, then there actually is something that prevents certain qualities being in certain places—in other words, there are true E propositions.

The confusion involved in the "stuff" theory is still clearly marked when Alexander passes from empirical universals to what he calls the most comprehensive of all universals—the categories themselves—which he says are *a priori* plans of configuration Such a doctrine of Highest kinds fails, of course, to get out of the difficultie of substantialism and having spoken of an "empirical" universal as a "plan of empirical determination" Alexander has to speak of the categories as the "key plans of all plans of empirical determination"—an expression which I suggests is meaningless.

He holds, incidentally, that while the other categories are universals, universality itself is not a universal anymore than the empirical universal dog is a dog (anymore than dogginess is a dog as we might put it). But the comparison, I would say, is not a fair one and if the categories really are pervasive characters of things universality would have to be a universal. In using the word "plan" to describe a universal Alexander distinguishes plan from configuration—speakin of a "plan of configuration for example, he says the configuratio of a person which varies from moment to moment remains within the limits of a plan which persists. But it may be argued that "plan" and "configuration are concepts we cannot really distinguish and more broadly that Alexander can't distinguish universals and particulars, a point which, as we saw, he recognizes at the beginning of the chapter although he afterwards goes back on it.

A plan, in fact, can be considered as much a particular as a universal. As Joseph pointed out we talk about particular plans (At Cambridge in 1926—Joseph instanced "but I was thinking of a plan to dye my whiskers green…" Discussion may be in one of the

Aristotelian Supplementary volumes).[9] This might be taken to be unfair criticism—we say that something is of a particular kind but we might be said to be using "particular" in a different sense from the sense involved in saying that something is a particular of that kind—but the general point remains that any expression Alexander uses to distinguish universals from particulars will admit of particularity as much as of universality. Thus, in trying to distinguish his theory from the theory of forms Alexander raises the question of the kind of reality universals possess and says:

> "half the difficult or possibly all of it disappears when it is admitted that particulars are complexes of space-time and belong therefore to the same order or are of the same stuff as the universals which are plans of space-time." (*STD*, Volume 1, pp. 220-1)

But if universals and particulars, plans and complexes, were of the same stuff we should have to concede that there was no difference between them—that there are no separate universals.   But if the distinction is retained universals will have to be treated as not themselves spatio-temporal—as not of the same structure as particulars and in fact they would not belong to the particulars—like the forms or like Moore's non-natural good they would floa or hover over the particulars (this is rough and metaphorical) and we should never be able to connect such and such a form with such and such a particular.

Thus, while on a propositional theory we see that the same thing can qualify and be qualifie can, if we care to put it so, be universal and particular, on a substantialist theory—on the doctrine that things are composed of a universal stuff—we can't give any account of qualificatio (qualifying) we cannot recognize or assert any sort of difference between one part of the substance and another. And these considerations bring us back to the point that just as there aren't separate universals so there aren't separate particulars—that when we are talking of a thing we are talking of a thing of some sort and when for example we say that a thing lasts for a certain time in that we see the same thing again it is only in terms of certain persistent qualities that we can say so.

Lecture 26   *(5th October 1949)*
The Category of Universality continued—Ranges—The Concrete Universal

We saw that there is no such thing as a pure particular—that there is only a particular X, a particular man or a particular colour. In these

---

[9] H. W. B. Joseph (1867-1943), author of Introduction to Logic (1906).

illustrations, of course, you have different meanings—a particular man being what we call an individual—that is a number of occurrences, of the sort manhood which form a single continuous history whereas a particular colour generally means something like "red", that is, a species of the genus colour where the various occurrences dealt make up one continuous history but there is a similar relation to the universal (what I call a universal for short) in the two cases—the relation of "exemplifying" as we might put it—and in both cases there is repetition—that is, what we call an individual is a species in that it is at once an instance of the universal and itself has instances even though these instances make up a continuous history which could itself be called an instance of the universal.

Ranges

Now on the question of colour Alexander makes a curious point, he is discussing the question of space of various curvatures in connection with his view that there are universals because there is a uniform or constant curvature of space as against the view that there is not this uniformity. He says then that:

> "...while there is a good meaning in the universal contained in the varying curvatures of curves in our Space it is difficul to see what is the universal element in the varying curvatures of the supposed Space which itself varies in curvature. [JA: Is this just a way of saying that the notion of curvature of Space is meaningless?] The supposed universal is rather comparable to colour in relation to the various colours, red, green, etc. There is no element colour in these of which red and green are variations. Colour is a collective name rather than a class one or a universal. Such a universal curvature is nothing then, as before, but a bare thought; and no conclusion can be drawn from the suppositions of my critics." (*STD*, Volume 1, p.216n.)

> If no conclusion is drawable then there is not really a supposition at all, but I am here more concerned with his remarks on *colour*.

We may ask why if red, green and so on have nothing in common we should collect them together and how we could speak of them by a collective name—how we could know what the name included and what the name excluded. What Alexander says of colour could be said of shape or any other universal—there is no element which we can pick and say that is the shape of the thing, and so on. No doubt we seldom say when we are presented with a thing it is coloured" (though we sometimes say "it is colourless") because so little would be distinguished from anything else by the general term "colour" whereas much can be distinguished, say, by the special term "red". But "red" presents us with the very same problem, namely whether it isn't a mere collective name for various shades of red (as we say) seeing that we can't extract an element from a space of red and say that is its redness and again we should have a similar problem regarding what we call an *exact* shade of red, namely whether this covers a certain range or is confine to one mathematical point on the spectrum.

The tendency to take the latter view comes with the association of rates of vibration with colours so that an exact shade would correspond to a precise number (namely of vibrations) but even if it were not the case (I would say that it is the case) that any colour name applies over a certain range however short—even if every time we said "That is X" we were referring to something whose rate of vibration was the number N without a hairsbreadth of deviation—there would still be variations—the thing being X would not be all about it as is indicated by our saying "these two things are of the same colour but of different degrees of brightness" and so on. I would say, then, that expressions like royal blue, salmon and even bright red always cover some range and that the theory of exact shades is of a Rationalistic character—that is, involves the doctrine of "whole natures" and this applies in general to Alexander's doctrine of the collective name—a doctrine which comes close to Stout's theory of universality—the theory of the distributive unity or disjunction which constitutes being of a certain kind.

> (i) It may be that in doctrine of the collective name Alexander is influence by Stout, although the Gifford Lectures are earlier than Stout's doctrine of universals, but they belong to a certain common line of thinking.
>
> (ii) "Whole natures", *cf.* Berkley's difficultie with "abstraction" in the Introduction to his *Principles of Human Knowledge*.[10]

The Concrete Universal

Coming to Alexander's discussion of the Concrete universal with general reference to Bosanquet, we can say that just as "plan" doesn't give us a distinction of universals from particulars so the notion of "law" does not—that you can have a particular law just as you can have a particular plan. When we speak of the laws under which a thing is acting we are referring of course to a thing's ways of behaving which of course is just the adverbial way as contrasted with the adjectival way of expressing predication—instead of saying X is just we say X behaves or goes on justly though perhaps when we speak of a law we are thinking rather of the whole proposition than specially of the predicate—that is

---

[10]George Berkeley, *Principles of Human Knowledge*, edited by T. E. Jessop. London: Thomas Nelson and Sons, 1945. Pp. 8ff.

we might say "All X are just" is a law but we would hardly say that justice is a law and to say in particular that it is a law of X is again to say "All X are just". But what we do not or cannot empirically mean by a law is a governing principle—something distinct from a way of behaving of certain things—something which rules over and determines this behaviour.

In the theory of the Concrete Universal we certainly have the notion of a governing principle—a principle which draws things together or unites them or which takes them as in reality unified—a being such that in any one we can see all the others. Thus, on Bosanquet's view, we do not see what is involved in attributing manhood to anyone unless you can see what are the capacities of men in general—that is what are all the things that a man can be and not just what are things any man must be ("the doctrine of Comprehension"). That is, human nature is not something attributable to each *man* but is the system which unites men—that of which they are all expressions—and we don't really understand one such expression without understanding all of them.

Alexander, of course, points out that such a system, such a uniting of all the members of the human race which is sometimes referred to as humanity, is not what we mean by the universal "humanity"—that is it is an individual (assuming that this total collection could be made or contemplated) and it would be false to say of that united entity "this is a man". At the same time, as I suggested earlier, Alexander himself is not entirely free from views that belong to the logic of the Concrete universal, what I was calling Totalistic views—and we will see this further as we proceed.

Bosanquet—in "Principle of Individuality and Value"—lecture on the Concrete universal, says:

> "The ultimate principle, we may say, is sameness in the other; generality [JA: is what is involved in the notion of class as contrasted with the notion of world] is sameness in spite of the other. Universality is sameness by means of the other".[11]

Thus he says:

> "the true embodiment of the logical universal takes the state of a world whose members are worlds".[12]

---

[11] Bernard Bosanquet, *The Principle of Individuality and Value: The Gifford Lectures for 1911.* London: Macmillan, 1912, p. 37
[12] *Ibid.*

A little later he speaks of the "power" of the Concrete universal[13]—its capacity in the way of unifying experience and a little later again:

> "the Universal is just that character of Experience which overcomes the "is not" by reducing it to an element harmonious with and corroborative of the "is". It is the self in the other... true inwardness is outwardness absorbed".[14]

> Nb. I am denying the existence of exact shades—even if exactly correlated with a certain rate of vibration (conversation with Anderson).

Lecture 27   (11th October 1949)
The Category of Universality continued

> Humanity is a whole, not a quality. We are talking about a certain collection of men (assuming that it could be made).

This notion of a total humanity, realized in all its parts or members, is analogous to the notion of a total mentality realized in every one of its acts—the notion of an "I" or Ego which is present in each of my acts. It is this assumption which permits the theory of Concrete universality, or universality as totality, to be formulated and the demonstration of the falsity of the assumption is clearly connected with the *cogito*—with the demonstration of the falsity of the theory of the ego.

> Bound up with whole Hegelian position—Stout, Cook Wilson will, on close inspection, be seen to approximate to Bosanquet. *Cf.* Kemp Smith on universals[15]

The leading example of a Concrete universal, is Mind as conceived by the Idealists—that is, mind is taken to exhibit what we may call through and throughness—the universal of mind is taken to run through and organise all mental manifestations. Now this doctrine has the emptiness of the *cogito*, that is, of a conception which has only a relational content and is fille in by the related terms and the position is that the possessor of various experiences is at once identifie with and distinguished from these experiences—is treated as abstract and also as concrete—as embracing the whole of experience. The doctrine of "the owner of experience"—the sort of theory conveyed by the personal pronoun—would be impossible without some qualitative reference—that is without there being some entity related to that experience which had a quality of its own (i.e., of the entities' own). That is required for the *distinction* but for the *connection* it is lost sight

---

[13] *Ibid.*, p. 41.
[14] *Ibid.*, p. 46, p. 74.
[15] Norman Kemp Smith, "The Nature of Universals I", *Mind* New Series 36(142) April 1927: 137-57; "The Nature of Universals II", *Mind* New Series 36(143) July 1927: 265-80; "The Nature of Universals III", *Mind* New Series 36(144) October 1927: 393-422.

of and we have the identificatio of what is an object of mind with what constitutes mind and here we have the common idealist doctrine in Hegel, Caird, etc. of the inseparability of subject and object—the rejection of what is called the "abstract subject" and equally of the "abstract object" and expressions like experience are used to cover the whole—being taken to have a subjective and an objective aspect. (This expression "aspect" by the way, is another idealist device for overcoming opposition, or unifying differences.)

Thus both the implicit distinction and the absence of explicit distinction (between mind and its objects) are required to make the theory plausible and the position is that "I" am the universal of all my experiences (as contrasted with the general notion of "experience of mine" which ordinary Logic would employ and which wouldn't imply any unity or collection of its subjects) and so the unity of all the experiences is supposed to be found in each of the experiences—they are supposed to run together—to belong to one another—to have a through and through connection—and on this view the universal is a distinct entity or substance.

There is, of course, a close connection between the doctrines of Hegel and Leibniz—Leibniz having the notion of each perception of a subject as an expression of that subject and hence as an expression of all the other perceptions, that is it is all or any of the others with a certain degree of clarity, and when Hegel praises Leibniz as the firs philosopher to make the fina step from substance to subject—from extensive unity to intensive unity—he means by "subject" this through and through expressiveness—each aspect expressing the whole, or being the whole raised to a certain power. But although these theorists speak about unity in difference they are left with just as many inescapable differences as those who continue to recognize bare and unmediated distinctions.

This doctrine of universality requires that the particulars be taken not just as separate instances of the universal but as forming a system or totality—as being collected in some way. Thus when I am said to be the universal or the unity of my experiences it is not a matter of merely a relation between this universal and any experience we like to take but of these experiences hanging together—making up various minor totalities within the totality and, starting from mind, the same notion of system or totality, or through and throughness, is found by the idealists in any subject whatever.

Thus, in enquiring into social facts[16] Bosanquet takes society as a Concrete universal—as something manifested in each social phenomena hang together. Now naturally we recognize certain connections among social facts just as among mental facts but we are doing violence to the facts if we treat them all as manifestations of a single entity and reject or explain away social or mental conflict or again relations of indifference in mind and society. The view I am criticizing treats opposition of interests and similarly indifference as something only apparent—something that has to be abandoned in a rational view of the matter and thus you get the Monistic view of mind or society as against the Pluralist view. Thus the treatment of mind as this sort of totality assumes one pre-eminent interest which is satisfie or for which satisfaction is sought in any mental act whatever and the notion of Reason, for example covers the reconcilability of all interests.

Now there is one obvious difficult about this view—the Idealist doctrine of universal man or humanity in which men are treated not as various instances of a certain kind but as forming a system or totality—namely that humanity is indistinguishable from society and in fact Bosanquet identifie social system or harmony with mental system or harmony and the Hegelians generally treat the social as mental, even when they call it "objective mind". There can't on this view be any real distinction between subjective minds and objective mind and this amalgamation of distinct question is inevitable, just because the alleged unities—at once totalities and principles—don't really exist and we can't then really distinguish them and this exemplifie the well known difficult Absolutists have in preventing the Absolute from absorbing every distinct thing that could be talked about—that is from doing away with what are supposed to be its distinct manifestation—just as in the Socratic theory it is impossible to prevent the Form of the Good from absorbing all the entities supposed to come under it and nullifying their differences.

Now, in spite of Alexander's rejection of the Concrete universal—his contention that a system or totality is a particular, not a plan of particulars—he frequently comes very close to this doctrine. For example, in discussing class-concepts "abstractions taken apart from all variations in things" and similarly laws of Nature as "abstractions of the common elements in the relations of things to the neglect of the variation of the relations" Alexander says that:

---

[16] *Cf.* especially the *Philosophical Theory of the State*, London: Macmillan, 1923.

"it is evident enough that useful as such abstractions maybe and are for
arbitrary or provisional purposes, they have nothing in common with universals
as plans or laws of construction, for these so far from neglecting the wealth and
variety of their particular instances are the formulae which hold the instances
together, not merely in our thinking but in fact". (*STD*, Volume 1, p. 231.)

and he goes on to say that in the actual practice of the sciences a class

"is not a mere collection of particulars which happen to agree in certain
important respects but a group determined by their constitutive formula".
(*STD*, Volume 1, p. 231.)

We might suggest that for Alexander as for Bosanquet and for that
matter for Berkeley the difficult is to show how such abstraction,
such inferior thinking, is even possible, how in Alexander's case we
can have a class-concept which isn't a universal; but at least we
can see here that there is very little difference between Alexander
and Bosanquet—Alexander might be said to take the universal as the
determining formula and Bosanquet as the group determined by the
formula or rather as at once the formula, and that of which it is the
formula, which in itself indicates how the two positions run together.

Lecture 28   *(12th October 1949)*

The Category of Universality continued

A recognition of species with their differences (what we call a
classification is not the universal—that is, is not the general character.
We can be said to be concerned with that character, or that sort of thing,
when we speak quite generally of the class—that is when we speak of the
class "men" as contrasted with the character "humanity" or "manhood"
we are distinguishing X or man as a possible subject from man as a
predicate, but these are the same term—we don't really have the class
on the one side and the universal on the other—we are not setting up any
system when we refer to the various things which have such and such a
character.

On the other hand when we do make a class or a division—when we
distinguish the species—then we are not simply expounding the genus
or universal, we are findin a set of relations between that term and other
terms and to make those other terms inherent in the given term (i.e., the
species inherent in the genus) is to adopt the standpoint of the Concrete
universal and to be unable logically to stop short of the Absolute which is
the universal of everything (*the* universal). Of course in the very doctrine
of space-time as a universal "stuff" we have something of the nature
of an Idealist Absolute—that is in Alexander's view that qualities are

inherent in space-time, that they emerge from space-time as such. In fact Alexander's optimistic evolutionism is a species of Idealism and to avoid the difficultie of Idealism Alexander would have to refer to the abstract universal—in the sense of what is common to a number of things and doesn't in any way embrace their variations or differences.

Stout's theory as an approach to idealism

Now Stout's theory of universality may be said to recognize the fact that there isn't a certain thing common to the various members of a class—that we cannot speak of the universal as a distinguishing and distinct part, the same part of this, that and the other thing, but then he proceeds to treat a quality as a number of different things—one in each members of the class—and he has to fall back for something common—for the possibility of speaking of a common feature—on his "distributive unity"—that is on a kind of system of qualities of things rather than of the things themselves. And even if this system is only distributive—even if it only allows rather than requires variations—still in order to say how far the variations extend, in order to have a position which isn't simply an arbitrary naming, we should have to have something like Alexander's "plan" or Bosanquet's "through and throughness"—that is, we should have to say that in this distributive unity taken as an object of thought lie all the variations which in other theories are thought to be inherent in the plan or system.

Now we have seen previously that Stout's theory evades some of these difficultie by the use of the vague notion of resemblance, we have seen also that this would make classificatio impossible unless it is a question of resemblance in a particular respect, in other words that the mere statement A is like B is simply the assertion of a subject A or B without a predicate and while the acceptance of the terms may be said to involve the acceptance of their opposites not-A and not-B, or of the proposition "not-A i not-B" [some not-A are not-B] is certainly not a characterization of A or B (it tells you nothing specifi about A and B themselves), and we still require to defin the likeness by some predicate (X).

It is possible, of course, to recognize likeness without being able to specify that likeness—to name it. We make assertions like "He looks like a Trade Union Secretary" or "This poem reminds me of Wordsworth" without being able to say just what the common qualities are in either case. But since we are saying that there are such qualities even if we have difficult   in precisely distinguishing them or conveying them to others in other words, what we are trying to bring out is made more exact when the quality is specified

We might say, then, that Stout is trying and failing to present qualities as relations and that there is more than a suggestion of the doctrine of system or concrete universality in the position. Alternatively, we can say that Stout is bringing out one aspect of the Idealist view, that is that there would have to be something relational in this account of universality—they would have to say, and they do say, these things belong together or work together and they can say this more definitel than they can say what it is that these things have in common, particularly of course in respect of the view that *all* things work together. In that way Stout's doctrine is akin to Idealism or can be taken as a variant of Idealism and Alexander's doctrine, again, has clearly marked Idealist features.

Stout's amalgamation of qualities and relations is seen again in his article "Things, Predicates, and Relations"[17] as, more broadly, the doctrine of relational properties may be said to identify different issues, and Stout's phrase "an enveloping relation" covers such a false identification—fo while in a sense we could say that the situation ArB envelops A and B we certainly can't say it characterizes or describes A or B—to speak of the enveloping relation is simply to say that the situation ArB exists.

---

[17]G. F. Stout, "Things, Predicates and Relations" *A.J.P.P.* September 1940.

5
The Categories II: The Mathematical Categories
Categories of Quantity[1]

Lecture 28   *(12th October 1949) continued*
The Table of Categories—Universality and Particularity
The Table of Categories

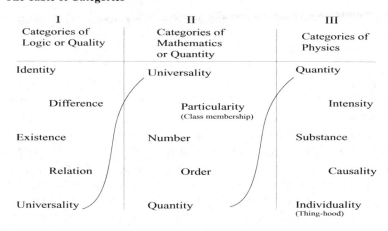

I	II	III
Categories of Logic or Quality	Categories of Mathematics or Quantity	Categories of Physics
Identity	Universality	Quantity
Difference	Particularity (Class membership)	Intensity
Existence	Number	Substance
Relation	Order	Causality
Universality	Quantity	Individuality (Thing-hood)

Figure 11.

Universality and quantity are link categories, and so each appear twice. Note also the alternation of "monadic" and "dyadic" categories.

One way of distinguishing these groups is to say that the categories of the firs group are necessary for, or are ways in which we can give an account of things, as in space and time or as in situations; the categories of the second group are ways in which we can give an account of things as spatio-temporal or even as spaces and times, and the importance of the second group is that they enable us to speak of space and time themselves along with things (this is just a suggestion of mine) thus helping us to see how there can be a theory of space-time although space and time aren't things; and the categories of the third group are ways in which we give an account of things as distinct from space and time—as

---

[1] The student notes err in describing the Mathematical Categories as categories of *quality* rather than *quantity*. Anderson's own notes are clear: "I want to come on to the second group of categories: what we may call the categories of quantity as contrasted to those of quality, or the mathematical as contrasted with the narrowly *logical* categories." (P.A.J.A. Lectures on Alexander 1949, p. 154. Series 43, Box 102.)

qualitative—as having what are loosely called secondary qualities (the so-called primary qualities being associated with the second group or being qualitative features of things).

(The larger problems of grouping and order I will have to set aside.)

Universality and Particularity

I said previously that the category of universality (expressed roughly, as if the categories were predicates) should not be taken as indicating that anything is of a kind, but rather as indicating that anything is a kind or is a quality. Now as far as the firs group of categories is concerned we needed to consider only the distinction of quality among propositions we needed only the form X is, or is not Y, without regard to what is called the quantity of propositions [all or some]—that is we were dealing with the thing in a broad way. (That is, relation is associated with incompatibility—this would hold however the proposition was quantified.

However, when we turn to the quantity of propositions which I have presented as bound up with the convertibility of terms (see Logic lectures, 1948, Lecture 1), coming in this way to the mathematical categories or categories of quantity we make the transition through the notion of universality—that is through the doctrine of a general predicate and a general subject, or, if you like, between universality and class, or alternatively between quality and class, both notions being covered by the notion of *kind*, man and men, but at the same time we have a sense of the difference—what I have called the difference of function between quality and class and this difference is made explicit in *division*—in recognition of species related in a disjunction—or in recognition of members of the class—what we call particulars and with the recognition of the possibility of such division or such membership we have the recognition of the category of particularity.

This division is connected with quantity, with disjunction, and the class view of the proposition may be said to be an attempt to reduce the proposition to a quantitative character—to treat any proposition as a division or as part of a division. Now as contrasted with this, definition involved in conjunction, can be connected with quality—that is we can call division a quantitative combination and definitio a qualitative Combination (extensive and intensive combination) and in these terms we can see some force, even without accepting it, in Alexander's doctrine of "plan"—in the consideration namely that the universality of a term is brought out in definin it—in indicating how it is constituted—and similarly its particularity in dividing it. We should remember, of course, that there is convertibility in both cases—that both the definition and the division are co-extensive with the given term, but we could roughly say that the one is so in a general way, and the other in a special way.

Lecture 29   *(18th October 1949)*

Universality as a Link Category—The Category of Number—Whole and Part as Substance

Conjunction: Combination of Predicates

Disjunction: Combination of Subjects

I have suggested that you could take the term *kind* to cover the two notions of quality and class and at any rate that you have the passage from quality to the various things having the quality—from intension to extension or from universality to particularity. Now without admitting the doctrine of special kinds of proposition having the "is" of inclusion or the "is" of class-membership we can say that the doctrine of such types of proposition is an attempt to grapple with these categories, but that what we need for the consideration of them is not a certain kind of proposition or a certain part of a proposition but rather a grouping of propositions under which might also come argument or implication as a certain way in which propositions are connected. At any rate we can treat disjunction or an assumption of likeness with which particularity is connected as a group of propositions—instead of saying All (A or B) are X we could simply say AaX and BaX—in other words a conjunction of truths in place of a disjunction of terms.

> I have always treated the disjunctive form All (A or B) are X as an inference from AaX and BaX, i.e., as a distinct proposition, but we could still say that implicitly AaX and BaX raise the question of grouping.

It might still be difficul to include universality among the categories of quantity but carrying it over into the second group, of making it common to the second group, at least reminds us of the importance of universality for all considerations of quantity since all quantity, all measurement involves singleness of kind—involves a common quality—something that the quantity is a quantity of—and similarly something that a number is a number of, for though we sometimes count things which we say are not of the same kind, e.g., enumerating the fruits on a plate where some are apples and some are pears the difference of kind is actually irrelevant to the enumeration—it is only the recognition of a common kind—of a common description that enables us to understand the counting or assigning any meaning to it when we have completed it.

The Category of Number

Coming on then to the discussion of number, I contend that considerations of number begin with integers (whole numbers) a position conceded by Russell in the *Principles of Mathematics*[2] (whatever he may say in later works) and that these integers are characteristic of groups (Russell's concession covers both of these points)—that is, of some recognition of number as linked with definit classes, or instances of a universal. Now to say that the theory of number starts with groups is not to fall into the error of the Pythagoreans of taking the discrete to be prior to the continuous, or the continuous to be built up out of separate units, because each of the so-called units is itself continuous and there is no question of an absolute unit—of what is just one—but only of what is one X—say in a given case one apple—and as such already exhibits spatial and temporal continuity—and it is on the rejection of the just one, or the absolute unit, that the Pythagorean theory has to be rejected.

The continuity does not arise out of original units, but, still, considerations of number arise in connection with separate members of a class—recognition of such membership being recognition of the truth of a proposition and the proposition already involving spatio-temporal continuity so that while we come from number to quantity—that is to theory of the numerical representation of something that has continuous graduations and doesn't change by units; on the one hand it is from groups that we get our numerical apparatus which we employ when we talk about a unit quantity and on the other hand there is no denial here of continuous graduation since continuity is present in whatever we take as a unit.

The unit by which we measure continuous quantity is, of course, arbitrary—we decide arbitrarily that such and such will be a foot or a pound but without such unity we can't measure quantity and we can still see them as not absolute units in the Pythagorean manner. However there is a distinction of types of consideration—there is the question of integers or whole numbers which takes its departure from qualitative description "This is an "X" and there is the question of quantity which

---

[2]Bertrand Russell, *Principles of Mathematics*, Cambridge: Cambridge University Press, 1903.

takes its departure from spatial extension, from things being alongside one another instead of qualifying one another or, if you care to put it so, from the compound as contrasted with the complex (a part is not the same as a quality) but there is no opposition between these two types of consideration—they are both covered by the theory of things as spatio-temporal.

All this is in line with the treatment of mathematics as an observational science like any other science and is opposed to the treatment of it as of a higher kind—perhaps intuitional—is opposed to the view that 2 plus 2 equals 4 has nothing to do with actual groups—nothing to do with recognizing say that 2 apples plus 2 apples are 4 apples. One difficult of such a doctrine of rational mathematics over and above how we could ever fin out that 2 plus 2 equals 4 would be that of applying mathematical knowledge to actual things, of knowing what the rational entity 2 means in terms of apples or any other observable entity. It would be possible to apply mathematical science to physical facts, I would argue, only if it was possible to refute mathematical theories by recognition of physical facts and that means that it is really with physical facts that mathematics is concerned. On the other view it would be impossible to replace or criticize any mathematical doctrine whatever—to make the least objection to anyone saying that 2 plus 2 equals 5 (on the assumption, of course, that such an assertion could be made at all).

Alexander on the Category of Number

In Book II Chapter 8 Alexander treats the two questions of whole and part, and number, that is to say he connects the notion of number with the notion of whole and part which is opposed to my connecting it with particularity, that is with quality in the firs instance even if we go on from it to take in the question of quantity.[3] Now here we may ask is "whole and part" a category at all and firstl , as far as it is a question of containing or including, we take that as equivalent to the category of quantity—that is, of what admits of more or less—in fact distinguishing quantity as continuous from number as working with the distinct unit we might particularly identify the notion of the more and less with the notion of quantity. Of course in speaking of the distinction it is important for mathematical theory to come on the notion of "real number"—to attempt a correlation of numerical values with continuously varying

---

[3] *STD*, Book II, Chapter 8: Whole and Parts; and Number. Pp. 312ff.

quantity as contrasted with what varies by ones. But that doesn't alter the fact that integers are the originally apprehended numbers and it may still be noted that the application of number to the continuous is never complete or exact—that you can't represent continuous variation numerically any more than the Pythagoreans could have a figur of the passage from one figur to another. Thus, even if we should describe the square root of 2 as a real number and consider it to have a place on a line just as definit as the place we could assign to 1 or 2, we could never exhibit numerically the passage between the point $\sqrt{2}$ and the point say 7/5 or 17/12—that is we could never represent it by a numerical expression but only by movement.

For that matter, we couldn't represent by a mathematical expression the passage from 7/5 to 17/12—we couldn't represent the passage between two rational numbers—which serves to bring out the fact that however we may apply considerations of number to continuous things there will be a limit to such applications—that there is, so to speak, no number for continuity itself which emphasises again that the continuous can't be built out of the discrete. But this is no reason for not recognising where and how numerical considerations apply.

But all this makes it very important not to confuse the two conceptions of quantity and number whatever connections there may be. This confusion, I suggest, is involved in Alexander's theory of the conception of whole and part as the starting point for a theory of number. Among integers we still have the relation of more or less but we don't have the continuous passage between the less and the more—and it is with quantitative continuity that Alexander is linking number when he says:

> Number is the constitution of a whole in relation to its parts; and it is generated
> in the concurrent or correspondent distinction of parts in space and time within
> a spatio-temporal whole." (*STD*, Volume 1, p. 313.)

and again when he says:

> All existents are numerable or possess number because in occupying a space-
> time they occupy part of space in correspondence with parts of time. (*STD*,
> Volume 1, p. 313)

But (i) this suggests a doctrine of unitary parts again; (ii) the notion of a whole is different from the notion of a class—there is no suggestion that members of a class are united—are alongside of each other.

Whole and Part as Substance

Well then, the confusion of number with quantity being one relevant misunderstanding there, is another possible sense of whole and part besides quantity or the distinction of what contains and what is contained, namely the sort of thing that Alexander recognizes in the category of substance and what we call the constitution or composition of a thing; and once these two categories quantity and substance have been recognized there is no need for a category of whole and part. This alternative sense of whole is indicated in the assertion that a whole is something more than a sum of its parts and this no longer seems paradoxical when we realise what a sum is—namely a disjunction of things which don't have to be spatially continuous at all so that even where we have things that are spatially continuous even where, as we say, we enumerate parts of a given thing, still even that is not a description of the thing as it is not an account of the thing as a whole.

Lecture 30   *(19th October 1949)*
Universality and Particularity Addendum—The Category of Number continued

In saying that universality is the point of transition between the firs and the second group of categories I suggested that while the firs set can be correlated with certain constituents of the proposition—particularly the qualitative proposition—in the sense of that which admits of the distinction of affirmat ve and negative—there was, e.g., correlation of existence with the copula; the remaining categories might be correlated with logical operations or procedures—with relations between propositions or groups of propositions. Now here the dual use of universality, of the transition to particularity, may be connected with the operation of conversion, with the convertibility of terms—that is, the passage under the head of Kind from quality to class can be linked with the passage from being a predicate to being a subject. On the understanding that any predicate can be a subject, and in treating being X as placing rather than characterizing we pass from X-ness to X's or all X—from the universal predicate to the universal proposition or from quality to quantity in the sense in which these expressions are applied to propositions and thus to the notion of class. In the same way we can connect the distinction of universality and particularity with the distinction of quantity of propositions—the distinction between all and some.

> When you are dealing with the class, the notion of particularity covers both (i) particular as a member of the class; (ii) particular as part of the class ("Some...").

The Category of Number *continued*

We have seen that Alexander in his treatment of whole and part confuses quantity and number and under the same heading he confuses substance with quantity and again with number. Now when we speak about a substance—a thing or whole of a certain substance—we are not speaking in numerical terms since a whole is not equivalent to a sum and thus there is no paradox in saying as is commonly said that a whole is more than the sum of its parts. But if, with Alexander, we confuse whole with sum—or with something enumerated—an enumeration of parts—there is a paradox, in fact there is a contradiction we can't get over. When we are using whole in the substantial sense—in the sense of make-up or constitution, an enumeration of parts is not a description of the whole—it leaves out the essential question how these parts, which of course are quantitatively included in the whole, are related to one another.

Thus interrelation of parts is one of the things we mean by that composition of a thing though we also mean an interrelation of qualities—of things predicable of the whole which a part is not.

"Arm" is not a predicate of Man—unlike, say, "Rationality".

Substance—involves complexity of qualities and compounding of parts.

The fact that an interrelation of parts is not what we mean by a sum disposes of the superficia view that 2+2=4 doesn't apply to drops of water since when you add two drops to two drops you get not four drops but one. Those who make this assertion don't indicate how we can take a pair of drops in the firs place without making them one but in any case we can say that if when two drops and two drops are run together they are no longer four it is equally the case that they are no longer 2+2 so that no exception has been found to the rule 2 and 2 are 4. The main point is that there is here a complete misunderstanding of the notion of addition which implies nothing as to physical contact or juxtaposition but is simply what is indicated by the expression "or" with the proviso that a mathematical sum differs from a logical sum (A or B) in that A has to exclude B (A or B where AeB—No A is B) which is not the case in logical disjunction (which doesn't *have* to exclude though it may).

Now if we say that a human body is composed of head and arm and trunk and legs logically—head or arms or trunk or legs are the parts of the human body—then that disjunction or addition is not the human body—the sum of these four things would be the same if the body were dismembered—if the parts were lying around in various places—but it wouldn't be that whole of interrelated parts—that substance which we call a human body. In general then, the introduction of this type of consideration only confuses further the doctrine of number which Alexander confused in the firs place by not distinguishing number from quantity.

Now having said that all existents are numerable Alexander goes on to deny that enumeration implies singleness of kind. He says:

> "It matters not whether the parts be equal or unequal, homogeneous or heterogeneous in their qualities; or whether the wholes are of the same extent of space-time or not, a group consisting of a man and a dog is as much a two as a group of two men or two shillings; though its parts are unequal in quantity and different in quality; and as much two as a group of two elephants or two mice which occupy as wholes very different quantities of space-time. To arrive at the number of a whole of individuals we have to abstract from the quality or the magnitude of the individuals—their number concerns only the constitution of the whole out of its parts or the resolution of the whole into them". (*STD*, Volume 1, pp. 313–14.)

Alexander is here assuming in a quite unempirical manner the absolute individual—assuming that there is a compelling reason for calling a man one and a dog one—and hence a man and a dog two—assuming in the Pythagorean style that that is the number of a man and a dog as against the view that there is no such thing as the number of things in a given situation—that the things in a situation could be numbered in any way whatever and that we call a man and a dog a pair only because we start from some at least vaguely conceived common quality—say animality.[4]

In disjunction, as we saw, we are not saying anything definit when we say A is like B or use the term (A or B)—nothing more definite as I indicated, than that A and B together aren't everything—we come to a precise issue only when (A or B)aX—only when we have found a quality in which the likeness resides and the possibility of numbering, I have suggested, is the same as that of disjunction. But there is no particular quality we have to use when we enumerate or form a disjunction and that is why we can have general propositions like 2 plus 2 equals 4—propositions which don't require the specificatio of a common quality but, on the other hand, don't involve the notion of an absolute individual or pure unit. In fact if you abstract from the quality you abstract from the individual—it is only in respect of some quality

---

[4] [DMA] Contemporary Set theory would support Alexander here. The members of a class can be heterogeneous (although such classes may be quite uninteresting.)

that you call a man one. Just as it is only by virtue of some quality as animality that you call a man and a dog two. While the laws of number are independent of what unit is taken they are to be understood as referring to things of the same quality and not to a pure unit abstracted from quality. Thus we can have statements like "There are 20 things on the table" for here there is no unit—any part of what we call a thing is also a thing whereas any part of a man is not a man.

There may be doubt about particular cases or cases may be settled in a conventional manner. If you say there are twenty pieces of wood on the table it might be said that a piece of wood can be divided into pieces of wood and so on but presumably the convention here would be that a piece of wood was something continuously wooden—without any such division as there is between what we call two pieces of wood even where they are touching.

This brings us back to the distinction made earlier between a quality of a thing which is a quality of any of its parts (like "being wooden"), a quality of a thing which is a quality of none of its parts (like "being a man"). Now while enumeration is not confine to individuals in this sense—that is, is not based entirely on qualities which belong to a whole and to none of its parts, while, as I said, we can have conventions enabling us to number things in other ways, at least individuals in this sense are important for the conception of the unit—that is, it is in this way that we distinguish being *an* X from simply being X, that is that we make at the second stage distinctions that we do not make at the firs stage of logic though we have to have a general logic—a logic of pure predication or pure quality—in order to go on to make this distinction.

Lecture 31   *(25th October 1949)*

The Category of Number continued—Alexander's Rationalist View of Mathematics—Frege-Russell Doctrine

While we can pass on from the theory of number to that of continuous quantity and while in treating of continuous quantity we can take any unit we like (even the units involved in continuous quantity are originally determined by something of a qualitative character like "foot") it is from the treatment of the qualitative unit that we get the theory of number and it is from that that we go on to give a numerical account of continuous quantity passing, of course, through the category of rational number, including fractions, on the way to the theory of real number—of the correlation of number with, say the points in a continuous line and while, as I said, in the theory of integers or whole numbers we are not setting up the discontinuous, in so far as each of our units—each thing we call one—is itself a continuous existent still there is a discontinuity or discreteness in the sense that the units don't run together in the sense particularly that addition doesn't mean physical coalescence but applies to separate units excluding one another and related by "or", but all of a common quality as far as qualitative enumeration is concerned. Thus we might be able to take one instance of the kind X (an X) as made up of several instances of the kind Y—we are not tied down to this or that unit or this or that class but in any concrete case we have to have the notion of one instance and, therefore, of what it is an instance of.

Another general way of putting the matter is that the approach to the quantitative characters is through the notion of inclusion (class inclusion) as indicated in the notion of "member of" or the distinction between All and Some but this not the same as inclusion simply in the sense of more or less—that is a question that we go on to in the Quantitative categories though it is understood that in the recognition of an existent the recognition of continuity and that of the general notion of more and less is implicit.

Alexander's Rationalistic View of Mathematics

Now Alexander tends towards a Rationalistic view—towards treating mathematics as concerned with other than observable things—he does say that figure in geometry and numbers in arithmetic are different kinds of empirical object but he also says that;

> "...however much the observation of collections of things may provoke us to attend to numbers and their combinations we no more derive arithmetical truths from the things in which they are embodied than we derive geometrical truths, such as that the two sides of a triangle are greater than the third side from the actual measurement of brass triangles or three-cornered fields" (*STD*, Volume 1, p. 315.)

This would certainly seem to suggest that mathematical knowledge is derived from something other than observation and that number is something apart from the enumerable.

> *Cf.* A. E. Taylor in his discussion of mathematics in commentary on the *Republic*. He talks of *The* Triangle—I ask which of its three angles is *The* angle.[5]

My contention is this, that a theory of number is in the firs instance a theory of integers or whole numbers embodied by different groups

---

[5] *Cf.* A. E. Taylor, *Plato the Man and His Work*, 6th edition. London: Methuen, 1949, pp. 290-1.

of concrete things and the fact that different groups of different things can have the same number creates no more difficult than the fact that different groups of different things can have the same quality.

Alexander's View that Unity is Subsequent to Multiplicity

Now Alexander rather curiously takes unity as subsequent to multiplicity. He says it is safe to say that "...unity is a notion posterior in development to multiplicity" (p.316) which would imply, for example, that we contemplate a 4 (a quartet) as a particular sort of thing before we thought of a unit or a one, and the point may be that we recognize certain patterns of configuration (say, as in this

Figure 12.

diagram) before we recognise things as so many ones or again that we recognize a group of six—let us say six sheep—as greater than a group of four sheep before we learn actually to count them, but we could never assign an actual number to either group without having decided on our unit. The unit is actually involved in such discriminations whether the discriminator actually explicitly brings it out or not. Otherwise the comparison would be of a larger extent and not of a larger group.

It is possible also, of course, to be interested in certain shapes—to be interested more in the shape than in the number of a collection but of course this doesn't support Alexander's view that multiplicity is prior to unity. It cannot be denied that number is a ground of classificatio but it is a secondary group of classificatio requiring previous recognition of the unit—that is, requiring recognition of kinds of things before recognition of kinds of groups. It might still be suggested that space or configuratio is a primary group of classificatio but it is with reference to a common quality of the stars—brightness or yellowness or whatever you may call it—that we are able pick out the constellation and even in recognizing a continually enclosed space we should be recognising some quality in the boundary.

Russell-Frege Doctrine of Number

Alexander then discusses the Russell-Frege doctrine of a cardinal number as a class of classes—the number N being the class of classes similar to a given class. Now all that this could defensibly mean is that the number two is any pair—not this or that pair but the general notion of a pair—but that doesn't justify the expression "class of classes" and if we look at that expression then referring to the general (first class as "a" and to any of the particular classes as "b" we can say that here the class "b" is being taken as a collection of a certain number of members—an aggregate—but the class "a" is *not* being treated in that way—there is no question of our making or being acquainted with a collection of all such collections—say an aggregate of all pairs—thus belonging to the class (a) of classes (b) simply means being of the sort of classes b—not a question of aggregates but of kind, and this in turn means "being of the sort of", more particularly "being the number of" a certain collection of unit members—it means, in other words being of a certain number, so that if we remove the ambiguity of class—if we don't treat a class as a collection we are left with the position that the number two is a pair, or a pair, using the "a" in the indefinit sense that Russell uses it in the chapter on denoting (*cf.* the "Principles of Mathematics"—also an article in *Mind*[6]). In other words that being of the same number two is being a pair and we don't have to bring similarity into the matter—that is the fact that any other pair has a one-one relation to a given pair so that the Russell-Frege position is not only needlessly complicated, but is actually confused, is not any sort of explanation of cardinal number—in fact is quite irrelevant to our seeing that a given pair is a pair.

It is important, of course, to have the notion of cardinal number and not to treat number as merely ordinal as simply amounting to a series

$$1, 1+1, 1+1+1, 1+1+1+1,\dots$$

and that may be part of what Alexander has in mind when he says that the notion of multiplicity is prior to that of unity and also part of what is involved in Pythagoreanism where a specifi number is identifie with a special figur which we can recognize without counting the units, but it is still the case that without the unit there would be no cardinal numbers so that—even if we could recognize 3=2+1 as a fact and not recognize it in the Leibnizian manner as analytic, or as it is sometimes put as simply the definitio of 3, even, in other words, if we cannot say that three is just the number that comes after 2 in the series of numbers (because that won't tell us that there is anything that comes after two in the series of numbers)—even so it is still the case that any cardinal number implies

[6]Bertrand Russell, *Principles of Mathematics*, op. cit.; "On Denoting", *Mind* New Series 14(56) October 1905: 479-93.

the unit and if it weren't so we couldn't make the ordinal arrangement
of numbers—we couldn't, as the phrase goes, form the number series.

> I don't think it is vital here that children learn the names of numbers in ordinal
> fashion—the point is that that sort of naming them wouldn't enable them to
> recognize a quartet (say) when they see it, but granted that, and granted the
> importance of the recognition of cardinal numbers, yet recognition of latter is
> still based on recognition of the unit.

Lecture 32   *(26th October 1949)*
Transition from Number to Order and Quantity—The Category of Order—Quantity as a Link Category

I said that in forming the number series, as it is called, we do require
the unit because we are distinguishing what are members of the series
in terms of the unit and while as I said we are acquainted with cardinal
number or with various positive number groups, it is in an ordinal that
we approach at least the higher numbers of the series—the members
above a fairly small initial range.   However the point is that along
with the notion of the group and its number we have the notion of
greater and lesser numbers and in connection with that the notion of
addition—though that, I suggested might be taken to be involved in the
original disjunction—but, generalizing that, that is considering addition
otherwise than by units, we also get the notion of subtraction—of
the difference between two members as well as the sum between two
members which of course could be given concrete form, on the one
hand, by taking groups together, on the other hand by removing a smaller
group from a larger group (as before this doesn't require any sort of
physical operation—it merely means that to think things together, or
think one thing away from another).

We have here, then, such relations of groups but the more specifi
question of groups of groups might be said to arise in connection with
multiplication—for instance 6 multiplied by 6 might be considered as
the number of a group formed of 6 groups each of 6 members and, of
course, when we generalise the operation of multiplication, that is when
we think of it as something possible with any two numbers, then we get
the correlated conception of division and this of course, leads directly
on to the conception of rational number—particularly of fractions where
we are led to think of a proportional part of a unit and thus to abandon
the simple conception of number in terms of units—to get an extended
conception of number further emphasizing the conception of quantity.
We now think of the class of numbers each of which is a ratio between

two integers and of course this class has an order of more and less just as the class of integers itself has—that is any rational number is greater than, equal to or less than a given rational number or if we consider always different rational numbers then any one is always greater than or less then a given one.

But since this series does not have quantitative continuity—that is in recognising continuous quantity we have to go beyond rational number in spite of the fact that there is a rational number between any two rational umbers, for instance the average of the two or the ratio whose numerator is the sum of the two numerators and whose denominator is the sum of the two denominators and it is from that, or rather it is in contrast to that lack of continuing, that we pass from rational number to real number.

Now here there is a difficult because if in place of taking a series of rational numbers you talk of a series of real numbers (where real, of course, includes both rational and fractional) you have to admit that there are no next real numbers—there are no two real numbers which are next to one another, or that between any two rational numbers there is a real number which means that it is improper to speak of the series of rational numbers and of such a series as giving continuity—the position would simply be this, that correlating greater and lesser numbers as before with points on a line we cannot have a movement from a rational number to another rational number through rational numbers alone but we can have movement from one real number to another real number through real numbers alone in the sense that any point through which the movement goes will be correlated with a real number.

But what is really important here is not that the conception of real number leads us to a continuity that we didn't have with the conception of rational number but rather that it is the conception of continuity that gives us the conception of real number and that anything we call a series no matter what it is a series of, implies discreteness—implies next or adjacent members so that, as I said before, we cannot speak of the series of real numbers or even of rational numbers and it could be argued further that the very conception of order as in the order of series implies continuity even though the series itself does not have continuity.

The general position is, then, that we do not build up the conception of order and continuity from the conception of number, though by working with, and partly in contrast to the conception of number we can clarify our conception of order and continuity. It may be noted that portions of the treatment of these categories has already come in Alexander's discussion of the relation between space and time—for instance in the notion of "betweenness", and this might be taken to instance my point that the categories of quantity or mathematical categories apply equally to space and time and what is in them.

A Note on the Category of Order

Alexander treats order subsequently to relation and not with any special connection with number (connected with the absence in him of a rigorous view on the order of the categories) but the most interesting point that he makes on the subject of order is that we shouldn't speak of an order among terms or an order in a certain relation (a relation having orders as we put it) unless that order is asymmetrical or irreversible as well as transitive, so that we could set up an order in terms of greater and less than but not in terms of "equal to". The interesting point here is that Alexander is here admitting that the transitive is not necessarily irreversible which reinforces our criticism of his account of the transitiveness of time in which he included irreversibility.

The Category of Quantity as a Linking Category

One point might be this that while the notion of quantity involves the notion of order (greater and lesser quantities) you might say that in another sense quantity hasn't order, or is contrasted with order. When for instance, you say that a thing has such and such a weight then you are getting away from any notion of before and after or succession—away from parts to something total and again even in saying that a thing is of a certain length you are not concerned say with taking it from left to right rather than right to left, you are concerned with a total once more, and thus in getting away from the question of parts or number which, however you may generalize it, as I said, takes its departure from members of a class.

But when we consider quantity as the point of transition between the second and the third set of categories we fin that the abstraction from quality is not complete, that is when we think of concrete quantity—quantity of things as contrasted with quantity in general which, as I said, could apply to space and time as well as to things—from the mathematical point of view quantity is just that which has continuous measurement, this being connected, as I suggested, with the question of real number—but from the physical point of view quantity or the continuous may be regarded as solidity—as what is meant by matter or, with the Greek Atomists, with the full as distinguished from the empty.

It may be remembered that Locke added solidity or impenetrability to the merely mathematical primary qualities of Descartes, and what I am suggesting is that it is a borderline case—that it may be taken as the point of transition between the mathematical or "primary" qualities and the physical or "secondary" qualities. This is not to say that matter is itself a quality—rather that matter cannot be a particular quality—that is, can only be space-fillin or solidity—which is against the view that when you have called anything matter you have described it—the point is rather that in order to be space-fillin anything must have come specifi quality—something other than spatio-temporality and thus, as I said before, the physical categories are those involved in the distinction of the things that are in space and time themselves.

Thus the doctrine of Materialism in taking matter as the actual substance of things is still untenable, and the very existence of chemistry as a science (without going on further to biology, etc.) shows that things are of different substance and takes almost all meaning from the question "what is it that all things are composed of?" to which the only possible answer would be that they are composed of this solidity or space-fillingness But physics can still investigate the characters and proceedings of things as space-filling insofar, that is, as they are independent of variations in chemical substance.

Mathematical categories concerned as much with the empty as much with the full.

In the matter of the distinction of the three sets of categories we might perhaps put it in this way, the firs set of categories are the categories of fact where the question is "is it so or not"; the second group of categories are the categories of situation with particular emphasis on juxtaposition or region or the subject; and the third set of categories are the categories of occurrence which specially emphasise activity or the predicate. These will be connected, that is they will not deal with entirely separate questions, but they indicate a set of distinctions that we do make between situations and occurrences and also between relation and quantities even if we fin both of these in any fact.

6
Categories III: The Physical Categories

Lecture 33 *(19th April 1950)*
The Category of Quantity continued—The Category of Intensity

Note the distinction between:

1. Quantity in a quite general way—applying equally to space-time and things, i.e., continuous extension.

2. Quantity applied specially to things—*something* that is continuously extended, that fill space. In so far as there can be an investigation of things as space-filling this is physics or a part of that study, but beyond that we are concerned with the peculiarity, the special nature, of things.

If we take quantity on the mathematical side we should be taking it as it applies to the void or the empty as well as to the full—to continuous space as well as to the space-filling There is, I think, no real opposition here—the mathematical quantity and the physical quantity of a thing would be in some sense the same, although, of course, we can't call a "quantity" like weight a mathematical quantity.

The Category of Intensity

I link quantity specially with continuity and, taking quantity as the firs of the physical categories to involve the notion of something that is continuous, I pass on to the conception of intensity or degree.

Now, once more Alexander discusses degree or intensity in no very thorough manner—he refers to but doesn't really elucidate Kant's theory of intensity. It might be suggested that the notion of degree comes very close to that of order and it is certain that it does involve an order or a range but I would say that it has a different sort of relation to quantity to that which order has—that even if we say that the members of a series must have something in common in order that we may recognize *that* series as distinct from some other series—so that, for example, we could speak of or distinguish the order of the benches in a room from front to back but couldn't speak of the order of the *things* in a room from front to back—still, the quality and the order are quite independent; that is, you can't infer place in the order from quality, or quality from place in the order. Whereas in the case of intensity there is taken to be a close connection between quality and order, whatever account we may be able to give of it, so that while intensity may be *correlated* with quantity—with quantitative conceptions like amount or distance—it cannot be *equated* with it and this means not merely that intensity is something more than quantity but that to recognize a difference of intensity is not necessarily to recognize a quantitative difference. For example, we speak of one note as higher in pitch than another and we accept the theory that the difference between higher and lower goes with a difference in the number of vibrations in a given time, but it may still be said that people can recognize difference of pitch—higher and lower notes—without knowing anything about rates of vibration.

It might be argued, of course, that the question is really one of greater or less exactness in measurement and that in distinguishing distances, for example,—that is, in making what might be regarded as a simply quantitative distinction—we are in the same position in distinguishing pitches, temperatures etc., that is, we see one distance to be larger than another without knowing exactly how much larger it is and similarly that we could call a difference of pitch a quantitative difference even though we cannot say exactly how much one note is higher than another or one thing hotter than another or one sound louder than another and so forth—in other words that in any of these cases we can make a judgment of greater and less even when we haven't, and haven't even attempted, to fin a unit of measurement.

I would still say, however, that there is a difference between merely spatio-temporal comparison as in "longer" and "faster" and the kind of comparison involved in those other cases. We could never express "hotter" or "louder" simply as a distance or as a rate or in merely spatio-temporal terms nor again (the point covers the same ground) could we express these differences in terms of one another—couldn't translate "hotter" into "louder" etc.—the point being that in each case some particular logic of quality is involved. There could, of course, be connections between various types of variation—a sheet of metal, let us say, could become brighter as it became hotter—but that wouldn't give us any common measure of brightness and heat, whereas if difference of intensity were simply difference of quantity it should be possible to fin a common measure to express hotter in terms of louder and so with similar pairs of terms.

I would still say (*cf.* my paper "The Meaning of Good"[1]) that there is a great deal of confusion in ordinary conceptions of degree and that

---

[1] John Anderson, "The Meaning of Good", *A.J.P.P.* 20(2) September 1942: 111-40. Reprinted in *Studies*.

it would always be wrong to speak as if, when two things had a given quality, one of them could have it in a higher or more eminent degree than another and that if it is proper to speak of X and Y as green, e.g., if "X is green" is a complete statement, then it would be improper to speak of X as greener than Y and, similarly, if we can say that A and B are simply good then we cannot say that A is better than Y—meaning that it has goodness more fully than Y has.

But granting this, granting that in general we cannot have a comparative of a strictly positive term, it may still be the case that where we can properly use a comparative qualitative, considerations are involved or, more accurately, that allowing that there are comparisons like "longer" that have a purely spatio-temporal meaning, there are others that also have a qualitative component and if we take "louder" as an example the point would be that if "louder" is significan "loud" is not a quality and "X is loud" is not a complete statement. But still when we say X is louder than Y certain qualities of X and Y are involved in this comparison—that is are part of the *meaning* of X's being louder than Y.

Alexander on Intensity

Alexander's discussion of quantity and intensity in Book II Chapter 7 is very brief and doesn't distinguish between the two types of conception that I have mentioned. He takes speed, for example, (rate of motion) which I have referred to as a purely spatio-temporal or quantitative matter as an example of intensity and we may also note in connection with his reference to green and greener that Alexander doesn't think there is any such thing as colour in general (cf. Alexander on universality) so that for him colour differences must be differences of intensity or differences of place within a certain range or scale comparable, in other words, to difference of pitch.

Lecture 34   *(26th April 1950)*
The Category of Intensity continued—The Weber-Fechner Law

Alexander on intensity (*cf.* his note in *STD* Volume 1, p. 307)—speaks of the difference of extensive and intensive quantity *both* in reference to difference of length—that is, he is saying that you could have an intensive or extensive problem, each of these in regard to the same subject.

The Weber-Fechner Law

The problem is what is sometimes called a psycho-physical one. That is, it is an attempt to measure sensation, particularly in relation to stimulus, and the law is that sensation varies as the logarithm of the stimulus or that while the stimulus increases in geometrical progression the sensation increases in arithmetical progression.[2]

Now this implies an exactness of measurement that it may be impossible to obtain in such investigation, the greatest difficult being that of establishing a unit of sensation, and the essential point is that what is really being investigated is people's powers of discrimination. First, then, there is the question of what is called the threshold of consciousness, that is of the amount or intensity of stimulus required for the occurrence of any sensation—that is in order that the object should rise above the threshold of consciousness, or, as we say, be noticed.

(1) Now it could be said that it was a different threshold that was in question according to the type of stimulus being applied. At the same time we can say that the noticing of a certain kind of thing can be closely connected with the noticing of some other kind of thing either helping or hindering it, so that we might fall into a confusion regarding thresholds or conditions of observation by taking each type of stimulus in isolation. And this would lead us to question the procedures of experimentalists, whether in psychology or physics, who think that progress is to be made by considering one factor at a time, psychologists in trying to separate, say, "sensitivity to red" from every other sensitivity and from other mental or physical conditions.

Here, of course, experimental psychologists go wrong in company with non-experimental psychologists, namely in their *cognitionalism*—in their assuming that cognitive powers can be taken by themselves—in particular can be taken apart from the emotional life, cognitionalism being characteristic of the whole trend of modern philosophy and psychology.

Well then, there is a different threshold according to the type of stimulus even though one sort of threshold may affect another; again there will be different thresholds for different minds and not only that but for different minds at different times—different powers of attention and discrimination according to, on the one hand, factors like fatigue which of course has been investigated to a fair extent and, on the other

---

[2]The Weber-Fechner Law concerns the discrimination in sensation of the intensity of physical stimuli and is based on early work by physiologist Ernst Heinrich Weber (1795-1878). In 1834 Weber asserted that the smallest increment in a stimulus required to produce a difference in the sensation experienced is not an absolute amount but is relative to the magnitude of the stimulus. The law was expressed quantitatively by Gustav Theodor Fechner (1801-1887). The suggested demonstration of mathematical regularities of mind was crucial to the development of experimental psychology. Fechner held that Weber had discovered the fundamental principle of mind-body interaction.

hand, to emotional conditions which have been considered more by the Freudians than by the ordinary experimentalists.

The rejection of cognitionalism would cast doubt on the ignoring of a particular value to a power of knowing or distinguishing this and that—would lead us to see that such powers could change independently of change in the apparatus—particularly the physiological apparatus.

(2) But even without that (i.e., even without challenging cognitionalism) we can fin objections to Weber's law. That is, while admitting quantitative measurement of the stimulus and its variation along a continuous scale, we cannot admit a similar scale of the side of sensation. We can only regard as arbitrary the decision that where a person can just distinguish two things of a certain kind the difference of the intensity of the two sensations is a *unit*—that is, that each of a successive set of discriminations while the stimulus is being steadily intensifie is "equal" to every other. In fact, the absence of continuity on the psychological side—the movement by jumps—is opposed to the very notion of units (I assume that all units are continuous and divisible).

Well then, what is suggested is that if you have a stimulus A and if say only a unit of the stimulus were added, the mind wouldn't notice the difference in stimulus, wouldn't discriminate, wouldn't say this is a greater stimulus until, say, we have arrived at A+B. Where that is the position, where A+B is the firs thing discriminated after A then, if the value X is assigned to the sensation given the stimulus A, given the stimulus A+B the value X+1 will be assigned and for any stimulus between A and A+B the value assigned to the sensation will still be X.

	1	2	3	4	5
Stimulus	A	A+1	$A+B\ (A[1+\frac{B}{A}])$	A+B+1	$A(1+\frac{B}{A})^2$
'Sensation'	X	X	X+1	X+1	X+2

Figure 13.

(First discrimination at 3, no discrimination at 4, second discrimination at 5.)

A great many factors could complicate this, e.g., speed—there could be different results for a rapidly increasing stimulus—the formula doesn't take account of this—if it is claimed that this would be a *different* sensation, then there are great difficultie (*cf.* 1 above).

Well then, when the mind notices a certain difference or makes a certain discrimination then we are said to have a *unit* increase in sensation but, of course, even if we didn't accept this treatment or the postulation of units we certainly do have points of discrimination which can be studied in relation to various physical processes like increase in loudness of noise or increase in amplitude of electric current—in all these cases you would have certain increases which the mind couldn't distinguish—couldn't say that an increase had taken place although, as I've maintained, this discriminatory power could vary from mind to mind, and in the single mind from time to time.

The suggestion of the Weber-Fechner law is that if in the same way you went on to a stimulus of A+B+1 you couldn't distinguish that from A+B and the point at which a further discrimination could be made so that we could say that we now had a sensation of the value X+2, which would be one where the new stimulus bore the same relation—that is the same proportion—to A+B as A+B bore to A so that the series of stimulus given: X, X+1, X+2…etc., would be A, A(1+B/A), A(1+B/A)^2…, in other words where A just gives the sensation X and A+B just gives the sensation X+1, then A(1+B/A)^2 would be the minimum stimulus for sensation X+2 and the decision to say X+1, X+2 and so on is made on the basis of the successive discriminations or noticings of increase.

I have suggested that it is arbitrary to speak of a unit sensation under these conditions and incidentally that it assumes there is an entity *the sensation* to be distinguished from mere knowledge of the stimulus, when actually the only fact we have at our disposal is that certain discriminations are made. To say then that we are just able to distinguish one stimulus (or one object in a certain range) from another gives us no ground for speaking of a unit sensation and the real outcome of the law, or what is important about it, is just that discrimination is in terms of proportions or ratios rather than of absolute or arithmetical differences, so that we distinguish two things of a certain class in respect of their amount or intensity when and only when the ratio of the larger to the smaller does not fall below a certain level and that, of course, is just what we should expect—that is we should expect things to be distinguished in accordance with the proportion one has to another rather than in accordance with the differences, though of course it is always possible that we should attend to that difference or should be more interested in it than the thing that had the difference—which would mean that in the two types of cases Alexander refers to it is true that different types of question that are at issue.

Now Alexander is talking about just perceptible differences of lengths of line as measured by the eye and he says that:

> "With lines of moderate length [this begs question I would say] the just perceptible difference follows Weber's Law and is approximately a constant fraction of the length. But when the differences of length are larger we tend to equate not fractional but absolute differences. For example the difference of 5 and 7 inches seem equal to that of 10 and 12 inches not to that of 10 and 14 inches as it should do if Weber's law held". (*STD*, Volume 1, p. 307 fn. 1.)

Now of course the difference between 5 and 7 inches would hardly be a just perceptible difference but for the range through which discriminations were made in terms of Weber's Law we should expect discrimination to be in terms of proportions; but, as I said, it is possible to think of an actual difference, say of an amount of projection, just as well as in proportions and, in these terms, we could equate 7 and 6 with 12 and 10 though if we were thinking of the whole of the lengths in question our equation would be 7 to 5 and 14 to 10. Although, then, we can consider things as other than proportions we are more likely to think of things as proportions than their absolute differences and this is illustrated in music e.g., where we have the recognition of a certain sort of thing, the musical interval where the same interval, or having the same interval, means having the same proportion between rates of vibration and where the developed account of measurement—the account in terms of the number of tones etc. has to be understood as measurement of ratios—for instance two tones—a major third—means 5:4.

I would suggest, then, that the geometrical relation is what might be called the natural one while the arithmetical relation is an artificia one; and it is certainly the case that having certain powers of discrimination and recognition we can recognize or fin repeated a ratio or proportion where we should be quite incapable of observing the repetition of a mere arithmetical difference.

Lecture 35   *(10th May 1950)*
The Category of Intensity continued—Qualities in Ranges

Expressions of degree, I have argued, are not just quantitative distinctions, there being considerations of quality also involved in them. Whereas you could speak of quantity (distance between two things, e.g.) without raising any question of quality—that is, the quality of that quantity (to say that two things are two miles apart doesn't involve thinking of the quality of the intervening space)—quality is not involved in the statement of the quantitative relation.

But even if intensity involves quality, that doesn't enable us to speak of the intensity of a quality in the sense of having the quality in greater or less degree. What we get is a number of quite different qualities which can be placed in a scale and correlated with quantities though of course we can recognise the range—the difference of intensity—without having any exact knowledge of the quantities. For example, differences of musical pitch were recognised before the Pythagoreans made their discoveries about the harmonic intervals and even then it was possible to recognise the relative quantities or ratios without knowing exactly what they were quantities of—that is to say, recognising them in terms of length of string without knowing anything or much about rates of vibration. And when we do know that it is a ratio of rates of vibration this doesn't mean that we know the octave—the difference of pitch—any better than we knew it before. Similarly, we could know a range of colours without having exact quantitative knowledge—knowledge of rates of wave motion—so that, in general, intensity is not to be reduced to quantity any more than it is to be equated to quality.

Do All Qualities Exist in Ranges?

Thus, on the one hand, if green is a quality there is no such thing as greener and, on the other hand, if there are relations of brighter and duller there is no such quality as bright. But it is still possible to maintain that there are close connections between such qualities and intensities and here we may ask whether intensity is bound up with *all* qualities—whether every quality exists in a range like the range of colours or the range of tones and pitches. However, if we take quality as just being such and such (being of a certain kind) it would seem that not all qualities exist in ranges and there might then be a quite important distinction between qualities which exist in ranges and qualities that do not. And this might coincide with the distinction previously suggested between qualities which if they characterize a whole characterize all its parts and qualities of a whole which characterize some part only, or even none of its parts—for instance when we say that a thing is yellow we would also say that any part of it is yellow (*Nb*. This would be denied on Alexander's theory of substance—there is no interpenetration.) But when we say a thing is human or is a man then we do not say that any part of it is human or a man. Now yellow is one of the qualities that exist in the colour range whereas there is no qualitative range in which humanity exists.

> *Nb.* certain biologists do try to make out there is a range, series of animal types put in order, but there is no real continuity in such a series—decisions of higher and lower would be quite arbitrary—unlike pitch or temperature.

Well then, its possible, I say, that the two distinctions coincide—that the qualities existing in ranges are what we call through-and-through qualities and the others not. And this might cast light on or help to account for the common distinction between substance and attribute—the through-and-through qualities being the ones referred to as attributes and the others as substances so that whereas asked what is the substance or composition of a thing we should never answer "yellow" but we might say that humanity is the substance or constitution of a man. (It might be suggested here that the range qualities are what are usually referred to as the secondary qualities—a loose usage, unlike Locke's precise usage.)

A similar point or a partly connected point, arose in my discussion of the *Theaetetus* (1948) where the inclusion of aesthetic and ethical characters among the categories, among the forms of comparison and reflection could be taken to indicate that in the Socratic, or Socratic and Platonic, aesthetic and ethical judgments are *comparative* judgments—judgments of degree of value and not qualitative (a point which might clear up a good many problems in regard to Socratic theory). But beyond that it might be maintained that for Socrates as represented in the *Phaedo* (particularly in the early part of the *Phaedo*) all qualitative judgments are comparative judgments—all so-called qualities are matters of degree and that that is just what distinguishes a quality from a thing or substance.

> *Cf.* Anaxagoras—"everything in everything"—every complex thing (bone etc.) is a combination of various opposite qualities *in different measures.*

Thus the soul is a substance and, as is argued in answer to Simmias, there is not a degree of being a soul or being psychic, but for qualities there are degrees of approximation to a standard and this is how qualities are to be understood. In this connection, also, we may remember Socrates' difficult in the *Parmenides* about whether or not there is a form of Man—where "man" might be taken as a substance rather than a quality.

Assuming, for the sake of argument, that this distinction is valid, the question might be raised whether such a substance could always be specifie by what we may call the *pure* qualities together with spatial and temporal relations between them, which would be to treat substance similarly to what I have called "relations in the extended sense", as contrasted with relations in the strict sense—namely spatio-temporal relations. Without then coming to any fina conclusion on the point, we might consider that our knowledge of what is here called a substance involves a knowledge of spatial relations—of juxtaposition and so forth and perhaps also of temporal relations—certain successions—in addition to a knowledge of qualities so that we would never look for a merely qualitative description of, for example, "man"—would never expect to identify a man by the mere enumeration of qualities. The point even in the rough definitio of a man as a rational animal being that "animal" would be a substance in the same sense as man (and whatever might be meant by rational.)

And the suggested distinction might cast light on the general theory of definitio and classificatio in that even if the genus and the differentia in a definitio have both the same class relation to the species—namely the relation of inclusion—still in a good distinction the differentia could be expressed in terms of what I have called the pure qualities, while the genus would be a substance in the suggested sense.

If our logical theory were developed in this way we are not really abandoning a propositional logic—setting up a hierarchy of terms or a distinction among kinds of predication—because, even if the distinction held good we could still use either of the terms in such a definin complex as a subject, and either as a predicate—taking QS as such a complex it would be just as proper to say QiS (some Qs are Ss) as to say SiQ (some Ss are Qs) and just as significant— ven if it were false—to say QaS (all Qs are S) so that the distinction is supplementary, not opposed to the predicative theory. It could be argued in general that unless there were *some* such supplementation at the firs set of categories—at the level of "is it so or not"—and that we can't go on beyond that unless we are going to establish distinctions and connections which are not indicated by the earlier categories though we still have to work in a manner from those earlier categories in order to arrive at the later and when proceeding to the Quantitative categories from the complexity of the propositional subject.

And if something like that can be made good it brings out an important point in the criticism of Rationalism—that the objection to Rationalism is not that it makes certain distinctions but that it makes them at the wrong place, or the wrong stage of logical theory—that they recognise kinds of proposition—variants of the propositional form instead of something supplementary to that form—that they don't see that the single propositional logic fully permits of the making of the necessary distinctions.

Lecture 36   *(17th May 1950)*

The Category of Intensity continued—Idealism as a Philosophy of Degrees—The Category of Substance

A possible distinction: qualities exist in ranges, substances do not exist in ranges.

Idealism as a Philosophy of Degrees

The distinction of quality and substance is not a distinction recognised by idealism. Idealism could be characterised as a philosophy of degrees or of perfections (to use the Cartesian or Scholastic term) so that "humanity", just like any quality, would be the expression of the absolute with a certain degree of adequacy. It would be reality raised to a certain power and anything whatever would come somewhere in that range—there would be a single range of reality—a single order or set of degrees of reality and both what I was calling qualities and what I was calling substances would have a definit position in the range (*cf.* Hegel and to some extent Bradley).

It would be impossible, of course, consistently to range all characters in this series just as it is impossible for Alexander to have a consistent theory of the various complexities of the various parts of space and time—a range of realities of the more and the less complex. That is, the position can't be logically worked out and Alexander has arbitrarily to determine his levels, his heights of complexity, by reference to the existing division of the sciences (we could say Alexander's Evolutionism is a variant of idealism.)

In the same way Leibniz can't really establish a continuous series of monads from the lowest to the highest, being faced not only with the difficult of treating any change as an interchange by two monads in the scale of being; but also by the regular difficult concerning relations and differences—the relation of two monads being not itself a point on the scale.

Idealism, then, I suggest, is a philosophy of degrees and Alexander would have to take the same line to be consistent with his Evolutionism. But, as I said, he cannot work out any general theory or present any general criterion of greater or less complexity and it would have to be quite arbitrarily that he can even speak, for example, of one category as being more complex than another.

The Category of Substance

There is a great deal of confusion in Alexander's discussion of substance (Book II, Chapter 6, Section A) and, as in other places, he may be said to confuse the category with several other categories, for example, with identity and with quality.

(1) Thus, at the beginning of the chapter, he proposes to take substance in a spatial sense while recognising that temporal questions are also involved. He says:

> "For simplicity and brevity it will be enough to speak of substance as a piece of space which is the scene of succession, without stating the same thing in terms of time in the reverse order." (*STD*, Volume 1, p.269.)

This means that he is treating substance as a piece of time which is spread out in space. And while we may say that if these two formulations are both defensible, it would have been better to work out them both in his expositions; we can say more broadly that in treating substance as the scene of succession—as a region within which various things happen—Alexander is making it indistinguishable from identity.

(2) Again when he says on the next page:

> "A thing or complex substance is then a contour of space (i.e. a volume with a contour) within which take place the motions correlated to the qualities of the thing and the complex substance or thing is the persistence in time of this spatial contour with its determinate motions." (*STD*, Volume 1, p. 270.)

We might say that in this notion of volume there is a confusion of substance and quality and also that the word "contour" is particularly misleading when it is a question of volume. But in speaking of the movements correlated with the quality yellow and other qualities being contained within the contour of the atom or molecule of gold he would seem to be coming back just to the notion of identity; and we could reject the view that when we are considering gold as a substance yellow should be regarded as merely within it—the point being rather that yellow helps to constitute gold and is no more within it than is gold itself.

I suggest then that we should reject the term "contour" and, in thinking of a substance as a complex of qualities should consider it as being a form or formula of combination—a formula which, in accordance with my previous suggestion, could cover not any qualities but spatial and temporal relations among them. For instance, we could say that H_2O is such a formula of combination and we could refer here to chemical theories of the spatial arrangement of what are taken to be the elementary constituents of things. And without accepting those particular chemical theories we can say that this sort of account is what is meant by presenting a substance—quite briefl that *substance is composition*, and if that is the position then the question of an extreme boundary or contour is of no special importance here.

> *Nb.* "motion correlated with quality"—we could say that this shows Alexander's failure to entirely shake off parallelism—quality as standing above what it qualifies—cf his account of mind in Volume 2.

Now Alexander's confusion is further illustrated in his reference to our own mind as a substance when he says that the acts of mind change from one moment to another according to the objects which engage it, where, in other words, he takes a relational view of mind and thus gives it an *in*substantial character—he is unable to describe it except in terms of a fiel of consciousness—that is in terms of its taking in various distinct objects of attention which do not really have any substantial unity. (We could say, moreover, that in taking space-time as "stuff" Alexander sets up an insubstantial substance.)

And this absence of a substantial unity is further illustrated in the view that he goes on to—namely that the qualities of a substance do not interpenetrate but that the substance is "a sphere of a certain contour, "stippled over with qualities," the qualities, in other words, or the motions correlated with these qualities going through the given space but all somehow missing one another. And if this were so, it would seem that we should rather speak of several substances—one for each quality—and not of a single substance within this space. In other words, in spite of all that Alexander says about complexity he really denies complexity and his position here may be occasioned by the remnant of Idealism in his thinking—exemplifie not only in the sort of correspondence doctrine in which a quality doesn't really belong to a thing but hovers over it—but also in the relational and hence insubstantial view of mind—and then in the treatment of even a non-mental substance as a sort of fiel comparable to the fiel of consciousness—as an arena through which various processes can pass just as ideas or trains of thought are said to pass through the mind. That is, you could only have such trains actually intersecting if you could fin something substantial in the mind itself—something not expressible merely in terms of its objects.

Nevertheless, the reason Alexander actually gives for holding that qualities don't interpenetrate is scarcely compatible with what I have just said. But actually it can hardly be called "intelligible" at all. He says:

> "The qualities of a substance do not interpenetrate. It can only be supposed that they do if qualities are treated as mental creations or ideas and, because they are such, are somehow regarded as not being in space or time." (*STD*, Volume 1, p. 275).

It would seem intelligible to me to say that things cannot interpenetrate because they are not in space and time but to say that they couldn't interpenetrate because they are in space-time seems simply wrong-headed.

Of course it could be said that in space different processes have room to miss one another but this doesn't seem to give the slightest ground for saying that a particular set of processes do miss one another, or again for saying that a set of processes which do miss one another are processes of the same substances. Rather, as I suggested, there would seem in such a case to be as many substances as processes.

While, then, Alexander's account seems to be entirely false—to be one according to which there is no such thing as complexity, we can see in his treatment of substance as a mere contour—as that within which there are various qualities—something similar to his treatment of space-time as the stuff of which things are made.

Lecture 37   *(7th June 1950)*

The Category of Substance continued—Interrelation of Qualities in a Substance—Transition from the Category of Substance to the Category of Causality

Alexander confuses substance with various other categories (*Cf.* also Kant—1st Analogy—substance as bare occupation of space—confusion with identity, quantity. Aristotle in the *Organon*—similar confusions.[3])

My account of substance as constitution or composition comes close to Alexander's account of universality as plan.

---

[3]Immanuel Kant, *Critique of Pure Reason*, *op. cit.*, "First Analogy: Principle of Permanence of Substance", pp. 212-17. Aristotle's *Organon* is the collection of logical treatises, *Categories, On Interpretation, Prior Analytics, Posterior Analytics, Topics* and *On Sophistical Refutations*.

Of course, I would say, there must on any view be diff culty in distinguishing the categories—they refer to the types of question that can be raised about any material whatever—but there are special difficultie if they are not brought into relation with the proposition—without this. We have no specifi foundation, they are taken at random, and we have no clear cut line between the different categories.

(3) Now Alexander, I would say, confuses substance not merely with the absolute identity from which most theories of Categories begin but with the concrete identity, with thinghood, with which on my view the list of categories would end.

Thus Alexander says,:

> "The identity of a substance is individual identity as persisting through a duration of time. Numerical identity was occupation of a point-instant or complex of them. Generic identity or identity of sort was the preservation of a plan of construction through repetition at different times or places. When the repetition of a plan is found in its varying phases, in the duration of an individual we have individual identity. We see now that substantial identity is equivalent to individual identity." (*STD*, Volume 1, p. 272.)

Here, then, Alexander distinguishes substance or substantiality from mere identity—mere power of locating—and identifie it with individuality. But in fact when we speak of identity of substance we don't mean individual identity. We say that two things are of the same substance when they are of the same composition or constitution—which would support my suggestion in an earlier lecture that substance is the make-up of a thing—that it is a certain relation of qualities in spatio-temporal relations. Now this is what Alexander calls universality or plan but the notion of plan or constitution seems a very forced interpretation of the meaning of being such-and-such—being of a certain sort. For instance when we speak of "being yellow" we don't seem to have any plan or build up in mind even though that which is yellow always *has* a certain composition. That is, we seem to have a fairly definit distinction between being of a sort—being predicable, and being of a certain constitution—having a certain interrelation of constituents.

Interrelation of Qualities in a Substance

Another question arising in Alexander's discussion of substance is that of the relation between the different qualities of a substance. He wants to argue that:

> "the multiplicity of properties of a substance is not haphazard but rooted in some simple state of affairs which enables many properties to belong together within one contour and to be in part simultaneous." (*STD*, Volume 1, p. 277.)

a view which Alexander connects with Locke's theory of primary qualities. In other words there has to be some *reason* why whiteness and sweetness, e.g., co-exist in a given substance—say sugar—and since that reason doesn't exist in whiteness and sweetness themselves because, of course, they can be found apart, there must be something else in which it does exist or in which it consists—some explanation of why the thing is both white and sweet.

Now, the argument is certainly not along the lines of individual identity. On the contrary, Alexander is at least approaching the notion of the constitution of something but he is doing so in a Rationalistic manner—that is to say if there is no reason why the white should be sweet or the sweet should be white we are certainly not going to fin a reason why X should be both white and sweet apart from the mere fact that X (which here would be "anything of the sort X") is both sweet and white. In other words we are going to fin that there are certain conjunctions of properties but not anything which explains why there should be such and such a conjunction. The whole point of recognizing the complexity of a substance (and here we may recall that Alexander would have special difficult in doing so when he considers that no two qualities interpenetrate) is that we have to admit the mere concomitance of a number of different properties; and what is supposed to be the explanation of that concomitance will either be the concomitance over again, perhaps in disguised language, or will be something superior to the properties—a power whereby that property exists. And in neither case do we have a clear and sound conception, in neither case do we have a possible explanation.

It is very important, of course, to see that certain properties of a substance do entail certain others—that is one of the things we have in mind in definitio and classification— ut however far we go in findin such connections or entailments we must always come back to the peculiarity of the given substance—to the fact that in it certain properties just do recur together.

Of course, in our inquiries, we can go from mere concomitance to entailment, $XY \longrightarrow XiY \longrightarrow XaY$.

This is the sort of thing that is involved in the notion of constitution or composition and there is no question of findin a formula which will explain all the features of the case—that is, a single reason why each of the properties will be found existing within one contour and perhaps

going through a regular sequence of phases. We do fin some actual
"balance of tensions" in the Heraclitean phrase but still we can't fin a
reason why it must be so. All we can say is that when we have a thing of
a given kind then these different characters or these different tendencies
are found within it.

I'm suggesting then that it is the concomitance of qualities *not*
entailing one another that constitutes that peculiar substance whatever
it may happen to be, and that there is neither the possibility of nor need
for any underlying unity. The so-called unity, in fact, would, in order
to be an explanation, have to exhibit the same disunity or variety as the
substance itself, which means that it wouldn't be the kind of explanation
asked for.

Transition from the Category of Substance to the Category of Causality

Now the notion of a balance of tensions or interrelations of tendencies
leads on to the point mentioned by Alexander at the end of his section
on substance, namely, to the question of the interaction of the parts of a
substance, an interaction which Alexander describes as "the reciprocal
action of different substances within the whole substance" and which,
he says, involves causal relations within the substance.

Now to say that a substance in this way embodies causal relations is
not to say that the category of causality is contained within the category
of substance. It must be possible in some way to pass from any category
to any other category but still the categories have to be distinguished
and I would say that when we are thinking of substantiality, even where
we are recognizing a succession of phases as well as an arrangement
of parts, even when we are recognizing opposing tendencies, when,
say, we are thinking of substantiality we are not thinking of causality
as such. And when we are thinking specially of causality then we are
recognizing relations between different things, different substances as
Alexander puts it, independently of the question of their falling within
a single substance. In other words from the point of view of substance
the question is of the internality of those things—of their being within
the substance we are talking about—from the point of view of causality
the question is of the externality of those things—their externality to
one another even if they can also be called parts of the same thing.
Or, putting it in terms we used earlier—in terms of substance we are
thinking of their togetherness, in terms of causality we are thinking
of their distinctions. But since in fact any consideration of a structure

of parts and phases inevitably raises the question of external action or influenc we can say that there is a natural passage from substance to causality.

Lecture 38   *(14th June 1950)*

The Category of Causality—Causality in Cartesian Philosophy: Descartes, Spinoza, Leibniz, Locke, Berkeley, Hume

In the case of Alexander since it is a spatio-temporal theory then he naturally emphasizes the part played by space in the matter and does not try to treat causality as essentially temporal in Kant's manner—the point being that it is not merely a question of succession but of replacing.

Causality in Cartesian Philosophy

If you take Cartesian philosophy generally—that is in Norman Kemp Smith's sense of Cartesian (the general line of thinking in Descartes and his successors) then you fin two main conceptions of causality—namely Creation and Comprehension. The point in Creation theories being that when we ask for the cause of a thing we are simply referred to some other thing and we are supposed to be satisfie with that—that is, with the simple dictum that A can and does bring about B. And of course this theory is not merely of an atomistic kind but is essentially dualistic—that is to say certain ultimate powers or agencies are set over various effects or outcomes. In causality as creation we have a division into active and passive entities. Now of course any Rationalistic theory—that is any doctrine that works with the Principle of Identity—must endeavour to overcome such a division—that is, for Rationalism, as I have put it, any relation is a form of identity or one related term is a form of the other and that is what leads up to the second conception of causality—the conception of comprehension in which the agent in some way embraces the effect or again in which the effect is deducible from the cause and is not simply set against it.

Spinoza

Now among the Cartesians both conceptions are operative. You have a position like that of Spinoza which attempts to work only with comprehension—in which in fact the only true substance is the all-comprehensive substance. But even such a doctrine has to introduce *modes* which are not in fact deducible from the total substance even though they are supposed to be, and which have to be treated as created by the substance—that is all we can really say about the relation of substance to mode is that the substance has the power of expressing or manifesting itself in this way. And it is only by dogma that we can say that the mode is a manifestation of the substance—only because according to the theory it must be so and not because any logical connection can be demonstrated between the two.

If Spinoza were to try to hold strictly to the doctrine of one great cause which has no effect distinct from itself then he would really be denying any sort of causality—any actual operation—nothing would happen. And even the supposed complexity of the substance would be unthinkable because if it had various parts and processes they would be bound to affect one another—this is to say there would be external action, what is called efficien causality. In other words a theory of causality as comprehension can't be consistently worked out, and among the Rationalists we have a swinging back and forth between Comprehension and Creation—that is we have no single and determinate view of causality.

Leibniz

Leibniz again tries to work out a theory of Comprehension—takes the effect to be comprehended in the cause in the way in which the predicate is contained in the subject that is his leading principle. But when he substitutes for the single substance of Spinoza a multiplicity of substances and yet rejects any action between them—when he puts up a doctrine of the *harmony* of all substances with one another—he can logically be forced back to the doctrine of a single substance not merely that of a supreme or highest substance. And in trying to work out the relation between the supreme substance and the lower substances—the universal monad and the particular monads he is forced to introduce external relation—to say, in fact, that at a particular point in time the supreme substance created all other substances.

Now Locke, Berkeley and Hume, on the other hand, tried to avoid comprehension and Locke and Berkeley at least, tried to uphold a doctrine of creation. But taking Berkeley as holding this doctrine in its most extreme form we fin that even he admits comprehension in the sense that the ideas which are effects are said to be in the minds which are causes.

Locke

We fin that Locke already recognises a point later emphasised by Hume—that cause and effect are two different things, as against the principle that it is a part or manifestation of the other; but he still attempts to explain causality by means of the conception of "Power"—in fact for Locke material things are made of so many "powers" to produce effects both on our minds and on other things. Locke says, of course, that some of the powers *resemble* the effects they produce but he is quite unable to demonstrate that this is so. And, logically, he could be brought to the position that anything that occurs does so because there has been a power capable of bringing it about, but we have no means of determining what this power is like—what it is in itself apart from its causal effica y. This is, of course, a necessarily inadequate account of causality because unless we have actually observed another one of the so-called powers bringing things about or something bringing things about we should not understand what was meant by causing or producing or bringing about.

Berkeley

Berkeley, of course, tries to avoid this difficult by saying that we do have experience of causes, only it is a different sort of experience from our experience of effects. We experience our own minds as causes—we have a *notion* of their activity—and we are aware of the images which are the effects of such activities. But, of course, if the experience of causes is a different kind of experience from the experience of effects there can be no single experience which will inform us that a cause A produces and effect B. And if there *is* such an experience then we cannot divide reality into the causing—namely minds—and the caused—namely ideas. Still, as I said, this theory that only minds can cause does involve a certain recognition of Comprehension—what mind is able to bring about is something in mind though we could say that even Berkeley's theory of images cannot be consistently stated in this manner because we don't have the image until after we have brought it about, and if we have to comprehend it in order to bring it about we should be forced to postulate images of images and so on.

Hume

Well then, Hume recognises as Locke and Berkeley tried to do that cause and effect are distinct. But taking this fact quite seriously Hume is able to argue that there can be no such thing as the "power" which is taken to exist by Locke and Berkeley and in all atomistic thinking. The main point is simply this—that granted that there is a cause A and an effect B, to say that there is in A a power to produce B is to say that B is in A, at least to the extent that by knowing A we already know B, its effect, and if that weren't so, we can't say that A has the power to produce B, but that, at most, A has a power which produces

B—that is the cause of B is not A but something X existing in A. And if we are not then to say that X is not A but something existing in A, and if we are not to say that X has a power to produce B and continue the argument indefinitel then we are forced back to the distinctness of cause and effect—we are forced back to Hume's position that apart from experience we might take anything to be the cause of anything else. Whether, then, it is A that produces B, or X, or A in respect of X, we simply have a relation between two different things, each with its own qualities and we can attach no meaning to the concept of "power".

> What is interesting here is that this criticism of "power" brings out the fact that every notion of Creation involves Comprehension.

Now for the concept of "power" Hume substitutes the concept of constant conjunction—that is he substitutes one bridge or tie for another and is involved in difficultie similar to those raised in regard to "power". Previously we had A, the power of producing B, then B. Now we have A, a certain mental transition, then B. But if this connecting link is not itself a "power" then we simply have the fact of sequence and Hume is not entitled to distinguish a sequence which is caused from one which is not caused. Hume in fact accepts the criticism applicable to Berkeley that we cannot take the cause to be of higher reality than the effect—that if we are to speak of the two as related in a definit manner then we must be capable of knowing the relation in the same way and by the same act. But what Hume has not clearly grasped is that the criticism must be carried further—that we must be capable of knowing the relation in the same way and by the same act as we know the terms of the relation. And that, I would say, is what Kant brings out, namely apprehending objects is apprehending them in space and time and in various relations including the causal. And this is the point that James is expressing more vaguely than Kant when he says that we know the connections between things along with the distinctions between things and both, of course, along with things themselves.

Lecture 39   *(21st June 1950)*

The Category of Causality continued—Hume continued—Causality in Kant

Hume *continued*

Hume's treatment of the question of causality is inadequate because he gives no account of the relation of cause to effect on the level of the things take to be related.   In fact he avoids having to give an account of the relation by making the distinction between internal and external impressions—a distinction which he is definitel not entitled to make—but which in any case strictly makes no difference because even if we could call a thing an internal impression it would be something known and in place of Hume's view which amounts to this: that firs we are aware of A, then a certain mental transition takes place, and then thirdly we are aware of B—instead of that he would have to say we are aware of a transition from A to B or are aware of A passing into B, though of course to say this would not be in accordance with the doctrine of simple ideas with which Hume began.

If however we say that for consistency the transition would have to be part of what is cognized and not merely a condition of cognizing, then it would appear that frequency or custom has nothing to do with the case because, on the one hand, no manner of repetitions of A and B unrelated would give rise to the conception of A and B related, on the other hand a single instance of A and B related gives us the relation we want, in other words the question is not how we have some to associate A and B, but of what we have in mind when we do associate them—what is meant by A and B associated—which here of course means related in a certain manner. And if it is admitted that the whole complex can be known by a single act of thought—failing which there could be no such thing as a judgment of causality—then the complex can be known even if repetition has not taken place—and that is actually the position in our experience, namely that in observing a certain sequence even if only once we take one feature of it to be the outcome of another—that is we observe causality (admitting of course that such observation may be mistaken—but then so may any observation).

Causality in Kant

Now what Kant may be said to do is to present in some detail this doctrine of an object of transition—not merely a mental transition between perceptions but a perception of transition as part of a situation. For him then the relation is of the same order as the terms related, though he considers this to be the phenomenal order.

But if his distinction between phenomena and things-in-themselves is found to be untenable—if the whole doctrine of things-in-themselves is untenable because they have relations of a different order among themselves—then we can say that there are no things-in-themselves in the Kantian sense or that what Kant calls phenomena are things in themselves in the only positive sense—namely actual existing things—and the kind of causality they exhibit is the only kind of causality.

There are in fact two strains in Kant's thinking—that involved in his criticism of the sort of distinctness referred to in Hume's two principles—and that in which he accepts this distinctness though with the view that it can somehow nevertheless be overcome. It is not merely then that Kant's phenomenal world is the world of science—that is where Kant's phenomena differ from Locke's ideas—but that any account that he gives of something beyond or independent of this world is in terms of the very categories that one takes to be peculiarly applicable to phenomena, and reduces it therefore to the phenomenal level (if there is any question of reduction that is to say). For example, to say that things in themselves are the source of phenomena or even to say that phenomena are the appearance of things in themselves is to refer to things in themselves in terms which are intelligible only in the phenomenal world—only to things as they are under the conditions of the understanding.

If we deny then, that there is any difference between things as they are in themselves and things as they are under the conditions of our understanding we can still fin in Kant's theory of phenomena a great deal that we can take to be strictly applicable to actual things with no question of anything other than actual things.

Now if we take the firs of Hume's two principles—namely that all our distinct perceptions are distinct existences we can say that Kant specificall denies this if it means that our diverse or various perceptions are unconnected—that they are separate essences—and maintains that the things we perceive are all connected in space and time and under the categories. That is, taking causality as the typical example, that by the very act of perceiving things we perceive them to have spatio-temporal and causal connections.

> Even an expression like "manifold" does imply connection—intelligible again only under space, time and the categories.

The Analogies of Experience

Well now, in the "Analogies of Experience" Kant tries to work out particularly a theory of causality and the way in which recognition of it is involved in any experience.

First Analogy: His doctrine of substance in the First Analogy is comparatively unimportant. We can recognize that any change is a change in something without having to say that substance is permanent and that the quantum of it in nature is neither increased nor diminished. All that we need to say is that in a given change A becomes B or A which is not B gives place to A which is B but this constancy of A thus met in that particular change implies no absolute constancy of A—A itself might be regarded as something which another fact or thing X had become or as equivalent to X's having become Y (X that is not-Y becomes XY) so that A on this view could cease if X became not-Y again. And there is in all this argument back from attribute to substance or from the changing to the persistent no reason for thinking that we should ever arrive at the absolutely permanent—that which was never substance and always attribute. On the contrary this substance could only be space or perhaps space-time—something which in an important sense is not substantial at all.

Second Analogy: The point of the Second Analogy is that all change takes place according to a rule. Now Kant discusses this in connection with the perception of time—that is he connects temporal irreversibility with what I was previously called material irreversibility, that being equivalent to change in accordance with a rule.

Lecture 40   *(28th June 1950)*
The Category of Causality continued—Causality in Kant: Second Analogy continued

One important point about Kant's theory, though it doesn't appear explicitly until the work of Alexander, is that in fact it is as spatio-temporal that things come under the categories and that though in connection with causality in particular his argument is conducted explicitly with reference to time it actually requires a reference to space also in order to be fully intelligible.

That is, for Kant, the recognition of an absolute order in Time, that is of temporal irreversibility, is bound up with the recognition of absolute order in phenomena or of a law of the succession of events—in other words with what I called in an earlier lecture material irreversibility—the fact that recognition of a certain kind of thing includes recognition of an irreversible sequence of phases.

If you take Kant's example of the boat floatin downstream, then there is nothing in the nature of the things that requires a boat to be firs higher up and then lower down—there is no essential order of this kind but on the contrary if the phenomenon in question were that of a boat being towed upstream or being rowed downstream or being carried up by a sail the necessary order would be from lower to higher and not from higher to lower. So that Kant, at most, is saying that our recognition of absolute temporal order is bound up with the recognition of an absolute order of priority among the phases of a process of a certain kind (whether for example, as I said, that that process was an upstream or a downstream order) is bound up then with the recognition of kind.

Now, I had suggested to you earlier that while causality may always be present in the situation in which there are such sequences, the sequence itself is not an example of causality—the sequence, so I said, is part of the constitution or substance that is in question in each particular case. However, granted that we have determined that the phenomenon we have observed is one of *floatin* then there will be that absolute order of phases—namely from higher up to lower down. It's important, however, to see how considerations of *space* come into the matter—that is, you have to have spatial *continuity*—you have to have the replacing of one situation by another and not simply their sequence before you have the regular order of which Kant speaks. In other words, even if the developing situation in question hasn't yet been shown to involve *causality*, it is only in respect of continuity in space as well as time that it exhibits the *regularity* on which Kant is insisting.

> We must have one thing replacing another within the same general region to have necessity.

Well now, in recognizing "floating say, we do recognize a necessary order—we see the boat firs higher up and then lower down and we say that these things have to be in that order—that we could not see the boat firs lower down and then higher up unless it were something other than floatin that were in question.

Now Kant contrasts with this necessary order in perception the absence of any such necessary order in our observation of the parts of a house. We could look firs at the front, then at the side, then at the back, then at another side without thinking that there is any necessary priority—that the front had to come before the back and so forth. Or similarly taking just the front we could look firs at the top and then at the bottom or firs at the right hand side and then at the left hand side without thinking that the top in any sense preceded the bottom and so on. But then the question arises if time is involved in all our perceptions, in other words, if there is a series of perceptions in any perception, and if the perception of time is bound up with the recognition of a necessary order, why are the two cases different? Why are we not bound to say that the passage from the firs to the second perception of the parts of the house is just as much a causal passage as the passage from the firs to the second perception of the boat? In one sense there *is* an absolute temporal order here—that is (allowing for exceptions that I will touch on in a minute) that there *is* an absolute order even in the objects perceived—that when we look firs at the top and then at the bottom the perceived top part *is* earlier than the perceived bottom part and so it would seem that we ought to say that it is the *cause* of the bottom part (taking cause in Kant's special way).

One difference that does exist is precisely that of *replacing*—we don't see the top part passing into the bottom part as we see the higher position of the boat passing into the lower position—so that space does have to come in to make Kant's theory complete or consistent. But what is further required is that even if there is not a necessary order in the parts of the house there is a necessary order in our *experience* of the parts of the house—that causality is involved in our *looking* firs at the top and then at the bottom—that is, that there is a necessary order in our lookings even if not in the things looked at. And this means two things.

First of all the distinction between our perceptions and the things perceived, that is the realist distinction which, I suggest, is not covered by phenomenalism; and secondly the treatment of the things distinguished as on the same footing—the treatment of them both as phenomenal to use Kant's term or of them both as actual occurrences to use the realists' expression which, I say, Kant is forced by the logic of his statements to adopt. In other words it is only by recognising the mind as one thing among others, known in the same way, that Kant can make the distinction he wants to make.

And this distinction is further required for the cases I said he was coming to where the observed order is *not* the necessary order—the case, for example, where we see the flas before we hear the report though we actually believe that the two are simultaneous, or cases in the observation of the stars, for instance, where we see later what we believe was actually earlier. The possibility of such beliefs, whether they are right or wrong in any given case, depends on our recognition not merely of so-called phenomena but of independent things distinct from ourselves (who are also independent things) and able to act out in the various ways so as incidentally to affect our perceivings. And here, of course, we have the notion of external action by which I suggest necessary or irreversible order had to be supplemented in order to give a clear account of causality.

Now one attempted line of escape on Kant's part is the recognition that there are specifi phenomena of the human mind—is the recognition of the empirical or phenomenal self as something alongside other phenomena—something however which is not to be equated to the transcendental self and which therefore doesn't undermine the doctrine of phenomena as such which permits us to treat the empirical self as in some way subordinate to the transcendental self while at the same time having a kind of connection with it that other phenomena do not have. And it is in this connection that we get the curious doctrine of Inner sense—a doctrine which treats mental phenomena as not subject to spatial externality because they have to be in some manner internal to the self but at the same time treats them as objects of sense and thus as not identical to the self to which they are such objects. This device, this treating of certain phenomena as in some way and in some way not identical with some specially intimate relation to the subject is no more successful than Berkeley's attempt to distinguish a particular set of my ideas as "my body". Strictly, on the theory of ideas, there wouldn't be any more mind than any other ideas, they would all just be passive objects to me. Similarly on the theory of phenomena no set of phenomena would be any more me than any other set, that is they would not even be a special kind of self or a special aspect of the self. But in point of fact the considerations already advanced are sufficien to overthrow the doctrine of the transcendental self. The interaction referred to involves action upon the very perceiver itself and the knowing subject and not just on something that could be called its inner phenomena.

I have here departed from direct consideration of Kant on causality but it is important to see that if perceptions are taken in a necessary order (although a distinction between perceptions and phenomena in this regard essential to Kant) we are involved in an argument that can bring down the doctrine of phenomena as such.

Lecture 41   *(5th July 1950)*

The Category of Causality continued—Causality in Kant: Second Analogy continued and Third Analogy—Causality in Alexander

Temporal view of the matter not enough, we need successive phases of a single process, which includes replacing.

If you take the examples Kant gives: (i) in the case of the boat there is continuous spatial passage, one phase supervenes and cancels out the previous one; but (ii) in the case of the house, parts do not cancel out one another or give place to each other (although *perceptions* do give place to one another in the mind).

Now as I said it is not merely replacing, but there is also in Kant's distinction of the two cases the conception of circumstance, that is to say we recognize all the parts of the house as existing at the same time and indeed as alongside one another—we recognize then as spatially different parts of a single structure and we don't think that the roof is the cause of the foundation or the front or the back because we have proceeded in that order in our perceptions though, on Kant's own showing, there is an absolute temporal order in the matter—there must be a succession of some kind involved, a certain regularity of sequence, and that, as I said, involves the putting of our acts of perception on the same level and having the same general relation as the things perceived, and it also involves the introduction of space in the account of causality.

Third Analogy: Now Kant's Third Analogy which he describes as the principle of co-existence according to the law of Reciprocity or Community, is formulated in this way:

> "All substances in so far as they can be perceived in space at the same time exist in a state of complete reciprocity of action."[4]

The main point here is not that action involves interaction, though that is important enough, it is the introduction of the concept of action itself. The Second Analogy was formulated as:

> "All change takes place according to the law of the connection of cause and effect."[5]

This of course is somewhat misleading as referring to *the* law of such connection, but is defensible as in accordance with Kant's actual exposition if understood simply to mean that all changes take place according to some law or that all sequences have some regularity. But that in itself doesn't involve the conception of "action", of the influenc of one thing on another, and in so far as that conception is involved in causality not only the concept of regularity or sequence but even the concept of replacing is inadequate as an account of causality. This is in

---

[4] Immanuel Kant, *Critique of Pure Reason, op. cit.*, Third Analogy: Principle of Coexistence, in accordance with the Law of Reciprocity or Community, pp. 233-38. Anderson is quoting from the J. M. D. Meiklejohn translation, London: J. M. Dent and Sons, 1934. Kemp Smith's translation of this passage is "All substances, in so far as they can be perceived to coexist in space, are in thoroughgoing reciprocity." (p. 233.)
[5] *Ibid.* Second Analogy. Kemp Smith: "All alterations take place in conformity with the law of the connection of cause and effect."

accordance with the view I previously put forward that the recognition of regular phases of a certain kind of process raises only the question of substance, so that the phases of infancy, youth, manhood and old age for example are features of the human substance ("human nature"), and while if causality is a category the things wouldn't be without causality (we couldn't have such phases) they don't in themselves illustrate causality but only character or regularity.

Causality in Alexander

Sequence and External Action: Now Alexander seems to waver between the view that would take replacing as a sufficien characterisation of causality and the view that in causality we have not merely a sequence of phases, in other words change in something, but we have that change as conditioned by something else, by what we call *external* action, by at least the second things coming into certain spatial relations to the firs thing.

Thus when Alexander says that causality is "the continuous passage of one motion or set of motions into a different motion or set of motions", he seems to be merely saying that causality is change and on my view to say that X becomes Y is merely to say what the effect is and not what the cause is and this is not a complete statement of a causal relation. But then again, he speaks of "the very different effect produced by one and the same cause in different substances", and he gives the example of a stone that would break a window but would only bury itself in a cushion or a mound of earth and here he seems to treat the cause as an external thing, a different thing from the affected but the occasion of the change in the thing affected.

In the main, I would say, that the point that he emphasises is that of one motion issuing in another—that is of change rather than of causality. However he actually treats the distinction as unimportant, saying:

> "It is immaterial, with our metaphysical conception of a substance, whether we describe a cause in popular language as a thing or substance affecting some other thing or substance producing an effect in it or, in the stricter language of the logicians, call the cause and event or process which precedes another event or process and without which the second event or process the effect does not exist." (*STD* Volume 1, pp. 279–80.)

Here Alexander gets credit for saying "does not" instead of "would not" exist because he says the only means of telling what would or would not exist is by seeing what does or does not exist. Now even if one said "would not" here we should simply be calling the cause necessary for the effect and not even sufficien which would be only one among the many deficiencie of the formula. But we are losing all suggestion of a causal connection if we simply say that the one doesn't exist within the other because this suggests only concomitance—that A and B actually do exist together or, more strictly, that they are actually two phases in a succession, and on this sort of showing anything might be the cause of anything else.

Alexander, of course, goes on to speak of the event not as an isolated occurrence but as a process which is continued into the effect or into which a cause is continued, but even if he could avoid in some such way the effect of the substitution of "does" for "would" it still appears that he is coming down on the side of mere change, the mere acquiring of a character by something, indicated by his calling his firs formulation a logical one and the second a popular one. And this is all the more remarkable because he later denies that change is a category.

Alexander's way of speaking thus obscures two points, that of external agency and that of universality (necessity and sufficien y) for as far as "being continued into" is concerned that might well be taken to apply simply to particulars and of course would rule out agency since we don't speak of the agent becoming the patient.

The question then is of a certain kind of agent coming into a certain relation with a certain kind of patient and the latter thereupon undergoing a certain change. And all of this, I say, is obscured by the doctrine of "continuance". It is in fact from the absence of a division between agent and patient and particularly absence of the notion of a "field that we get the doctrine of causal chains exemplified for example, in Kant's Antinomies (the Third) and in particular in the notion of a firs cause as against a general doctrine of contingency and interaction—the view that wherever we begin in any enquiry it will be with something that has various influence operating upon it and variably influencin other things.

Now Alexander, we saw, at firs treats agent and patient as merely popular expressions but later on we fin him saying:

> "But the cause does its work not by a change in itself but by leading on into something else. A cause might well remain unaltered for a time and then findin its patient, produce its effect". (*STD* Volume 1, p. 298.)

a view expressed in the language of external action and not compatible with the simple doctrine of continuance. And yet Alexander goes on immediately after this to say that,

> "continuity is the conceptual formulation of motion itself, and hard as it may be to say where cause ends and effect begins, yet if the cause is itself a process and effect another and different one, the relation between the two is the translation of the one which is earlier into the later motion or group of motions." (*STD* Volume 1, p. 299.)

One could show other quotations exhibiting the same vacillation. The major concept is "continuity" but Alexander couldn't quite deny interaction and external action.

Alexander tries here, as he often does, to make some allowance for all views, agree with everyone.

Lecture 42   *(12th July 1950)*

The Category of Causality continued—Causality in Alexander continued—Immanent and Transeunt—Change and Causality—Reciprocal Determination

Causality in Alexander *continued*

We fin Alexander, then, using a phrase like this:

> "Causality is thus the spatio-temporal continuity of one substance with another" (*STD* Volume 1, p. 280.)

and again that the cause is transformed into the effect. (He modifie this by saying the transition is only an instance of causality—causality itself an irreducible notion—hence it is difficul to pin him down.) But still the predominant conception is that of change and not of transactions between different things.

Immanent and Transeunt Causality: Now this leads to the question, as Alexander puts it, whether causality is immanent or transeunt, that is whether it falls within the development of a particular thing or involves a going across from one thing to another. And while at firs Alexander seems to reject immanent causality he goes on to treat the difference between immanent and transeunt as merely one of convenience in description. The suggestion is that if we took our system wide enough we could always see causality as immanent, a matter of inner development, the working out or unfolding of something, which I has take to concern substance rather than causality.

Now firs we never could take our system wide enough to rule out external influence affecting its development and second when we treat the development of a thing causally it is by taking its parts as different things and considering their action on one another in terms of their peculiar characters and not of characters of the whole system. (A matter of *sorts* of thing—Alexander, as noted, obscures the question of universality.)

Change non-Categorial: Reverting then to the question of change versus causality we fin Alexander saying that causation is the continuity of existents within continuous space-time as subsisting between substances which are themselves motions or groups of motions—this being just passage or replacing— yet on the very next page (p. 285) he insists on the difference between cause and effect, contending that mere continuance of the same uniform motion is not a causal connection; though it seems curious, if causality is categorial, that there should in some situations be change and in other situations no change and, therefore, no causality. But apart from that special point Alexander will certainly fin it hard to explain why there is change in some cases but not in others, or, putting it from the other end why there is ever change at all. And this problem, I would say, is insoluble in terms of continuity alone and requires consideration of external action or of *exchanges* as in the Heraclitean theory in which persistence is seen as a special case of change and not an exception to change, or a different kind of thing.

On this view, even when we get a balance so that no changes are apparent to us there are changes—there are givings out and takings in so that change can be regarded as inherent in motion. Of course if we were considering in some detail the history of a persisting thing over a period, if we were considering the facts of causation involved then, whatever persisted, we should constantly fin changes in it, we should fin that however much a certain general character was retained some characters were lost and some were added. But this distinction itself couldn't be maintained or alternatively we should have a dualism, a logical division, unless even the *persistence* is describable in the same terms—that is, unless it also is a sort of change.

Reciprocal Determination of Cause and Effect: I have suggested that Alexander's discussion is exceedingly loose, that is, showing both indefinitenes and inconsistency, and this comes out again in his treatment of the question whether effect determines cause as much as cause determines effect. Alexander says that this is so only in a logical sense—that we can only mean that when the cause and the effect are precisely stated they are reciprocal:

> "... when the cause, that is, is purged of what may indeed occur in a particular case, but is accidental to it, and when the effect is stated in terms so precise as to presuppose one cause only, and not a choice of several, when, to take the familiar example, the death from drowning is distinguished from the death by hanging and the two not linked together under the general designation of death. The reciprocity of cause and effect means then that unless there were the precise effect, there would not be the precise cause. But such determination is logical and not real determination, and effect cannot be interchanged with cause except as a basis of inference." (*STD* Volume 1, p. 287.)

He concludes,

> "We can't say in any real sense that the future determines the present for the future is not yet and a past event introduces the order of Time. In that order the future does not determine but is determined." (*STD* Volume 1, p. 287.)

Again Alexander is neglecting the universality of causal connection—he is speaking as if what were causally linked were simply two particular events when in fact there can be no account of causal connection unless we take the events to be linked as an only as events of certain sorts. And, in that connection, "death by drowning" is as much a sort of thing, admitting of variations, as is death in general—and the same would be the case no matter how much detail we gave—however precise, to use Alexander's terms—we made our description. As I pointed out ("The Problem of Causality"[6]) the question always is "What is our problem?", "What is the field? and "What is the property to be acquired?" and from that point of view the solution could be called just as precise whether what we are trying to account for is death merely or death with special features. And of course we get the universal element and also reciprocity in the conception of the solution as one of necessity and sufficien y, even if there are also non-reciprocal and in fact irreversible relations in the situation—irreversible relations such as order in time between cause and effect.

Now, when Alexander distinguishes between real and logical determination he seems to be suggesting that there is some opposition between the recognition of a symmetrical relation between two things and the concurrent recognition of an asymmetrical or irreversible relation between them. But of course this is not the case and thus to say that the effect cannot precede the cause, that the two have an irreversible temporal order, is no reason for saying that the relation of determination

---

[6] John Anderson, "The Problem of Causality", *A.J.P.P.* 16(2) August 1938: 127-42. Reprinted in *Studies*.

or determining cannot hold equally in both directions. In popular usage, of course, "determines" and "causes" are equivalent but it is not in the least apparent from Alexander's account why a necessary and sufficien precedent condition (of X) shouldn't be described as determining (X) any more than a necessary and sufficien subsequent condition should be described as so.

More broadly Alexander may be said to deviate from realism in distinguishing logical from real determination—apparently meaning by logical determination that which permits us to infer or to use the expression "therefore".—a position illustrated again when Alexander says:

> "the only necessity which philosophy can recognize is that of inference but there is no necessity in things except fact." (*STD* Volume 1, p. 291.)

Nothing is added to the causal relation by the adjective "necessary". And its illustrated once more when he says:

> "Real grounds are to be distinguished from logical grounds though they may coincide". (*STD* Volume 1, p. 297.)

when he goes on to say, after describing the real ground as

> "a complex of motions of which the event or fact is the outcome. But logic... is the science of truth or of how our beliefs as expressed in propositions are to be systematised into a coherent whole at the guidance of reality." (*STD* Volume 1, p. 297.)

It is not indicated what a belief would be, or for that matter what a fact or event would be if it were not in a propositional form. But if a propositional form is something inadequate to the events then it is just a falsificatio of them and, incidentally, it is not apparent how reality could guide us in the use of such forms. And if logical grounds are not real grounds then there are no such things at all.

When Hume tries to give an account of causality as what we assert when we make the transition from one idea to another—when we infer—the realist answer is that we are not just passing from some ideas to others but are recognising the passage of some things into others. In other words that the relation is part of what we know. So in the case of inferring in general the realist has to say that the relation of implication is part of what we know—is part of the real or objective situation otherwise he would have to deny that there is any connection in the case—that there is any such thing as logical grounds.

Lecture 43   *(19th July 1950)*

The Category of Causality continued—Sequence and External Action
continued—Transition to Individuality

Note Alexander's curious view of, use of, "logical". His view of logic and truth is normative, anti-realistic. *Cf.* Book III —almost a social view of truth—a function of communication—treats propositions, as distinct from things, anti-realistically, a correspondence view.

Coming back to the more general point, Alexander's wavering between causality as change and causality as involving something that can be called external action, the important point to realise is that internality, or the development of a thing out of its own resources, doesn't cover the ground, that you could never get a Leibnizian "notion" whose content would embrace the whole history of the thing. In giving an account of this you have to recognise external action or contingency—not in the sense that there are exceptions to the rule that every event has a necessary and sufficien preceding condition—but in the sense that there could never be a single principle from which the whole history of a thing is derived, a single explanation of it, that there will always be "collocation" (Mill's term), the coming together of an irreducible multiplicity of factors.

In line with this contention I would say that when Alexander, following Hume, rejects the notion of power or force he is rejecting, along with the metaphysical or rationalist conception of it—that is, the conception of "that whereby" something happens—also the *logical* conception of it, the conception of *agency*, the operation of independent factors in the bringing about any result. And what we empirically call a force or agency is just *a thing, considered as capable of affecting other things*, and it is along these lines that I link the fina category of individuality or thinghood with the conception of force—that is, use the notion of an agent as elucidating the meaning of that category and, of course, linking it with the previous category, causality.

What I take to be Alexander's deficien y in this matter is connected as in the case of other theories of causality with the notion of the *fiel* —of the distinction between two sets of considerations, consideration of the agent and consideration of the thing acted upon, both of which could be roughly described as precedent conditions of the effect—what happens. In other words it is because such thinkers don't see in detail the nature of a causal problem that they fail, for example, to distinguish between a question of change and a question of causality—and that Mill, as I mentioned in "The Problem of Causality"[7], has difficult in showing why we don't call night the cause of day or day the cause of night. In my view the distinction is absolutely essential and you never would get causal laws, that is you never would get invariability, if you make it a question of what kind of situation is followed by what other kind of situation or what phase of a developing situation is followed by what other phase instead of recognising, on the one hand, the changing thing—the member of a field—and on the other hand, the external thing, the agent or occasion.

And here it is quite interesting to recall Hume's contention that causality is the only basis on which one can argue from one thing to a different thing, this of course being distinguished from ordinary syllogism in which we argue from some property to some *other* property of the same thing. This latter type of argument, I have suggested, brings in only the category of substance no matter whether the properties are concomitant or successive, whereas the former type brings in the category of thinghood or individuality conceived particularly under the head of force or agency. (A thing is what can act.)

And from this point of view it is wrong to say that immanent and transeunt causality are different ways of regarding the same events. On the contrary, causality will be necessarily transeunt and anything that we could call immanent development would fall under the head of substance. The Leibnizian "notion" is an example of immanentist theory, and of course, the doctrine is characteristic of Hegel for whom the essential point in any development is development from inner resources, is the Idea working out its own potentialities.

> *Cf.* my review of "Textbook of Marxist Philosophy"[8]—the denial of external action is used by Marxists for political purposes—the Socialist state has unlimited resources which it can develop from itself—denial of Trotsky's view of taking the matter on a world scale. However, denial of external action breaks out again in the Marx-Trotsky view, that is, for Marx, society or world history are unenvironed—a matter of society realising itself. But, the former view is an arbitrary drawing of the line, not justifie by Marxism even if there are parallels in Marxism.

The conception of causality as transeunt is quite vital but we could connect Alexander's confusion here once more with his doctrine of space-time as the "stuff" of things, a doctrine, that is, that can scarcely avoid immanentism, a doctrine in which space and time must "involve"

---

[7] *Ibid.*
[8] John Anderson, "A Textbook of Marxist philosophy: review", *The Australian Highway* 20(1) February 1938: 13-17.

everything—reality must be spun out of space-time because there is nothing outside space-time which could be the agent of its changes. And this is one of the main lines along which one would argue against the conception of a Universe, namely that there would be nothing to act upon it and so it couldn't change. That is any universe would be a block universe, assuming the treatment given of causality is true.

Alexander, of course, admits novelty or emergence, he admits that we can't predict the later stages, couldn't say from the beginning what was going to be unfolded. But this concession to Empiricism doesn't alter the fact that if you take up a monistic position you are really denying the possibility of any unfolding. It is along these lines, also, that one would reject the doctrine of a single all-embracing evolution. And here Hegelianism and Evolutionism are akin in that for each of them anything that happens is an actualisation of potentialities, is an unfolding or evolving. Such theories, then, I regard as really meaningless. You can say after the event that things were capable of becoming this or that but if you say that things become this because they had it in them to become this you are not giving any explanation at all—you are merely obscuring the fact, recognised by Hume, that the effect is different from the cause.

Lecture 44   *(26th July 1950)*

*The Category of Causality continued—Alexander on Reciprocity—The
Category of Individuality*

Alexander, like other writers, distinguishes the relation of cause and effect from the relation of ground and consequent, but he goes further and takes the latter to be an evisceration of the former—namely by the omission of the temporal element. In fact he says that implication is a notion posterior to causation. Now clearly if we recognise necessity and sufficien y in causal relations we are recognising implication, in other words we are able to say "therefore", but we don't in the least need to go to causation for this, we fin it already involved in quantitative arguments, such as arguments involving equality. It should be remembered here that Alexander actually discusses quantity after discussing causality, in other words that he hasn't presented what I call the Extensional categories before the Intensional, or, using the alternative expression, the Mathematical before the Physical categories.

But whatever order Alexander may follow in his exposition he cannot deny that in the order of the sciences mathematics is regularly put before physics and that mathematics is studied for the most part, though not entirely, without employment of the category of causality, that we can consider the interrelated properties of a triangle, for example, without raising any question of what makes a thing triangular in a temporal sense—what brings about triangularity and that the absence of a temporal factor from these calculations—from the content of geometrical arguments—is not in general felt to be a defect. It might, of course, be contended that the history of mathematics has been linked with the history of mechanics, it might be maintained, as it is by Sorel in *The Utility of Pragmatism* that it is essentially from the problems of engineering that mathematical problems come to be formulated, but the fact remains that their solutions are not worked out in mechanical terms and that the properties of a triangle do not have a temporal order and yet can be recognised as necessary and sufficien for one another so that the treatment of implication as something abstracted from causation doesn't seem to be justified [9]

Alexander on Reciprocity

Referring next to Alexander's treatment of Reciprocity, Kant's treatment of which I had suggested fill out his theory of causality, we might expect to have a more definit recognition of agency in external action connected with the category of thinghood. But once more we fin Alexander obscuring the position—saying for instance:

> "The transaction into which two substances enter, so far as they constitute a closed system is a two-sided and not a one sided transaction. It is one in which each partner is cause and effect in turn. The situation which is the relation of the two substances is from the point of view of the firs an effect on the second but from the point of view of the second an effect on the second." (*STD* Volume 1, p. 300.)

And again,

> "there is thus only one total situation arising from the relation of the two and it appears as an effect in B of A and an effect in A of B." (*STD* Volume 1, p. 300.)

As before Alexander is failing to keep apart or distinct from one another the question of change and the question of external agent, of the thing effecting and the thing effected, for, when we do distinguish these questions, that is when we recognise the field we see that the question of A's action on B and the question of B's action on A are different questions even though there are connections between them and that it is not a matter of a passage of motions in A in to motions in B and *vice*

---

[9] Georges Sorel, De L'Utilité du Pragmatisme, Paris: Rivière, 1921. Second edition 1928.

versa but of a passage or change in A into which B does not enter and *vice versa*. It is of course the whole point of the doctrine of the fiel that the effect of B on A depends upon the sort of thing A is as well as the sort of thing that B is, but that is not the least reason for confusing the effect of B on A with the effect of A on B; not the least reason for saying that these two are the same things from two points of view, whatever, in any case, that might mean. We are brought back to the general criticism that Alexander's emphasis on continuity makes him unable to distinguish change from causality or causality from change and the neglect of the notion of the external agent.

The Category of Individuality

Individuality and Substance: Before going on to discuss individuality, which I am identifying with force or agency, I would like to say something arising out of Alexander's confusion between individuality and substance, and, firs of all, that while there may be a use of substance in which it was idenfifi with thinghood (it would I think not be the most defensible usage historically) but we should if we accepted it simply have to fin another expression for what he has called substance and treat it as the central one of the third group of categories—for example, we might use the expression *structure*.

Aesthetics and Logic: I have taken the conception of structure to be the leading concept of Aesthetics and it might be argued that the categories of aesthetics fall within the physical categories but stop short of the category of causality—that even in the art which takes time, that is, where the work isn't presented all at once (as in plastic art it is) the question is not one of tracing causal connections but the bringing out of the character of the subject through its successive phases, just as I have argued against Alexander that the mere succession of phases or stages without reference to an external agent did not raise the question of causality but was still a question of substance.

Now if in this way the artist rules out causality, if he tries to present the development of something in its own terms or to treat it as self-contained it is not that he really believes that such things are impervious to external action but just that he is concentrating on a certain character, bringing out what we may call its elements or leading features and thus proceeding as we do in definition—tha is giving a number of features which are necessary and together sufficien for a certain kind of thing. In other words the scheme of interrelated properties which the classifie recognises is equivalent to the series of phases in which an artist works out a theme or the various features by which he builds up a structure.

But such a structure can of course be invalid, we can have the intrusion of other features and the breaking up of the character in question, we can have *history* as opposed to art—the sort of thing James Joyce is referring to when he says "History is a nightmare from which I am trying to awake";[10] but when the artist intrudes other factors, when, in Joyce's terms again, he is concerned with kinesis rather than with stasis, then he is a bad artist, he has fallen away from the aesthetic standpoint as in the case where the work is taken to have some social reference, some "purpose" and so on, and not as just self-sufficient

I am suggesting then that when we complete the third group of categories, when we bring in interaction or external agency, then we pass from the Aesthetic to the Historical. Though this use of "historical" could be quite opposed to that of Croce who considers that history is definitel a non-causal study, who holds that causality is alien to History, who thus treats history in the manner I have referred to the category of substance, that is, as the unrolling of a certain subject through its successive phases.[11] That would seem to be a view of a Hegelian type and seems to be scarcely in accordance with Croce's rejection of a single-track development and particularly of a regular progress because the recognition that there can be reactions as well as advances seems to me to imply distinct and interacting (conflicting factors.

Under the category of substance aesthetics has its special connection with logic.

Under the category of agency epistemology has its connection with logic

This doesn't mean that the development of these subjects is to be treated simply as a logical matter, but each does have a logical category of special importance to its own subject matter—but there are many difficulties many problems here.

Lecture 45   *(2nd August 1950)*

The Category of Individuality continued—General Note on the System of Categories

I identify individuality with agency, or being an agent, and that sort of view is connected with or can be further clarifie by the view put forward by in a number of articles on ethics (e.g., "Realism versus Relativism in Ethics"[12]) where I have taken it as equivalent to treating good as a force and treating it as a thing. The reference is specificall to good but more

[10] James Joyce, *Ulysses*, London: The Bodley Head 1960, p. 42.

[11] Benedetto Croce, History as the Story of Liberty, London: George Allen and Unwin, 1941. Translated by Sylvia Sprigge. Cf. Chapter IV, "The Historical Meaning of Necessity", pp. 27-31.

[12] John Anderson, "Realism vs Relativism in Ethics", *A.J.P.P.* 11(1) March 1933: 1-11. Reprinted in *Studies*.

broadly to human or social affairs and it is particularly in connection with social theory that it is important to reject the view that there is anything at all which is a mere resultant, which is an epiphenomenon or after-effect or which exists in subordination or relative to something else. That is, I argue, that anything that can be produced can also produce and it is in emphasising the capacity of thing for acting as well as being acted upon that I refer to them as *forces*. Thus in "Realism and Relativism in Ethics" and again in "The Meaning of Good" the point is made that goods, if they exist, must be agents, that they can't be only attached to something else but must have their own modes of operation and this will be the subject matter of ethical science.

Now it might be suggested that the series of categories has come in full circle—that the last returns to the first—tha individuality is the concrete or practical form of identity. But there is still a distinction, because in identity we are concerned only with locating, whereas in individual identity we are concerned with activity, with something dynamic or as I put it intensional as contrasted with the extensional categories of the second group. Nevertheless if we were speaking specificall of a certain subject we would be considering it as an active being capable of affecting other things not merely as locating activities, being a region within which they occur, but as having these activities, operating in these specifi ways. In other words the subject is that whose acts these predicates are.

Now this is not, I would say, a departure from the distinction of functions in the proposition but is simply an insistence on a connection, or the fact that the activities are the subject's activities; and, on the one hand, this doesn't mean that we have to look for some force or power additional to the activities themselves, on the other hand, it doesn't mean that the subject is merely general, is a mere sort or kind—in other words it is vital while recognising the distinction of functions to recognise the convertibility of terms. (*Cf.* 1948 Logic course.)

I have pointed out to us the way in which individuality can be treated as a species of universality, for example, Socrates being an individual. The Socratic character is repeated or has various instances throughout the history of Socrates. But there is still the peculiarity that such instances form a continuous series which the members of an ordinary class, say, "men" do not. Now it might be argued that even in contrasting individuality with universality, instances that form a continuous series, with instances that do not, we are equally in both cases employing the conception of *an* instance, an individual or single instance, and thus using the conception of individuality.

General Note on the System of Categories

But it would not be a real objection to any view to say that according to it we use the later categories to explain the earlier because the point of the whole doctrine of categories is that they are all involved in any sort of discourse and even when we distinguish one from the other and present them in a certain order there is no question of our not employing them in that part of the argument in which they haven't yet been formally presented and discussed any more than there is a question of our not employing syllogism before the presentation of that part of the logical theory which comes before the presentation of the theory of syllogism itself, or the logic of syllogism.

In other words we are not involved in the Hegelian position in which to think about a certain category, or it might be better to say to think a certain category, is equally to think *with* that category, trying to think the whole of things under that conception. So that firs of all we try to think things simply as being and the attempt breaks down and the conception of not-being intrudes, a category which from its antithetical character clearly cannot be used to think everything and so we try to think everything under a category which synthesises or amalgamates being and not-being and so on indefini ely. Instead of trying to think with such a conception *alone*, allowing each conception to generate its own world, so to speak, we have from the very beginning of our empirical logic recognised propositions, recognised a variety of facts. And our later procedure at no time calls that starting point in question, at no time tries to do away with the proposition or with the variety of propositions, it merely elucidates that starting point, bringing out characteristics and relationships of propositions which remain as distinct as they were to begin with.

I am suggesting in fact that any totalistic view like Hegel's, any doctrine of the totality of things, not merely runs things together but runs categories together, makes it impossible to have any clear and determinate theory of categories. I have mentioned the peculiarity of Hegel's theory of categories, that every category comes round three times, once at the level of being, once at essence and once at the notion (distinctions which, without discussing the matter, I would suggest can't really be sustained) but it can also be argued, and I would argue, that even in so far as Hegel does make distinctions, does get distinct categories, it is because of a propositional treatment that he doesn't acknowledge, that even the very firs movement from being to non-being, thence to determinate being can be understood only in terms of the proposition—of the distinction and connection within it.

What makes an empirical logic, then, more concrete, more capable of being grasped than a totalistic logic is just this pluralistic starting point—starting with the proposition or complex situation—and not just with the conception which couldn't give us any sort of movement—while at the same time I have argued that this sort of thing is clarifie and amplifie by the identificatio of a propositional treatment of things with a spatio-temporal treatment of things.

Now the last account that I gave of the grouping of the categories was that in the firs group we are giving an account of things as in space and time, in the second group as spatio-temporal (and thus giving an account of space and time as well as of things) and of the third group as distinct from space and time or as qualitative. Now another way of putting that might be to say that taking the place/ character formula to refer to the firs group, the second group may be regarded as further specification of place and the third group as further specification of character. The two groups, then, are quantitative and qualitative respectively, or extensional and intensional.

But if we can allow such a notion of further specificatio we can at any rate see that it would be impossible with the general reference to space and time and, what may come to the same thing, without the pluralistic view of the proposition, without the recognition of connections and distinctions within it with which we began.

It is especially then in terms of the constituents of the proposition that I have been able to give what we may call propositional support to the doctrine of categories I have put forward. What I haven't done, or not to more than a slight extent, is to connect them with relations between propositions though I think the theory could be developed in that direction. The doctrine of a *class*, for example, is really a doctrine of relations among propositions. Another thing I have not done—I hope to do it but will have to think it out afresh—is to give any account of the *order* of categories, that is, why the categories should have an order—what we could mean by saying that one was more elementary than another—and whether we can regard as in any way satisfactory a statement in terms of "intelligibility"—that we can understand them better when we have them in a certain order. But the doctrine of specificatio does at least suggest one way in which the order I have given might be defended and I myself think that it is a logical and not a pedagogical order.

Appendix 1
Additional Notes

[Ed.] These notes in John Anderson's hand were appended to Sandy Anderson's student notes. They include a full re-writing of Lectures 1 to 4 (14th to 22nd June 1949); Lecture 9 (12th July 1949); Lecture 14 (27th July 1949); additional notes for Lecture 43 on substance and causality (19th July 1950); a single page added to Lecture 44 (26th July 1950); and a fuller concluding section following Lecture 45 (2nd August 1950).

Lectures 1-4

1 (14th June 1949)

Course concerned with Alexander's "logic" (theory of reality)—with Space-Time and the categories; not with most of Vol. II of *Space, Time and Deity*—material on knowledge and "values". On this last question, Alexander hasn't really advanced from his position in *Moral Order and Progress* (published in the nineties), where his ethics, with a certain foundation in idealism (Green), is of an *evolutionist* character (cf. Spencer). Some general remarks may be made on Alexander's evolutionism as it enters into his Space-Time theory. As regards his ethics, I take it to be incompatible with a thorough Space-Time view. His position may be compared with Plato's; in the later dialogues there is a definit advance on Socratism in *logic*, but in ethics and politics Plato substantially preserves the old position and this reacts on his logic so as to prevent a thorough working out of it—leading to a *compromise* between empiricism and rationalism. Thus rationalism appears in the doctrine of the "highest kinds", which is incompatible with a propositional logic. If this remnant of a *hierarchical* theory (coming over from politics) were dropped, the logic of the *Sophist* would be of a thoroughly empiricist kind.

Alexander was influence by the later dialogues (particularly by Burnet's presentation of them). It is with regard to this that he speaks of our having "two consummate guides" to the categories, "Plato and (with modifications Kant". He makes no reservations as far as Plato is concerned, and he is thinking especially of the *Sophist* but perhaps also of the *Timaeus* in which a theory of Space and Time is adumbrated. (Burnet's account is taken for granted.) In Kant's case also we see a reactionary effect of his ethics on his theory of reality; it is particularly in his desire to preserve an absolute morality (*right*) that he adheres to the doctrine of things-in-themselves—though Adamson contends that this doctrine is also influence by the remnants of representationism in him, that "things-in-themselves" have something in common with Locke's "matter". In this connection Alexander goes beyond Kant, wipes out representationism, and treats Kant's *phenomena* as things in themselves, as actual things and the only realities. Kant of course was influence by both Hume and Leibniz, and the latter is the source of most of Kant's *rationalism* (e.g. his rationalist ethics). If we get rid of absolute morality, then the main support of "things-in-themselves" disappears; the representationist division is easily seen to be otiose. Yet Alexander clings to one of the main bases of this division, the Cartesian *cogito*; this seriously confuses his psychology and in turn affects his logic in some ways. (Doctrine of "enjoyment"; hence "perspectives", etc.) (Cf. my review-article on Alexander—"The Non-Existence of Consciousness", *A.J.P.P.*, March 1939.)

Alexander's other writings are not of much importance for his main position though some articles in *Proceedings of the Aristotelian Society* give preliminary statements of it. *Cf.* also *Spinoza and Time*, in which he compares Spinoza's "attributes" of *thought* and extension with *Time* and Space in his own theory—considers how Spinoza's position would have been affected if he had seen that thought is something empirical (a *particular* set of phenomena) and had realised the importance of Time. (There is an important firs statement of Alexander's *psychological* position in "Foundations and Sketch-Plan of a Conational Psychology", *British Journal of Psychology*, December 1911.)

Alexander and the *realist movement* in Britain: began (about 1903) with Moore's "Refutation of Idealism". Alexander and Moore weren't very close in their views, but Alexander would have to be recognised as belonging to the realist movement—accepting the realist doctrine that the object is in no way constituted by being known. Important to remember that this "independence" of knower and known is not just a doctrine of *knowledge* (epistemology) but is part of a theory of *reality* (logic) (*cf.* "The Knower and the Known"). Moore and Russell didn't realise the full implications of the doctrine, clung to rationalist assumptions, and have got further and further from realism. *The New Realism* (especially the contributions by Marvin and Perry) is also important in the realist movement. These thinkers were influence by James, who upheld a partially realist position in *A Pluralistic*

Universe, Essays in Radical Empiricism (including one entitled "The
Non-Existence of Consciousness"), and the (earlier) *Principles of
Psychology.*

Reverting to the influence affecting Alexander's theory of categories
we may note that he does not include Hegel among his "guides";
yet the way in which he begins his list (*identity* and *difference*)
shows the influenc of Hegel.   In regard to Space-Time and the
Categories, Alexander differs from Kant not only in taking these to
be *forms of things* instead of just forms of our knowledge, but also in
rejecting the view that they have two different sources (Kant's "forms
of *sense*", Space and Time, and "forms of understanding", categories),
in holding that Space-Time is the source of the categories, that they are
"determinations of Space-Time" or, as I would put it, features of things
qua spatio-temporal; that it is in respect of their being spatio-temporal
that we know or can give an account of the categories.   However, as
far as Kant's doctrine of separate sources is concerned, we have to
consider what he calls the *Schematism of the Categories* which gives
them, at least as they appear in our thinking, a *temporal* character—and
it would be quite easy to argue in that connection that they must equally
have a *spatial* character; e.g., considering the Second Analogy, we
can easily show that causality, which Kant there closely connects with
time (taking, that is, our consciousness of causal relations to be bound
up with our consciousness of temporal succession), has also to be
connected with Space to make the discussion intelligible).

Hegel, on the other hand (*cf.* "The Place of Hegel in the History of
Philosophy", *A.J.P.P.*, June 1932), starts from the other side, i.e., from
the *categories*, as the various forms of the Absolute Idea, and the most
that Space and Time could be would be particular forms or examples of
categories—though in point of fact we can't even say that; for Hegel
Space and Time are general conceptions, at a lower level or of less
generality than the main categories. (Kant's "Transcendental Aesthetic"
gives the classical refutation of the Cartesian view that Space is just a
general conception—similarly with Time. Hegel is reactionary here.)

One point in which both Kant and Hegel are superior to Alexander is
in connection with the *classificatio* and *order* of the categories. After
starting off with Hegel's (Plato's?) identity and difference, Alexander
seems to take his categories quite at random, to decide under various
influence that such and such conceptions are categories but not to give

any reason why this should be so, why there should be so many and no more (though *Hegel* multiplies categories beyond all credibility). In Kant, in the Metaphysical Deduction, the categories are enumerated with reference to the *forms of judgment* (or, as we should say, forms of *propositions*), which is at least a definit method; and Hegel, though not so explicit on this matter, though he speaks of successive forms of *The Idea* from the most abstract to the most concrete, nevertheless really does get his starting-point from the proposition and is really working on the basis of what is *involved* in the proposition—in particular, the firs categories of *being* and *not-being* can be regarded as the affirmat ve and the negative copula; it is in terms of the significanc of the copula (thus, of the proposition in general) that the step is made from affirmatio to negation or from being to not-being.

2 (15th June 1949)

Alexander professes to uphold the empirical method, and by this he means the method of hypothesis. But his Space-Time theory (with all its special features) is put up as a hypothesis to be considered in its general intelligibility or coherence, instead of being attacked from the outset. If the Space-Time theory were a hypothesis in the ordinary sense, one would, in order to test it, have to know whether certain of its consequences were true or false: which means that a direct knowledge of facts is required—i.e. that we can fin facts in the fiel and don't have to be content with proposing hypotheses (which we may fin vaguely to "make sense"). In other words, the empirical method, in the philosophical as in other fields is *not* simply a hypothetical method but embraces observation or direct knowledge—so that a given argument in the fiel might not involve hypothesis at all, though no doubt we should be prepared to *test* a particular contention of ours if someone else challenged it.

The Socratic method in the *Phaedo*, similarly, is not just a method of hypothesis. It is empirical, as Socrates applies it, in so far as it is a method of explanation by *propositions*—not by *forms*. But its empirical character doesn't depend on its being hypothetical. Even where a hypothesis is put up, the procedure of testing it is empirical all the way; the other premises to be combined with it are finding of experience, and it is by experience that we go on to determine whether the conclusions are true or false. If the procedure were *hypothetical* all the way, i.e., if the other premises were hypotheses and if it was as a hypothesis that we put up the truth or falsity of the conclusion, there would be no *test* at all; the proposed explanation wouldn't explain anything and we should be no nearer *knowledge*.

Now in *logic*, of course, we are subject to special difficulties to the difficult of any theory that professes to deal with things in general as contrasted with dealing with a particular subject-matter—the difficult , e.g., of saying that "proposition" or "term" is itself a term, that a "sort of thing" is a sort of thing—a difficult which may lead to the suggestion that logical propositions (statements in the theory of logic) are not matters of fact at all; a difficult apparently avoided but actually only evaded on views of an idealistic character which take logic to be concerned with *thought*. Certainly we should have to admit that there is a class, e.g., "sorts of things contemplated by me" or "sorts of things contemplated by some mind", even if there isn't a class "sorts of things"; similarly that there are "things proposed by me" (or by someone) even if there isn't a class "propositions". That is to say, on the theory that a significan term has a real opposite, one can distinguish between things I assert and things I don't assert, even if one can't distinguish between propositions and non-propositions. But, while this is a real distinction for us, it isn't for the idealist; what we call propositions he calls *things thought* or judgments—and so for him there *wouldn't* be an opposite of *things thought*.

This, apart from the plausibility of any particular hypothesis or theory in logic, indicates the difficult of justifying a position in logic at all; and it might be suggested then that a fairly vague or loose criterion like intelligibility ("making sense") was the most we could hope for, that we fin we just *have* to say certain things even if we can't explain how we can say them, (incorrigibility) and that the test of a philosophical theory is whether in the long run it leaves us comfortable, leaves us feeling that the things we are saying are things we have to say and that they enable us to proceed in our thinking without difficulti s—or at least with a minimum of difficulties But it could be said in reply that this is still the idealist theory—a test of general coherence or satisfactoriness, without any exact testing of details; and so Alexander's procedure would be along the Idealist line, viz., putting up a complete view of reality and then findin that this satisfie our requirements of coherence or intelligibility. It is clear that along these lines not much philosophical discussion would be possible, that we would need something a little more exact if we were to distinguish, or express a preference, between the positions of Alexander and Hegel—that to be real is to be spatio-temporal and that to be real is to be thought.

I consider it at least an approach to logic, or a firs description of it, to say that it is concerned with discourse and that its problems are presented by discourse and are settled by reference to discourse—by enabling it to proceed, to *get over* difficulties But though this is the approach to logic, the *solution* of the problems arising in discourse has nothing specially to do with our discussions and inquiries; we are dealing with a *subject* which does not depend for its existence on our existence or our proceedings. Thus we have in discourse the problem of consistency and inconsistency; that problem would be insoluble if we took it to be a mere question of our procedures, i.e., if inconsistency were merely something that some people avoided and other people didn't avoid but fell into; that would be no ground on which to *defend* consistency, no ground for saying that there is something *wrong* with inconsistency. And we can make it appear that there *is* something wrong with it only by saying that thought is not something by itself but is concerned with something else, that it is seeking to know reality, to "lay hold of" *what is*: the point being that, though what is thought or said can be consistent with what is thought or said, what is cannot be inconsistent with what is. Thus, whatever sort of proof there can be of a logical point, and even if the point *arises* in discourse, it is only by reference to reality, or *what is*, that there is any problem at all. And this incidentally applies to those who try to make philosophical problems problems of language: viz., that it is only because to speak is to speak about reality that there are such problems—even though, once we recognise this, we can distinguish from other problems problems about the specifi thing we call *language* (or the use of language).

The problem then is one of reality and yet it can be expressed in terms of discourse: i.e., we can take our logical theory as showing what can be believed or contradicted or proved or understood, what sort of statements and arguments have significance—i other words, a theory of the significanc of statements and arguments can be presented in discourse so long as we understand that what propositions and arguments do signify (their "objective content") is reality or what is the case (propositions or arguments as the *words*, or *what the words mean*?). Along these lines Alexander's logic is a logic of events (to be is to be spatio-temporal) and this logic will be supported by showing that events are the subject of discourse (are what discourse is about) and that it is in terms of events or in spatio-temporal terms that disputes and inquiries can be settled. Then we can say that some other logic, e.g., the logic of substance, cannot solve the problems of thought and action (of what can be asserted and brought about), that it leads us to insoluble problems, such as that of the *simple and the complex* or of the constant and the changing, which were so marked a feature of Greek philosophy though they recur in Modern Philosophy. But Alexander does not work out such a contrast, does not show how a logic of events solves problems which a logic of substance cannot solve; he does not even give a logical basis for the hypothetical method he professes to employ, does not show that *testing* is possible only on a logic of events. At best we might piece together from Alexander's argument the sort of argument required; but it might rather be said that we have to supplement and correct him where he falls short of a logic of events (or a philosophy of process).

One way of putting this suggested criticism (a way of linking it with the question of discourse) is to say that Alexander ignores the proposition, does not see that the sort of logic he requires is a propositional logic, that to treat things as spatio-temporal *is the same* as treating them as propositional, that the Space-Time theory is important precisely as clearing up problems of the proposition—on the other hand, that the propositional theory is important in showing of what sort of problem the Space-Time theory is a solution.

3 (21st June 1949)

Alexander, if he does not entirely ignore the proposition, certainly treats it as of little importance; in particular, he regards the process of "putting into logical form" as trivial and artificial In my view, any theory of logic requires to recognise a definit number of *types of assertion*, just as a space-time theory will recognise a definit number of categories; and I have suggested (for later amplification that a treatment of things as spatio-temporal is identical with a treatment of them as propositional.

In the approach to this problem the position of William James is of interest. He also may be said to neglect the proposition; for him the question is one of "concepts", as is natural enough for one who comes to philosophy from psychology—though it should be noted that this sort of psychology has itself been determined by earlier idealist and representationist philosophy. Still, James attacks the problems (particularly in *A Pluralistic Universe*) in a way clearly enabling us to see the relevance of a propositional theory to their solution.

What James calls "vicious intellectualism" (which is similar to what I call "rationalism") amounts to the separating off or isolating of some aspect or character of things, the assumption being that it excludes any character that could be distinguished from it—which is closely connected with the principle on which Berkeley bases his criticism of "abstraction", viz., that it is impossible, or at least wrong, to think separately of what cannot exist separately, this being an example of rationalism, of the position that unless we are thinking of a thing in its essence or "whole nature" we are not thinking of *it*. This attitude would make theory impossible, (if we can't say something without saying everything) in particular would make propositions impossible, and it is from the side of the proposition (from the fact that rationalists have to use propositions, which on their theory would be meaningless, in order to present their theory) that rationalism can be most strongly attacked.

So "vicious intellectualism" can be attacked as making theory impossible. Taking the outstanding example of *distinction* and *connection*, James shows that if being distinct excluded being connected there could be no account of distinct and connected things; but, according to James, the only reason that could be given for believing in this exclusion is that *saying* that things are distinct is not the same as saying they are connected. It is, of course, not on the mere basis of words or usage that rationalists have come to believe in what Hume calls "distinct existences". But it is still important to observe that to recognise that calling A and B distinct is not calling them connected does not lead to the conclusion that things could *be* distinct without being connected or vice versa; and in fact they cannot be. In terms of the main contention of realism, (See "The knower and the known") a relation has two terms, and those who attempt to uphold "distinct existences" are always flounder ng in the confusions of self-relation. In the same way, the fact that to say X is a cause is not to say X is an effect is not the slightest reason for saying that there are causes which are not effects or vice versa; and indeed the space-time theory, or more broadly *logic*, shows that these things are not the case.

In the notion of "connection" there is commonly confusion between *being related* and *being the same* (*cf.* the expression "unity"). "The unity of A and B" can be taken to mean that A and B, which were thought to be two, are actually one (are not different things); alternatively, it can be taken to mean that A and B are joined or *united* in certain ways—which is a different matter. However, in idealist theory the two notions are run together. If we take Hume's problem, particularly the principle that the mind sees no real connection among distinct existences, we can see that this depends on the use of "connected" as meaning "not distinct", or, more broadly, that Hume's difficult arises from the treatment, on the one hand, of distinct as simply meaning *different* and as meaning *isolated* or unrelated, and a corresponding treatment of connected as merely *related* and as *identifie* or being *one*.

In the controversy between James and Bradley (see James, "The Thing and its Relations") Bradley assumes that to have a different relation means to be a different thing, i.e., he starts from a conception of what must be and takes this to determine or to override what we fin actually to be. The question whether having a different relation makes a thing different is a confused one. On the one hand there is the question whether merely to say a thing has a different relation *means* that this is a different thing; on the other hand there is the question whether entering into a certain relation does in fact change a thing or at least is an occasion of its being changed. It is acceptance in a certain measure of the latter possibility that often leads people to accept, or be confused about, the former.

Now it is a fact that some changes of relation are accompanied or followed by certain changes of character. But some changes of relation *do not* lead to changes of character in some respects; some things are indifferent to certain environmental changes, i.e., certain changes of relation make no difference to certain characters; and again acquisition or loss of some characters does not affect others, so that in terms of the latter we can say it is the same thing and in terms of the former that it has changed. If identity meant absolutely no change of character, nothing would have identity; a so-called "identity" could not enter into any situation and so no question of a change in its relations would ever arise. Bradley is dictating to experience, imposing on it a conception of what must be (here, of what "identity" must be), whereas in actual experience what we call "the same thing" is a thing which retains certain characters over a period, while changing in other characters and in its relations to other things. When we think in this way of identity or sameness, we realise that there are some conditions or changes of environment which would bring that identity to an end; there would no longer be that kind of thing in that place. But that would not affect what we mean by saying that it was *the same thing* (a particular thing of a particular kind) while it lasted.

On the general question of connection and distinction—if we believe in "essential distinction"(i.e., in being *distinct and nothing else*), then we could not say of distinct things that they are connected, or even that they are not connected; and similarly, if we believe in "essential connection". But such essences are not what we mean by distinction and connection, and what we do mean by these expressions are not exclusive of one another. Nevertheless, it is in spatio-temporal or propositional terms that we can see this fact, see the non-exclusiveness or non-opposition of connection and distinction, see that two different things can be in the same spatial situation, i.e., connected while remaining distinct, and that two terms can be connected in a proposition without ceasing to be different terms.

4 (22nd June 1949)

The terms of a proposition are both distinct and connected. That is not the same as saying that the terms of a relation (e.g., beside) are both distinct and connected, but it illustrates the same sort of logic, a situational logic or "logic of events".

James's general point regarding "vicious intellectualism" is that, even when *saying* that a thing is X is not the same as saying that it is Y, that is nothing against the same thing *being* both X and Y. But, as regards connection and distinction in particular, there might be some point in maintaining that to call things connected *is* to call them distinct or that being distinct is involved in being connected and being connected is involved in being distinct: i.e., being distinct at least involves being in the same situation (say, the situation AeB). However, the situation might be covered by saying that distinction and connection are bound up together or are themselves distinct and connected in all experience. This would prevent Bradley from asking "*How* are things at once distinct and connected?" if this is to be understood as a "difficulty or as suggesting that there could be anything *but* experience (i.e., the way in which we fin things) to which we could appeal to settle the question. All we can say is that in a situation or proposition things *are* distinct and connected, and there is no other manner in which they can be so, or in which we could show that they can be so.

This takes us back to the point on Alexander that to treat things as spatio-temporal is the same as to treat them as propositional, so that the answer to the question, not "How can things be distinct and connected?" but "How are things distinct and connected?", is "In space and time" or "In the proposition" (i.e., in situations). This would link closely with Kant's solution of Hume's problem, his overcoming of the difficultie of a doctrine of "distinct existences", even though for him the solution (overcoming of difficulties is only for "phenomena" or things as they come under the conditions of our experience and not for postulated "things in themselves" or things as they do not come under the conditions of our experience—i.e., things for which we have no evidence at all, since anything we might say about "things in themselves" *would* be something coming under the conditions of our experience. Apart from this weakness in his position, Kant's answer to Hume is that what we call "distinct things" are connected in space and time and under the categories, and that amounts to saying in Space and Time and in propositions; and if further, in Alexander's manner, we take the categories as inherent in Space and Time themselves, then we have a single answer, though it may be variously expressed ("spatio-temporally" or "propositionally"), to the question "How are things distinct and connected?"

But Alexander ignores the proposition, he does not, like Kant, work out the categories in relation to the forms of propositions, and he equally ignores it in connection with a general theory of space and time, and this gives an unnecessary arbitrariness to his account of the categories and to his theory in general—this is the main direction in which his position needs to be corrected.

That is so in spite of the fact that in the section entitled "The Clue to Quality" (at the beginning of volume 2) he gives what amounts to a propositional account of the body-mind relation, taking mentality (or being mental) as a quality of certain bodily processes. There are still weaknesses in his position here. Even while maintaining that the mental and the neural are *in the same place*, which we might take to mean that they are the same process, he still treats the mental as "higher" than the neural (mentality as higher than vitality); thus he returns to a position in which what is supposed to be a predicate of a subject does not really

inhere in that subject but somehow hovers over it or is its "spirit" (*cf.*
Moore's treatment of *good*), and so he creates insoluble problems and
loses all the value of the propositional treatment in which, while saying
"Some bodily are mental" (and understanding at the same time that some
bodily are not mental), we also say "All mental are bodily"—so that the
one is no more a subject than the other, nor is the one any more a quality
than the other: hence there is no question of one being "at a higher
level" than the other. (Note that the doctrine of levels is connected with
Alexander's evolutionism—emergence.)

The "clue to quality", then, is that mentality does characterise certain
bodily processes, is one of their characters in the same sense as
any others they possess (their so-called "physical" properties), and,
correspondingly, being bodily or physical is one of the characters of
what is mental, the point being that on a propositional theory there is
no difference between the class of *subjects* and the class of *predicates*,
and to say there is a difference is to fall into "vicious intellectualism"
or rationalism.   An even more important, a quite central, example
of the same confusion in Alexander is his doctrine of space-time as
"stuff", as that of which things are made, in other words, as the ultimate
subject of which everything else, every term of a less general character,
is predicate—a position which, in spite of Alexander's protestations,
amounts to substantialism; and, even further, space-time is taken as
the subject of which the *categories* are predicates, i.e., it is essentially
subject and they are essentially predicates even if in fact they apply to
everything. If predicates they would be subjects (things) as well. And
so once more we are confronted with terms that have no opposites, with
predications that have no intelligible contradictories.

The doctrine of space-time as stuff is contrasted with that of space-time
as medium or space and time as media, i.e., of things in general as being
in space and time instead of *being* space and time; and the difficultie
of that position (the difficul y, in particular, of taking space and time to
be in some sense things and in some sense not things) are once more
to be solved in terms of a propositional logic—the solution, roughly
formulated, being that space and time are involved in any assertion
whatever that we make.

Lecture 9

9 (12th July 1949)

The question of the relation between uniqueness of time and uniqueness of distance or direction (straightness) between two points. (Kant somewhere remarks on time as prototype of straight line—or spatial *direction*.)   If we make it a question of knowledge, if we say that it is awareness of time that enables us to *know* direction (shortest distance) between points, we are faced with the difficult that, according to space time theory, it is awareness of time that enables us to know *anything whatever* (i.e., that we can't know the non-temporal). Empirically, however, it is clear that we connect (in regard to *motions*) a shortest distance with a shortest interval (minimum of time taken) between given points. Perhaps it is best to say that, while there is a "correlation" between space and time in this manner, the evidence that there *is* a "shortest distance" lies in our experience of space; i.e., that in that experience we have the notion (the *knowledge*) of *direction* and that this notion itself involves the notions of uniqueness and of straightness, so that we *fin* "straight lines"—whatever the connection may be between that uniqueness and the uniqueness of time.

The appeal to direct experience, to what we simply *fin* , is opposed to any attempt to base geometry or knowledge of space on logic (sort of thing criticised in "Empiricism").   In the case of the "axiom of parallels" (Euclid's fift   postulate), it is asked how we can *prove* that two intersecting straight lines can't both be parallel to a third straight line, and it is contended that if this can't be proved then we can have alternative geometries—the Euclidean in which the postulate is accepted, and others, non-Euclidean, in which it is not. But the point is that we are concerned with a question of *fact*, not with an arbitrary manipulation of symbols which wouldn't be theory at all, and if we are asked how we know which of the two contradictories *is* the fact, it is quite possible to answer that we *see* it (as I would say, see the "axiom" to be true), and to deny that we can see such a thing is to deny that we could be empirically aware of an E proposition and, finall , of a universal proposition.

We could say that our recognition of the Euclidean fact is bound up with recognition of *direction* and *difference of direction*; i.e., in knowing that a line has a certain direction we also know that other lines have the same direction and others again have different directions—we recognise *intersection* and we recognise *being parallel*—and so we can see that to deny the postulate is to say that two directions are at once the same and different. Whether this is considered *proof* or not it is at least empirical; and anything at all that *can* be called proof must be empirical—must . start from premises which we simply fin to be the case. So, in regard to straightness or spatial direction and temporal successiveness, it could be said that they are *found together* in our experience; and this empirical view is opposed to Alexander's procedure of starting with abstract Space and abstract Time, the point being that even in talking about "pure Space" (Space without Time) we should already be thinking of it as within the Space-Time system (thinking of it in terms of a logic of events), and so when we force back Alexander on an empirical procedure (on what, according to his own view, must be what we *fin*) we have to reject his method of abstraction as anti-empirical or rationalistic.

It will be in similar terms, in terms of a logic of events, in terms of what is involved in the knowing and in the being of motions (in what we fin in motions), that any connection there may be between the other characters of time and a second and a third dimension of space can be upheld; and I would say there is a correlation, but not in the way Alexander presents it. He fails to establish these other connections, and in particular he fails in his argument from the characters of time to a three-dimensional space, for he has to show not merely that an additional dimension is introduced when we recognise a succession as irreversible and that is also done when we recognise a succession as transitive, but that these additional dimensions are distinct from one another: i.e., not that each character adds a dimension to a firs dimension, but that one does so and then the other adds a dimension to this *two*-dimensional system. This is not done by Alexander. His only argument to show that the dimensions implied by irreversibility and transitiveness respectively are independent of one another is that irreversibility and transitiveness (or "betweenness") have been shown to be distinct and therefore the dimensions they imply must be distinct. (Obviously *doesn't follow*: cf. A is different from B; A *supports* something, X; B supports something, Y; therefore X is different from Y.) (If XaY$\longrightarrow$XiY, YaX$\longrightarrow$XiY.)

First, Alexander's argument to show that the two characters as he define them are distinct is not a sound one; secondly, even if it were sound, he would require to treat one of them as adding a dimension to *two* dimensions, and he does not do this. One basis of objection to his argument is that it proceeds in terms of "point-instants"; it can be objected (1) that the use of this hyphenated term implies that intimate relationship between Space and Time which it is the object of the argument to establish; (2) that it involves the assumption of *units*, of the point as the ultimate constituent of an extension and the instant of a duration, as against the view that all constituents of an extension are extensions and of a duration are durations, and that there is no such elementary unit as the point or the instant or the point-instant. But the conception of point-instants is useful to Alexander here because it enables him to treat the units or elements of a motion sometimes as spatial and sometimes as temporal, and by this ambiguity to reach results that don't really follow from his data.

Thus, in his argument regarding "betweenness" (*STD*, pp. 54-55) he uses the illustration of pendular motion to show that transitiveness and irreversibility are independent—in particular, as an example of a succession having irreversibility without transitiveness. But the series or succession he is describing as irreversible but not transitive cannot be the series of *instants* in the motion of the pendulum, i.e., can't be the temporal series (*time*), because there would be no sense in illustrating *that* by a pendulum and, on his own showing, the temporal series is both irreversible *and* transitive, these being characters of time. Either, then, it is the series of *points* in the path of the pendulum, or it is the series of "point-instants", i.e., of *correlations* of points that the motion goes through with the times at which it goes through them (a series of times which have both a spatial and a temporal coordinate). If we take the points alone, then *transitiveness as Alexander understands it* does not hold, but equally irreversibility does not hold (the motion which has gone from A to B comes back from B to A). The fact is that Alexander has define transitiveness so as to *include* irreversibility; instead of simply taking the formula for a transitive relation "If A is before B and B is before C, then A is before C", he wants to add "and C is not before A"; i.e., he wants to include an *opposition* between A's having the relation to C and C's having it to A—in other words, he wants to treat the relation as irreversible. Thus the reason why the series of points does not exhibit transitiveness in Alexander's sense is *simply* that it doesn't exhibit irreversibility; so that Alexander hasn't got an illustration of *irreversibility without transitiveness*. But what he does is this: having proved the absence of *his* transitiveness (i.e., *irreversible* transitiveness) by reference to the points, he shifts his ground and proves the presence of irreversibility by reference to the *instants* or to the temporal character of the "point-instants"—and, if this ground is taken, we have a series which is not merely irreversible but *also* transitive, even in Alexander's sense.

To sum up: Alexander relies on the *instants* to assert the irreversibility of the series and he relies on the *points* (on the fact that the pendulum passes through a given point many times) to deny the "transitiveness" in the special sense of asymmetrical or irreversible transitiveness—which really means to *deny* the irreversibility of the series. It is just by confusedly including irreversibility in transitiveness that Alexander makes transitiveness appear the more advanced or complicated character, whereas if we take transitiveness in the ordinary way in which we speak of a transitive relation (such that if A has the relation to B and B has it to C, then A has it to C—without any implication as to whether C has it to A or not) then pendular motion with respect to the points (which recur) gives an illustration not of a series which is irreversible without being transitive but of one which is transitive without being irreversible. Of course (as previously indicated), with respect to the instants or to the "point-instants" in consideration of their time-component it gives a series which is both irreversible and transitive; but then this is a question of the time-series itself and the pendulum is irrelevant.

My contention, then, is that transitiveness (in its ordinary sense) comes *before* irreversibility and can be correlated with a *second* dimension, while irreversibility can be correlated with a *third* dimension.

Lecture 14

14 (27th July 1949)

I had argued against the treatment of categories as relations, i.e., as *between* things, that this is open to the same objections as the treatment of space and time as between things and not of things, or of the *proposition* as between things (themselves not being propositional). The view I am supporting is that things both are *in* situations and *are* situations, so that there is no pure quality (or nature) but the qualitative is itself relational (has interrelated parts and "aspects"). Thus a situational theory of things is alone *logical*, since it alone applies to everything and doesn't try to *separate* "things", "qualities", "relations", etc., (logical atomism).

Now the view of modern philosophers that mind is not spatial goes with a doctrine of *internality*, mind being conceived as a "thing in itself" or "unity" embracing all its characters and relations, so that mind is the supreme *unit*, that to which the notion of "individuality" is specially attached. (Leibniz is the leading exponent of the view that a thing's "notion", or essence, involves its whole history, and of individuality or "intensive unity" as the supreme category; but the same view is at least implicit in other idealistic theories.) Given this doctrine of internality we meet with various forced attempts to deal with the problem of *externality*, e.g., with the fact that there are *many* minds; and here we fin mystical theories of *identificatio* , the view that "we are members of one another", which, according to Russell (*Problems of Philosophy*?), would have been the consistent position for Berkeley to adopt and which is certainly a feature of Hegelianism—for various minds (individuals), being manifestations or "powers" of the Absolute, could be described as manifestations or powers of one another. (The doctrine of the Absolute is that for which internality is the supreme principle; (to know) the nature of anything is (to know) the nature of everything.)

In this connection, we may note that Alexander refers to space-time as "an infinit given whole"—though he goes back on that formula in Book II, chapter X ("The One and the Many") where he denies that any of the categories, of which he takes "whole and part" to be one, applies to space-time as such. But in spite of this retraction his substantialism prevents him from adopting any line other than the *totalistic* one, belief in space-time as a totality or whole—which is opposed to the recognition of the *infinit* of space and time; a character which could be roughly expressed by saying "All wholes are parts" (in other words, there is no Absolute or totality). (On the other hand, any situation is known against the background of "all space and all time".)

To say that things exist in space and time is, I have argued, to say that they exist *in propositional form*—an assertion which requires a distinction between the functions of subject and predicate which is overlooked or denied by idealists like Bosanquet for whom *symmetry* is a mark of the ultimately real and for whom, therefore, the solution of a problem makes the original *statement* of the problem meaningless, (*cf.* "'Universals' and Occurrences"; also review of Campbell's "Scepticism and Construction") and also (overlooked and denied) by the Cambridge followers of Keynes in taking the proposition to be an assertion of existence or of non-existence.

In distinguishing the functions, I say that the function of the subject is to *locate*; this means that without reference to space there would be no distinction of function—and this applies to *mind* too; any statement of a mental process must state that something goes on *somewhere*. And, though we seem to be involved in paradox in saying that what locates is located and *vice versa*, that no term gives *absolute location*, still in any given proposition we distinguish something which locates from something which is located, and thus location or spatiality is an ingredient in whatever we take to be the case, and it is this, and not the ability to fi a place once and for all, that we mean by referring to the *absoluteness* of space.

We can argue similarly about time and the *categories*, which could be called "pervasive" (though not pervasive *predicates*) only if they are involved in *being propositional*, apart from the peculiarities (i.e., the *material*) of any given proposition. Alexander's confusion (as before) is connected with his substantialism, with his belief that even the materials (empirical qualities) are *made of* space and time, a belief which would be opposed to their intractability (e.g., the irreducibility of *red* to anything else) and, at the same time, opposed to any distinction between the categorial and the empirical because there could be no special features of special situations. On a substantialist view, then, all features (if there *could* be any) would be categorial and all categories would be features (of the "substance": here, space-time), but this leads to impossibilities—the impossibility, e.g., as in *Parmenides*, of distinguishing the substance itself and its "features".

There is the same weakness in the *Sophist*, the doctrine of the "highest kinds" being a treatment of the categories as pervasive *characters*, and indicating the incompleteness of Plato's emancipation from the theory of forms, emancipation from belief in the *unhistorical* with consequent insoluble problems of relating it to the historical. Considering what is *meant* by "the historical" (in the logical, not the social sense), we can see that in order to treat things historically we have to have some view as to what history itself is and that this (what history is) is something that does not itself have a history—a point indicated in Heraclitus's reference to the "eternity" of his *word* or doctrine, even though it is a doctrine of universal flux It has to be possible to have exactly the same type of questions (*logical* questions) about any material at any time.

It is here that we get the distinction between logic and science and the impossibility of settling logical questions by science. We fin scientists maintaining, e.g., that inquiry into causality (the "causal principle") is on the same footing as inquiry into any particular fact or connection of things: i.e., that we get verification of the hypothesis of universal causality, we get various experiences that bear it out, and after a period of such verification we come to accept it—or, adopting it as a tentative hypothesis and conducting inquiries in terms of it, we are led by the success of such inquiries to have at least a stronger belief in it. The point is that what belongs to experience as such is not specially supported (built up into a certainty or a matter of "high probability") by a series of particular experiences. Unless there is a "causal principle", unless such a principle is accepted in advance, the conjunctions that occur in particular experiences are no evidence. *The presence of X when Y occurs* is of evidential value only if the principle is accepted: i.e., it could confir the view that X is the cause of Y, provided Y has a cause, but it could not confir the view that Y has a cause if *that* were the issue in dispute. As far as causality can be argued for, it has to be argued for as belonging to the nature of existence; and the "evidence" of the scientists is beside the point, it assumes, is *meaningless without a belief in*, what it is supposed to support.

Lecture 43 (Substance and Causality additions)

43 (19th July 1950)

Additional material on (a) Substance (b) Causality.

From Victor Dudman notes (based with additions on Tom Rose—omitted by Sandy Anderson.)

In discussion of substance I had brought out a number of difficultie in Alexander's notion of *contour*—i.e., in his treatment of substance as region or arena—also, way in which, for him, the qualities of a substance "dodge" one another; point being that, if this were so, there would not be complexity at all but just a lot of different (and simple) substances.

Quotation (*STD* p. 272)—"The identity of a substance is individual identity as persisting through a duration of time. Numerical identity was occupation of a point-instant or complex of them: generic identity or identity of sort was the preservation of a plan of construction throughout repetition at different times or places. When the repetition of a plan is found in its varying phases in the duration of an individual we had individual identity. We see now that substantial identity is equivalent to individual identity."

Alexander is here distinguishing substance or substantiality from mere identity, i.e., mere power of locating, and now he is identifying it with individuality. (Of course, as noted, he treats the categories in a very curious order.) But when we speak of *identity of substance* we certainly do not mean individual identity; we say that two things are "the same substance" when they are of the same composition or constitution, which would support the view that substance is the *make-up* of a thing, is a certain arrangement of qualities in spatio-temporal relations. Now that is what Alexander would call universality or plan, but this seems a very forced interpretation of the meaning of universality, of being such and such; e.g., when we speak of *being yellow* we don't have in mind any plan or build-up, even though the thing which is yellow has one (*qua* yellow). And there would seem to be a distinction between being of a sort or description and being of a certain *constitution* i.e. having a certain interrelation of constituents. The above passage, then, reinforces the view that Alexander confuses different categories: in some ways, he fails to distinguish substance from identity and in some ways he fails to distinguish substance from quantity. But it seems clear in the present instance that what we call substantial identity, i.e. being of the same substance, should not be identifie with individual identity, i.e. being the same thing.

There is a further point in Alexander's discussion concerning the relation among the different qualities of a substance—a point that does not seem to harmonise very well with the doctrine of non-interpenetration or the absolute (substantial) separateness of the various qualities. What Alexander now wants to argue is that "the multiplicity of properties of a substance is not haphazard but rooted in some simple state of affairs which enables many properties to belong together within one contour and to be in fact simultaneous." Thus there has to be some reason (that is the argument) why whiteness and sweetness coexist in a given substance, e.g., sugar, and since that reason doesn't exist in whiteness itself or in sweetness itself, because, of course, the two can be found apart (neither "entails" the other), there must be something else in which that reason resides, some single explanation of why sugar is both white and sweet. This is certainly coming nearer to the notion of the *constitution* of a thing, but it is doing so in a rationalistic manner, because if there is no reason why the white should be sweet or the sweet should be white, we are *certainly* not going to fin a reason why something X should be both sweet and white. All we will fin is the fact that X *is* both sweet and white, i.e., we will fin conjunction of properties, and without that we certainly could not speak of *a certain substance*, but we certainly won't fin any property *or* [as a?] condition of there being such a conjunction. (*Cf.* doctrine of "natural kinds" in *scholastic* philosophy.) The supposed explanation of the concomitance of a number of different properties would either have to be a furthei concomitance (another bunch of properties) or else (would have to be) a mysterious power, a "that whereby" the given concomitance existed. It is no doubt very important to see necessary relations among properties, to see that the possession of some properties does entail the possession of certain others (*cf.* definitio and classification but however far we go in findin such connections or entailments, we always come back to the peculiarity of the given substance, the fact that in it various properties that don't entail one another just do occur together. (That is a point of criticism of a view of Alexander's; but we can also see, I think, just how haphazard his views are—no coherence. *Cf.* universality is not a universal. Piecemeal.)

Now we could say that this *constitution* or *structure* is analogous to the "harmony", the balance of tensions or interaction of tendencies, which Heraclitus find to be characteristic of any particular kind of thing. And that leads on to the question, mentioned by Alexander at the end of his section on substance, of the interaction of the *parts* of a substance which he says is the *reciprocal* action of different substances within the whole substance, and involves causal relations within the substance. Now to say that a substance in this way involves causal relations is not to say that the *category* of causality is contained within the category of substance. In some way, of course, every category must involve every other category, but still they have to be distinguished; and the point is that when we are thinking of substantiality, even when we are recognising an order of phases as well as an arrangement of parts—even when we are recognising *opposing* tendencies, which must mean tendencies which affect one another—we are still not recognising causality as such. And when we do recognise causality within a substance, we are as Alexander says recognising relations between different substances within the substance or, more exactly, relations between different *things* within the substance, because, from the point of view of the substance

we started with, these things are internal, and we are not at the point
of view of causality until we have introduced externality, until we are
considering the interaction of different things, things external to one
another, whether or not they could also be called parts of the same thing.
It is the cohering, the *togetherness* of these things, that we are thinking
of when the category of substance is involved. It is their *distinctness*
that we are thinking of when the category of causality is involved. But
still here is a natural passage from substantiality to causality, in so far as
consideration of a structure of parts and phases *inevitably raises*, even
though it does not settle, questions of external action or influence (That
may clear up question of substance: proceed now to some more material
on category of causality.)

We had been discussing Kant's doctrine in Second Analogy, and I had
argued that the questions he was concerned with could not be dealt
with in terms of time alone but required reference to space—that it
was not enough to talk about a succession but we required the notion
of *replacing*, the notion of *substantial* (*spatial*?) continuity even to
see what was meant by the irreversible orders of phenomena that Kant
distinguishes from reversible orders. But this is still not a complete
account of causality—replacing does not give a sufficien description
of it, because that is already found in the conception of substance, in the
recognition of regular phases, of a typical kind of process, so that to take
the hackneyed example (used also, I think, by Alexander) the phases of
infancy and youth and manhood and old age are features of the human
substance, of human nature, even though you have a passage from one to
the rest; and although, if causality is a category, such passages couldn't
be without causality, they do not themselves illustrate causality, but only
character or regularity.

Now Alexander seems to waver between the view that replacing is a
sufficien account of causality and the other view, the view that causality
involves *external action*—not merely a *sequence of phases* or *change* in
a thing, but the conditioning of that change by a *different* thing—by, at
the very least, this other thing (this external thing) coming into certain
spatial relations to the firs thing. Thus when he says that causality is
"the continuous passage of one motion or set of motions into a different
motion or set of motions", Alexander seems merely to be saying that
causality is change, whereas I should argue that to assert that X changes,
that X becomes Y after being non-Y before, is merely to say what the

effect is, viz., *X's now being Y*, and not what the *cause* is, because we certainly cannot say that *X's previously not being Y* is the cause of X's being Y now. (Cf., again, night and day.)

Again, Alexander speaks of "the very different effects produced by the same cause in different substances", e.g., by a stone which would break a window but would only bury itself in a cushion or in a mound of earth, where he seems to treat the cause as an external thing, a different thing from the thing affected, one which, as we say, *produces* the given effect in the thing operated on or, as I say more broadly, *in the fiel* . And actually Alexander says quite early in the section on causality—"It is immaterial, with our metaphysical conception of a substance, whether we describe a cause in popular language as a thing or substance affecting some other thing or substance and producing an effect in it, or in the stricter language of the logicians call the cause an event or process which precedes another event or process and without which the second event or process, the effect, *does not* exist." (Alexander is stopping short there of the account I give of causality as involving a necessary and sufficien precedent condition—he mentions only a *necessary* precedent condition.) Alexander takes credit for saying "does not" instead of "would not", because, he says, the only means of telling what would or would not exist is by seeing what does or does not exist. However I would say on this that it is losing all the force of a causal assertion to say that without the firs event the second does not exist—that suggests only concomitance, that A exists with B, or that the two of them exist—it loses the *universal* element in causality, the fact that there is a question (the question is?) of a certain sort of thing being followed by another sort of thing, and this is what the expression *would* is pointing to (even if it doesn't convey it very clearly).

Of course Alexander goes on to speak of regarding the event not as an isolated occurrence but as a process which is continued into the effect, so that we are not to take *any* two successive events as cause and effect, though that is not what the earlier formulation, or the substitution of "does" for "would", appears to imply. But in speaking of this continuance, and even in his distinction of the logical from the popular way of speaking, he seems to come down on the side of causality as mere change, the mere acquiring of a character by something. And this is the more remarkable since in a later chapter he denies that change is a category. In any case, his way of speaking obscures the position of universality, or necessity and sufficien y, in causality, because this question of universality is quite distinct from the question of *being continued into* something, which may be taken to apply simply to particulars: there is no question in causality as a general relation of the agent's *becoming* the patient—the question is of a certain sort of agent, an agent of a certain description, coming into a certain relation with a certain sort of patient. The doctrine of continuance, I say, obscures that point, but it is just where agent and patient are not distinguished, and where the notion of the fiel is not brought explicitly forward, that we get talk about a *causal line* or *chain of causation* (e.g., in Kant's Antinomies), talk which becomes pointless when the notion of a fiel is treated as an essential of the causal situation—and the field of course, is just the patient, just the sort of thing acted on. And equally pointless is the notion of a firs cause, as contrasted with universal contingency and interaction, with the *complexity* of anything we choose to begin with in a specifi inquiry, and the fact that various influence are operating on it.

In the firs place then, or as far as we've gone, the distinction of agent and patient is treated by Alexander as merely popular language, but towards the end of the section we get an impression of the other view, when he says that "the cause does its work not by a change in itself but in leading on to something else. A cause might well remain unaltered for a time and then findin its patient produces its effect". Now if that, coming nearer to the notion of external action, is Alexander's own position, then he has fallen into inconsistencies. And if the agent-patient formulation is allowed, then (that of) *continuing into* or *issuing in* is quite inadequate; it is as before the treatment of causality merely as change. But yet again Alexander ends the section on causality by saying: "To repeat an often-stated proposition, continuity is the conceptual formulation of motion itself, and, hard as it may be to say where cause ends and effect begins, yet if cause is itself a process and effect another and different one, the relation between the two is the transition of the one which is earlier into the later motion, or group of motions"—where once more Alexander would seem to be abandoning the notions of agent and patient, and where he is ignoring the fact that we would regularly *deny* that a cause or what produces an effect comes to an end when the effect begins but would rather maintain that it can go on existing independently alongside the effect. (That, I say, is the last assertion in the section, so that it seems that Alexander favours on the whole the conception of causality merely as change—cause and effect are simply earlier and later stages in a process—involved just in *substance*.)

Going back to some earlier points, we fin Alexander using phrases like: "Causality is thus the spatio-temporal continuity of one substance with another" or again (same passage) saying that the cause "is transformed" into the effect—though he qualifie this by saying that transformation is *only an instance* of causality. But the predominant conception is still simply that of change and not of *transactions* between different things (the sort of *cycle* referred to in the theory of sense-knowledge in the *Theaetetus*—with, of course, a reference back to Heraclitus). Now this leads on to the question whether, as Alexander puts it, causality is *immanent* or *transeunt*, i.e., whether it is something that just (merely) *falls within* the development of a particular thing or involves a *going across* from one thing to another. And while, to begin with, Alexander seems to reject the conception of immanent causality, he goes on to treat the difference between the immanent and the transeunt (immanent causality and transeunt causality) as one merely of convenience in description—in other words, to suggest that if we took our system wide enough we could always see causality as immanent, as a matter of inner development, as the working out or unfolding of the character of a thing (what I have taken to be involved in the category of substance rather than in that of causality). And the points of criticism would be that, on the one hand, we could *never* take our system wide enough to rule out external influence affecting its development, and, on the other hand, when we do treat such developments in a causal way or from the point of view of causality, we are thinking of the parts of the given system as *different things* and we are thinking of their action on one another in terms of *their* characters and not of the characters of the system of which they are parts.—I am contending that this sort of question is obscured by Alexander's not recognising, or at any rate not bringing out, the *universal* character of causal relations—by his treating it as a question of *this* causing *that* instead of as a question of *this sort of thing* causing a *given sort of change* in *that sort of thing*.

Alexander's main view—causality simply as change—is illustrated again on page 284 when he says that causation "is the continuity of existents within continuous space-time as subsisting between substances, which are themselves motions or groups of motions"—where, in spite of the reference to substances, we are merely directed to the phenomena of replacing, the passage of some motions into others. And then on the next page Alexander insists on the difference between cause and effect, contending that mere continuance of the same uniform motion is not a causal connection. But we may ask, if causality is categorial, how that is compatible with change taking place in some cases and not in others, where the latter would not on Alexander's showing involve causality. And over and above that, we can ask how Alexander is going to *account for* the difference between the two types of cases, account for the fact that sometimes there is change and sometimes not, that some motions go on as they were and other motions go on in a new form. Or again we could put the question in the form—Why is there ever change at all? And I should say that the problem cannot be solved on the basis of continuity alone, that we have to take account of external action, that we have in fact to adopt a Heraclitean theory of exchanges and see persistence as a *special case* of change and not as an exception to change or as a different kind of thing. In other words, we would have to argue that change is *inherent* in motion but that in some cases we get a *balance* of changes *in such a way* that no alteration is apparent to us, a balance, at any rate, such that we say "this is the *same thing*" (same person or whatever it might be) and yet we *know perfectly well* (feel quite certain) that changes have been going on in it all the while, that in physical terms it has been constantly taking in and giving out energy and therefore its persisting or remaining uniform (within the limits, of course, in which it does remain uniform) would involve causality just as the most striking change in it would do.

Now in all these cases, in all the causal connections we recognised or postulated, the cause would be different from the effect and the thing acted on would have changed and still we could see in terms of a Heraclitean or near-Heraclitean theory how this is compatible with what we call the persistence of an individual: whereas, along the lines of Alexander's argument, we are simply recognising two types of occurrence, viz., the *maintenance* and the *loss* of uniformity, neither of them categorial and with no indication either of their common ground or of the basis of the distinction between them. And these considerations, I would suggest, strengthen the case for recognition of *external action* as essential to causality. In fact, we might view the third group of categories as categories of *action* and take them as starting from externality in the form of impenetrability or space-filling

Again we fin a looseness in Alexander's discussion of the question whether effect determines cause as much as cause determines effect; he says that this is so only in a *logical* sense, that we can only mean that when the cause and the effect are precisely stated they are reciprocal: "when the cause, that is, is purged of what may indeed occur in a particular case but is accidental to it, and when the effect is stated in terms so precise as to presuppose one cause only and not a choice of several; when, to take the familiar example, the death by drowning is distinguished from the death by hanging, and the two not lumped together under the general designation of death. The reciprocity of cause and effect means then that unless there were the precise effect there would not be the precise cause. But such determination is logical and not real determination, and effect cannot be interchanged with cause except as a basis of inference." He goes on to say: "we cannot say in any real sense that future determines the present, for the future is not yet and a future event introduces the order of Time. In that order, the future does not determine but is determined." Now as far as this goes we might as well say that it cannot be contended that the *past* determines the present because the past is no longer, and so we would be reduced to saying that only the present can determine the present, or that the present determines itself. Alexander in fact is giving some concession(s) here to the notion that the future has a peculiar logical status (as when people argue that "the law of excluded middle" does not apply to the future, and so on), and the point is that, irrespective of how we can *know* this or that event, it can be contended that a later event is *in fact* necessary and sufficien for an earlier event just as much as it can be contended that an earlier event is necessary and sufficien for a later one.

Now there may be some people who maintain the reciprocity of cause and effect while denying the absolute reality of time, so that being earlier and later would not affect the *content* (e.g., Absolute Idealism would take this sort of line) but, broadly speaking, those who speak of this reciprocity do not mean by "determination" *causing* so that they (would be) saying that when A causes B it is just as much the case that B causes A: what they are saying is that when A causes B it is just as much the case that A can be *inferred* from B as that B can be inferred from A. And in fact a point we have already noticed again affects this part of Alexander's discussion, viz., that he is neglecting the *universality* of causal connection—he is speaking as if what were causally linked were simply two particular events. But we are giving no account of causal connection unless we take it that the particular events are linked *as and only as* events of certain sorts. And here it may be noted, with regard to Alexander's examples, that death by drowning is just as much a sort of thing, admitting of variations along with the common character, as is death in general. The question is then of treating causal problems as a particular class of *problems in general*, where the prior question always is "what is the *fiel* , and what is the *property* to be acquired". Only when we have specifie the fiel F and the property P can we give an account of the conditions under which an F which was not P *becomes P* (or acquires the property P), this being distinguished from the problem of what *marks* distinguish those F which *are* P from those which are not P, because in the latter type of problem we are talking about two species of a genus, one with a given property and one without that property—we are not talking about how anything comes to *pass* from one of those species to the other, still within the genus or field But when that distinction is understood, when it is seen that causality involves *change* and not just differentiation, there should be just as precise a solution when we are trying to account for *death merely* as when we are trying to account for *death with special features*.

So (as said) Alexander neglects the universal character of causality, the fact that it involves *necessity and sufficienc* , which is certainly a reciprocal relation, granted that there are elements in the situation, features of the relation of causality, which are *not* reciprocal, like the relation of earlier and later. And here in referring (as we noted) to "the order of time" in connection with his distinction between real and logical determination, Alexander seems to be suggesting that the recognition of a symmetrical relation between two things keeps us from recognising at the same time an irreversible or *a*symmetrical relation between them. It may be quite true, then, that the effect cannot *precede* the cause [in a given "causal sequence"] and yet true that the effect *determines* the cause just as much as the cause determines the effect. We have to note here the popular usage in which "determines" and "causes" are used as equivalent or interchangeable, but why a necessary and sufficien precedent condition should be held to *determine* any more than a necessary and sufficien subsequent condition does is at least not apparent from Alexander's account. And he can be said to deviate from realism in distinguishing logical determination from real determination, apparently meaning by the former "that which permits us to infer or to use the expression *therefore*"—a point illustrated again when he says that the only necessity which philosophy can recognise is that of inference but there is no necessity in things except fact, nothing is added to causal relation by the adjective *necessary* (here he just plainly doesn't see that in causal assertions we are affirmin a number of universal propositions), and again when he says that "Real grounds are to be distinguished from logical grounds, though they may coincide" and where, after treating the real ground as "a complex of motions of which the event or fact to be explained is the causal outcome", he refers to logic as "the science of truth, or of how our beliefs, as expressed in propositions, are to be systematised into a coherent whole at the guidance of reality".

Just what a belief would be, or for that matter what a fact or event would be, if it were *not* in propositional form is not indicated; but Alexander's remarks above certainly seem to suggest that the propositional form is something *added* to beliefs—or at any rate to the facts (or events) that are the objects of beliefs—but, if that is so, it is a *falsificatio* of the facts (events); just as, if "logical grounds" are not real grounds, then there are no such things at all. And here we may note as one of the conditions of Alexander's not taking a propositional view of things, or not identifying it with a spatio-temporal view, a certain persistence of a *correspondence* view, because it is beliefs, and not facts, that are taken to be expressible in propositional form, but if the facts themselves are not in propositional form, then it is not in the least apparent how facts or reality could guide our beliefs or show how they were to be systematised.

The position is comparable with that of part of Hume's account of causality where he treats causal relation as what we assert when *we* make the transition from one idea to another, i.e., when we infer—*the point being* [the line of attack being the realistic one] that we are not just passing from some ideas to others but are *recognising the actual passage* of some things into others: i.e., the relation is part of *what we know*; and failing that realistic line, there would be more point in calling one sequence *causal* than in so calling another—it would not mean anything to contrast causal sequence with mere succession. So with regard to inferring in general the realist has to say that the relation *implication* is part of what we know, is part of a real or objective situation, just as much as *causation*, or causing, is: for if he didn't do that he would have to deny that there is any connection at all, to deny that there is any such thing as "logical grounds". Alexander's whole view of logic and truth is normative and anti-realistic. He tries to treat propositions, beliefs etc., as distinct from things, as being *in our minds* or not definitel located: i.e., he holds a correspondence theory.

Now coming back to the question of Alexander's wavering between causality as change *simply* (merely) and the recognition of external action, the point is to recognise (realise) that what might be called "internality" or the development of a thing out of its own resources (the development of a thing's own resources, the unfolding of its potentialities) will not cover the ground. For example, the Leibnizian *notion* would not provide the whole history—would not provide a *single conception* whose content would cover all the events of anything's history. *Leibniz* could not provide, or say he had, a notion from which the whole history of Alexander the Great could be unfolded: and in saying that *God* could have such a notion, he is still indicating that *we* could not, and that the assertion that God has such a comprehensive notion does not help *us* to make actual discoveries concerning Alexander's history or to work it out in any other terms than those of contingency, of his *environment*, of things that he collided with or that confronted him and on the character of which, as well as on his own, the outcome depended—where there is no question of embodying in a single formula the operations of Alexander and the operations of the things he encountered, but we just have to recognise *external action*. Now the recognition of contingency in this sense does not mean that there is any event which does not have a necessary and sufficien precedent condition: all it means is that there could never be *a single principle* (any single set of conditions) from which the whole series of events—what we call the "whole history" of Alexander the Great or of any other person or thing—could be derived. We have to admit (the mere fact of) *collocation*, accidental concurrence—which means the admission of an irreducible multiplicity of factors in operation in any region or in the development of any "single" thing. And when Alexander, following Hume, rejects the notion of power or force, he is rejecting along with the *metaphysical* or *rationalistic* conception of force (of "that whereby" something happens) also the *logical* conception of force, the recognition of *agency*, of the operation of independent factors in the bringing about of any result.

Here again Alexander, like other theorists, does not distinguish the
fiel from the agent, and so does not see at all the nature of what I've
been calling a *causal problem* and thus the distinction between a mere
question of change and a question of causality. And we've seen, of
course, that Alexander neglects, or does not seize the importance of,
the question of universality: i.e., that the solution of a causal problem
involves at least two universal propositions, besides the distinction of
the fiel or thing acted on, the agent or thing acting, and *the change that
takes place* (or the property that is acquired).

In my view, then, the distinction between consideration of the agent
and consideration of the patient (in other words, recognition of the *fiel*)
is absolutely essential, and you never would get causal laws (i.e., never
get invariability) if you made it a question of what kind of situation
is followed by what other kind, or what phase is followed by what
other phase of a developing situation, *instead of recognising* [to get
invariability or *regularity* or *laws of nature* you have to recognise on the
one hand,] the *changing thing* (the member of a fiel or genus), and on
the other hand, the *external* thing (the agent or occasion of the change).

Lecture 44 additional

44 (26th July 1950)

[Ed.] Additional note to be inserted on p. 149 above (following quote from *STD*
pp.300-01).

In this passage (*STD* pp.300-01) we again fin Alexander wavering
between different views—he identifie the different effects, or says they
are "the same thing from different points of view", and sometimes he
speaks as if the fact that the nature of the changes depends upon the
characters of *both* the acting thing and the thing acted on were a reason
for taking the two changes as not distinct. Now, even if there is confusion
here, there is at least some indication of the distinction between agent
and patient; but, as was apparent in his general account of causality (as
distinct from reciprocity), he has this other view of causality as simply
change, because here again he is insisting on continuity, on the earlier
thing *becoming* the later, to the neglect of the conception of the external
agent. Now that, as before, is bound up with the "stuff" theory; if you
start with pure Space-Time, it's at most going to be a question of the
unfolding of inner resources, it's not going to be a question of *external
action* or *interaction*: so that, as seen in other connections, in whatever
way he may approach an empirical philosophy—even if the doctrine of

space-time (extensional-intensional: *external-internal* (?)) drives him in that direction—his *stuff* theory (or stuff *formulation*) drives him in the direction of *Idealism*. (Hints of an empirical theory, complicated—or contaminated—by *rationalist* conceptions.)

In his chapter (Book II, chapter X) entitled "The One and the Many", Alexander says that "Space-Time is the source of the categories, the non-empirical characters of existing things, which those things possess because of certain fundamental features of any piece of space-time". We have the similar view of Kant that things-in-themselves are the "source" of phenomena; the objection to this being that if you affir   that relation, *being a source of*, between things-in-themselves and phenomena, you are bringing those things-in-themselves under the categories, i.e., you are making them phenomena, if the Kantian line is to be followed—and some such relation would have to be postulated or the whole distinction would be pointless. Similarly you have *matter*, in Locke's view, as the "source" of "ideas", of what we immediately perceive, but *being a source* has meaning only in terms of what we perceive or are aware of, and unless matter were perceived we could not possibly call it the *source* of ideas.

So far as I have indicated a *source* of the categories, it has been *the form of the proposition* or, as it might be put, *the distinction between location and description*, which, I have argued, is bound up with the distinction between space-time (space *and* time) and what is in *space-time*. I have pointed out that the second group, the mathematical categories, are concerned with what is *common* to *space-time* and what is in it, taking as point of departure the convertibility of terms (i.e., of location and description)—so that, since any term can *locate*, it can be treated as quantitative or extensional—or as so much space-time, i.e., that in so far as we are thinking extensionally (or in terms of extension) we can think indifferently of the spatial characters of things and of space without reference to the things. On the other hand, the third group (the *physical* categories) are concerned with what is *peculiar* to things, with what does not belong to space and time themselves (e.g., *agency*, and similarly *substantiality*). It is his failure to see this that is one of the major weaknesses in Alexander—his treatment of space-time as *stuff*, as actually *making up* concrete things, and again his suggestion (though this is not meant to be quite precise) that things are made *out of* space *by* time—his attribution of agency to time itself.

I have taken the third group to start with quantity and to go on, through intensity, substance and causality, to the category of individuality: and now I am suggesting an identificatio of this last category with *force* or *agency*, or at least its assimilation to that notion—the category of individuality being conveyed in the notion of *an agent*, where agency is something above mere *sequence* and, on the other hand, is something distinct from mere *implication* or necessity and sufficien y.

Lecture 45

Concluding Section

[JA] Concluding section (Victor Dudman)—*fuller* than concluding section of either Tom Rose or Sandy Anderson.

I mentioned that Alexander, among other confusions, seems to confuse substance with individuality; and there might be a usage of substance, though not, I think, the most defensible historically, in which it was identifie with individuality or thinghood—*being a thing*. But even in Leibniz's doctrine of individual substances or monads, it might be doubted whether he really identifie their individuality with their substantiality. At any rate we do require, whatever expression we use, to have some distinction between agency and what I've taken substance to be, viz., *structure*, and this is in line with the quite common contrast between substance and function.

As indicated, I take the conception of structure to be the leading conception of aesthetics, and if that were so then we might argue that the categories of aesthetics are part of the physical categories, that the general theory of aesthetics, then, is part of this section of logical theory—a point in which it would differ from ethics, though I've argued elsewhere (course on *Criticism*) that the major problems of ethics are actually the problems of causality; that to clear up the question of causality, and particularly the question of freedom, is to get rid of the commonest ethical confusions and to *lay the foundation* for a positive ethical theory, even if not to work it out. In that way, then, there might be a very close connection between the theory of ethics and the category of causality, though it is questionable whether it is as close as the connection between aesthetics and structure.

To say that aesthetics is specially concerned with structure is to say that for aesthetics we stop in this group at the category of substance and are not at all concerned with the category of causality—that in what you might call *non-temporal art* you are concerned with a balance, and even in temporal art, art with a temporal order, in the working out of a theme through successive stages or phases, the question still is of bringing out the *character* of the theme or subject—the phases are still taken as making (up?) a certain structure, and not as *causing* one another. And in that way, though you can't say that the author rules out causality in the sense of denying that such a thing exists, he is at least setting it aside theoretically—he is setting aside the question of external action and is considering the working out of something in its own terms, as if it were self-contained. And even in the temporal sequences he is only bringing out what may be called the "elements" or *leading features* of the subject, conditions which are necessary and together sufficien for the existence of that sort of thing: i.e., he is doing just what the logician does when he *define* . That is to say, the scheme of interrelated properties which a person definin and classifying recognises is equivalent to the phases in which an artist works out a theme or to the features by which he builds up a structure. But such a structure as it exists in nature can be invaded (broken in on); we can have the intrusion of other factors and the breaking-up of the character in question. And in this way we have *history*, but it is *still* antithetical to art, this opposition being the sort of thing that Joyce is drawing attention to in *Ulysses*, when he says "History is a nightmare from which I am trying to awake". History is concerned with *external action*, and art and aesthetics are not. And the same sort of point is made in the *Portrait of the Artist as a Young Man* when the artist is taken to be concerned with the *static* as contrasted with the *kinetic*, and he falls away from the artistic standpoint when *kinetic things* intervene, e.g., social forces (or) works (when the work is taken to have some social reference (some *purpose* etc) and not as just self-sufficient)

I am suggesting then that when we complete the third group of categories, when we bring in interaction or external action, then we pass from the aesthetic to the historical, though this view of history would be opposed by Croce who considers history a definitel non-causal study, who holds that causality is alien to history, and thus equates the historical view of things with what I call the aesthetic view (the point of view of substance or structure) (treats history as the unrolling of a subject ("liberty") through its successive phases). Nevertheless it does not seem to be a view that could be very easily maintained (i.e., history without interaction) and it would scarcely be in acccordance with Croce's own objection to a single-track development, and particularly (to) a regular progress, because the recognition that there can be retrogression as well as advance would seem to me to imply distinct and interacting factors. (We could also connect epistemology with this set of categories, and the line here would be that knowledge involves *interaction* and not mere *confrontation*.)

On the question of individuality and [or?] agency, I have spoken in "Realism versus Relativism in Ethics" of [*certain*] things as *forces*, and, in my argument, that is *equivalent* to treating them as things (e.g., *goods*): i.e., I am rejecting there as elsewhere the view that anything could be a mere resultant or could exist only relatively to something else; I am arguing that anything that can be produced is itself capable of producing; and it is in emphasising this activity of things, the fact that they can act as well as be acted on, that I refer to them as *forces*. I am making the same sort of point when I speak of the *independence* of things, and the special point I am making in "Realism versus Relativism" (*cf.* also "The Meaning of Good") is that goods, if they exist at all, must be *agents*: that they cannot be merely attached to something else, can't merely exist in dependence on mind, or as things which minds may or may not bring about, but they must have their own modes of operation, and that otherwise there is not a subject of *ethics* at all.

In that way, then, i.e., in the linking together of agency and independence, we can have this particular conception of individuality; and it could be argued here that the theory of categories has come full circle, that the fina category of individuality is just the firs one, *identity*, over again. But even if you were to say that individuality is the concrete or practical form of identity, still the distinction is there, because in identity we are concerned only with the function of locating (a thing has identity in so far as it can *place* something or other), whereas in individuality we are concerned with *activity*, with something dynamic, something *in*tensional as contrasted with *ex*tensional (second group). And yet it is such an active being that we would refer to specificall as a *subject*, as something capable of affecting other things, something which not merely *locates* (or is the region of) certain activities but, as it is commonly put, *has* those activities (operates in those specifi ways), something whose acts the various predicates are, i.e., the subject is that whose acts these predicates are. (This is not a *departure* from the distinction of functions in the proposition but simply an insistence on their *connection*.) Because, as pointed out earlier, the "location" formula is defective; it is only a rough indication of the function of the subject, in so far as literally it suggests simply *falling within* or *being contained in*, and yet we do not call what is contained in a subject its predicate (not invariably, at least), i.e., we don't call *parts* of a thing *predicates* of that thing, nor do we call things which that given thing simply (merely) *surrounds* predicates of it; so that, useful as the antithesis "location" and "description" may be, it doesn't cover the ground, it doesn't distinguish *having as an activity* (X's having Y as an activity of its (X's) etc.) and merely having as a part or even as a tenant.

To think, then, of a subject concretely, even if we still said that we were thinking of the subject's *identity*, would be to think of its various activities; and this seems to me to give a distinction between the *identity* of a thing which can still be recognised by its mere place and the *individuality* of a thing which is a matter of its being of special sorts. We should still, of course, have to reject the notion of a *totality* of characters or qualities of a thing, the notion of it as having some character, called *its individuality*, which included *everything that could be said about it* (or "all about it"). This is just something that hasn't any meaning; even to think of it as an agent is to think of it as an agent along certain lines and not to think of everything that it could possibly do. At the same time, we are not looking for some sort of power, agency or force *additional* to the activities themselves—it is just the activities themselves that we are speaking about when we say that this is an agent of such and such a kind.

I *could have said* (did say?), on the *relation* (question?) of types of philosophical or near-philosophical inquiry that are linked with this last group of categories, that just as aesthetics is bound up with substance in the sense of structure, and ethics is bound up with causality, so individuality or agency is bound up with the study of history. The important point here would be to see, on the one hand, that there are independent agents, which would be connected with the fact that there is no such thing as *the course of history*, no single track such as is postulated by Marx and which *involves history as having* a single subject and as the unwinding or unfolding of that subject, *spun out* of its own resources—we have to recognise the fact of mere collocation, we have to recognise interaction, which means that there is no single factor which we could ever *devise* (?) to give an account of (to account for the whole history of?) human society, or of anything else. But then at the same time (on the other hand?) we have to reject the notion of "individuals", of *ultimate* agents, of a special *initiatory* class of things, which is the way in which many philosophers think about persons: a *person* is that which can start a process *ab initio*—a point connected again with Kant's doctrine of freedom and made specificall by Kant in the Transcendental Dialectic. This notion of the pure or ultimate agent is opposed to the conception of *internal* exchanges as a condition of any *external* exchanges, opposed to the conception of *interaction all the way*, and of course it is just because of those internal movements, internal tensions and activities, that the thing, the "individual", can impinge on outer processes or have outer processes impinging on it, because even when we distinguish the external agent from the order (the sequence) of processes in the thing acted on, it is only because of the way in which this external process can become continuous with the internal processes that this *acting upon* is really possible. Thus it is possible to talk as I have done about movements passing through an individual, or certain types of activity outside him contributing to and indeed being necessary for the continuance of the same types of activity inside him—a relation which could obviously be reversed; we can think, i.e., of the movement passing through the person and at the same time of the person's making a distinctive contribution to the movement. But we cannot think of him by an act of will or in any other way setting such a movement going, we cannot think of the type of activity we call *inquiry* springing from the decision of some person, "I will inquire". So that once more, even if "individuality" might not be the best expression for this condition, it is the fact of *exchange*, of the *continuity* between internal and external tensions and *interactions* (activities?), which is the question we are concerned with here; and I am suggesting that this is the object of historical study. Of course, as theory has (actually) developed, history is (actually) the study of *society*. But, accepting the notion of things as historical, i.e., as *spatio-temporal*, then history could, formally at least, be extended; history would equally be the study, e.g., of the solar system, and not just of human society. We cannot, however, have ultimate agents, one point being that such ultimates are quite indescribable, and if you're going to talk about the *agency* of anything, it is its agency *as a thing of a certain kind* which is what enables it to enter into specifi processes with other things of specifi kinds, and not any *pure agency* that it possesses.

And a good many of Popper's confusions (e.g., his view that questions of demand are quite separate from questions of fact) are connected with the lack of positive description of the mind which makes the demands. When we get on to the positive characterisation, the discovery of the actual content of what is the agent in each case (the particular "motive" as I used to call it), then it becomes (purely) a question (just) of fact, of natural processes, and there is no question of setting matters of demand apart from matters of fact. But of course when Popper gives *no* concrete characterisation of that which demands, this lends support to what is his prevailing view (even though he hedges), viz., that anybody can demand anything—because the I or ego or personal pronoun has no concrete character assigned to it which would determine its movement in this direction rather than that. And as another part of the same confusion, Popper (in *The Open Society*[1]) takes anything as possible in social organisation; he considers that we should never take anything as impossible of achievement—we should always think that what we want to use for a certain purpose *can* be used for that purpose, we should (always) keep on struggling for what we think *desirable* (*relativism* here again) and never allow theory to say that certain things cannot be done. Which of course amounts to saying that we should not allow any *universal propositions*, because a universal proposition does indicate directly that certain things are impossible—$XaY > Xe\overline{Y} > X\overline{Y}$ are impossible. And if we don't allow universal propositions, then we just don't have theory, even though some people do confusedly think that all facts are particulars.

Now connected (along) with this rejection of ultimate agents, its rejection as quite indescribable and therefore as quite unidentifiabl as *the* agent in any particular change, goes the rejection of individuality in the sense of *totality*, of an aggregation of all the characters that anything has, because *within the thing* (*cf.* the question of *substance*), just as between the thing and other things, we always have to recognise accidental collocation, and we never could have *all that this thing (or "individual") is*, all the characters that it possesses, as a single and intelligible conception. Nor in particular could we conceive such a "whole nature" *as an agent*, could we *identify it* in other words (just as before) as the thing which was responsible for this particular development. If we know a thing at all, and if we talk about its agency at all, we know it (and we talk of its agency) as a thing of a certain sort. It is in that way, in terms of *types of activity* within and without the thing, that we can give any account whatever of its agency. Otherwise

[1]Karl R. Popper, *The Open Society and Its Enemies*, London: Routledge and Kegan Paul, 1945.

it is a matter of mere guesswork: we say without any possibility of indicating the concrete relationship, that *this* is responsible for that, (though even to indicate "this", we have to give some *general*, and not any "total", description) and we are back at the position where anything might bring about anything else, where there just would not be any laws or regularities.

Another way of putting this is that anything that we can call a *thing* is also an *arena* or fiel of interrelated operations. And this would indicate once more the coming back of the fina category to the firs one: at least, that we require the notion of subject as *region* in order to grasp the notion of subject *as agent*.

While in this way we get a difficult at (some) times in distinguishing various categories—while they must all indeed be closely related as involving types of problem in which any material whatever is involved (or is concerned)—we can still make certain formal distinctions. We do make the general distinction between the odd and even numbers in the category series that the even ones are all "dyadic" or require two terms for their formal setting out. But of course we are not limited to that particular distinction, and it is clear, I think, that the contention that it is only by treating a thing as of a certain sort that we can regard it as an *agent* in a specifi case, regard it as having a specifi kind of effect or impact on something else, still doesn't mean that it is merely general (doesn't mean that individuality is reduced to universality), because, as previously indicated, while what we call *an individual*, like Socrates, must be regarded as a kind, must be regarded as having instances, if there is to be any theory at all of either his history or the knowledge of him, nevertheless these instances are different from the instances of the ordinary universal, (different) in so far as they (do) form one continuous series, run continuously into one another in time in a way that the instances of the *universal* (term) "man" do not.

There is a possible objection here that, even in contrasting the instances which form such a continuous series with those that do not, we are in both cases employing the conception of *an instance*, an individual (or single) instance, and are thus using the conception of individuality in distinguishing individuality from universality. However, it doesn't seem to me that this is an at all serious criticism: by *the instance* we simply mean *the subject* and are not concerned with its singleness. (So "part of the extension of X" does not mean an *atom*.) And to say that the

later categories can help us to understand the earlier, help us to clarify
their meaning, or for that matter that the earlier categories can help us to
understand the later ones, is not important in a theory according to which
all the categories *occur everywhere*—or problems expressed in terms of
any category occur whenever (wherever?) problems expressed in terms
of any other category occur. And in particular there is no question of
our not employing the later categories in the earlier stages of discussion,
any more than there is a question of our not employing syllogism in
the arguments we present in that part of our exposition of logic which
comes before our presentation of the logic of syllogism, or indeed of
our not employing it in the early part of our discussion of syllogism
itself—before we have completely set out our syllogistic theory. That
means that we are not involved in the Hegelian problem of treating each
category as a conception under which we endeavour to think the whole
of reality, so that we begin by trying to think of everything as *being*,
(and nothing else?—being as anything's "whole nature") and then that
breaks down (and the conception of not-being intrudes) and we have to
think of everything as *not being*, and then we try to get a category from
the synthesis of these two, and so on. There is no question of trying
to think the whole of things under this or that conception; there is, on
the contrary, the fact that we can be using any of the categories when
we think at all, and consequently that even in working out a *theory of
categories* we certainly cannot limit ourselves in our thinking to the use
of the category which we happen to be investigating at the time.

The three groups of categories could be described by reference to
the fina category in each set: you could take the firs group as the
categories of universality or quality (being of a certain description),
the second group as the categories of quantity, which would be
essentially *categories of location*, and the third group as the categories
of individuality, which would be the categories of description but now
in the form of complexity or complex activity. (*Cf.* Aesthetics—3rd
group as qualitative). These are the historical categories, the categories
of *occurrence*, as contrasted with the categories of *situation* which
are the second group. While the firs group are just the more general
categories of *predication* (of *fact*?) This may not be greatly different
from what I have said already: that the firs group should be understood
by reference to the *place-character* formula, the second group gives
further specificatio to place or location, and the third group gives

greater specificatio to character or description—or you could use the expressions *extension* and *intension* to refer to this distinction.

One point that might be made here is that even if we could not accept the general Hegelian formula of thesis, antithesis and synthesis, the third group could be considered as a sort of unificatio of the firs two groups, or taking the reference by the fina category, individuality could be regarded as combining quality and quantity, because when we consider the distinction of the individual from the class, the distinction of what is still a general term, but one whose instances all belong to a single temporal sequence, from a general term whose instances *don't form part of* a single history, then we might say that in the case of individuality we have a general expression which nevertheless applies to only one thing. You could not say from any given combination of characters that there must be one and only one thing that has it, and yet we do believe that there is one and only one thing which does have a certain combination of characters, that there is a combination of characters which serves to *identify* what we call an individual (leaving it possible, of course, that there are a number of alternative combinations which would so identify it—not merely possible but *necessary*, in fact, if we take it that any term has many possible definit ons). Thus, when we know Socrates, we know him as of the sorts X, Y and Z, and *XYZ* is a quite general description (one which "could" apply to any number of things), and yet we think (that), whenever we come across the combination XYZ, *this must be Socrates*. As I say, there is nothing in a (logical) combination or *conjunction* of characters to compel us to think this (nothing in the combination as such to say *how many* things are describable by it), and yet we *do* think it: we do think that there are never two distinct spatially separated things which both are of this complex character. That might be why we fin something not merely embarrassing but slightly eerie when we are confronted with identical twins: (notion of "eeriness": against *logic*, against the "laws of nature") although as we become *more* or better acquainted with them we always do discover differences. We could often be (and are often) mistaken in this sort of judgment: we can have mistakes in recognition from taking a certain combination of characters *not* to occur in two spatially separated instances at the same time, when in fact it does; ("This must be X—X can't be elsewhere—because the combination of characters ABCD could not possibly occur in two distinct places—it's an adequate "identification"—an it's occurring *here*") and thus we "recognise" some person, as we think, when in fact it is not that person. But the fact remains that when we do have recognition, it is always of the occurrence of *a thing of a certain sort*, though we *think* that that sort is not duplicated.

When we are involved in *formulating*, (making?) a judgment of that kind, then we are saying that our judgment of quality does carry with it spatial identificatio (i.e., carries with it something *quantitative*): that it *contains* (*combines*?) these *functions* of quality and quantity: and that indicates what we mean by individuality. Though it still cannot be that a certain quality (*qualitative character*, group of qualities) dictates a certain quantity (how many or how extensive—a limit of its own—i.e., the quality's—*range*). And, as said above, it is at least closely connected with what we mean by identity—it *gives us* (?) a possibility of identificatio which the ordinary recognition of characters, even of combinations of characters, doesn't give us. But even so, we would still have to distinguish identity in the original sense (by which we merely meant having the function of locating) from identity in this complex sense, where we are thinking of *a specifi entity*, a definit agent (as I was putting it earlier), *with a continuous history*.

It is such concrete individuality that we are concerned with in all historical inquiry. Though that "history" suffers which is not combined with a general *social theory*. And it is in terms of such continuous agency that we could pursue such inquiry, though that is not in the least to say that there is any special type of entity, type of *conjunction of characters*, (i.e., special *way* of "being conjoined") to which the notion of agency, or of individuality in the sense I've been indicating, should be peculiarly attached. For example, as already indicated, the most common error in historical study, or in the study of human affairs, is *individualism*, is the notion that a *person* is in some peculiar sense an agent and an individual, that he has a sort of *unity* (ambiguity of unity: between (1) one or the same, and (2) united or joined. Attempt to amalgamate the two so that the joinedness of the terms makes them one term. Aspects (expressions or manifestations) of something—different and not different. *Cf.* "enveloping relation" G. F. Stout) that no non-person could have, that he has an *initiatory* power that no non-person has: whereas, if we take the question to be just that of a logical principle, then there could be "individuals", subjects of a continuous history, of which this person was merely a part, and equally there could be subjects of a continuous history which were merely parts of this person, which operated within him as distinct and recognisable things and which were as much *individuals* as he is. In other words, anything that we could call an individual would still have to be thought of as a fiel or arena of interconnected and sometimes conflictin activities (in fact, as *containing* individuals and as *contained in* individuals) and not merely as something that is *in* a field something that could have relations to other things but is itself a pure unit, because this brings us back to the Pythagorean difficultie and to the Heraclitean rejoinder that it is only because a being is an arena, only because of its internal exchanges, that it can have external exchanges. This then is *what I've suggested* about individuality; and such individuals are the external agents which I took to be involved in any worked out theory of causality; though of course they could also be patients, they could also be things which agencies (agents) external to them acted upon. In fact this *would* always be the case: any agent is a patient, and any patient is an agent.

But while the third group of categories culminates in this notion of individuality, we cannot say that this category is involved in the whole (group)—in each member of its group: in the case of structure or substance, e.g., we are concerned with *internal complexity* but not with the *absence of repetition* ("duplication"). On the contrary, when we talk of something as of a certain substance, we imply that there are other things of the same substance (or, as I put it, of the same *structure*). And that is one of the difficultie of aesthetic theory, viz., that while the theme is a certain general character—as you might say broadly that wrath or anger is the theme of the *Iliad* and its being the wrath or anger of Achilles means only that an illustration of the theme has to be given in order that the theme may be concretely presented (or again that exile is the theme of the *Odyssey* or of *Ulysses*)—still it has to be presented in a specifi case, and the difficult is to avoid confusion between special characters *of the instance* and characters involved in the theme as such. But while there is the danger of this confusion, it is still something general that is the theme, and the notion of exile is not in itself illuminated by its being the exile of Odysseus or of Leopold Bloom or of Stephen Dedalus. Substance or *structure*, then, is something that we are interested in in its generality. But nevertheless the notion of structure, i.e., of a variety of characters variously interrelated, does help us to understand—indeed is essential to our understanding of—the sort of external and internal exchanges that are postulated in the remaining categories: causality and individuality.

I said about this third group that it involved or emphasised the *distinction* between *space and time* and the things that are in space and time, and this was the point I emphasised with regard to the two senses of *quantity* or the two lines of thinking regarding quantity: viz., on the one hand, simply a spatial thing and, on the other hand, a space-*fillin* thing. And here I would say that it is in regard to these historical categories that Alexander's treatment of space *and* time as the actual stuff of things, as *fillin* themselves so to speak, is involved in his most striking error. That is, his major error is in treating space and time themselves as forces, instead of merely as a medium or arena within which forces operate.

And that is connected with his general *unhistorical* view of things, not merely the relativism but the individualism of his ethical and aesthetic *theory* (theories), and his general *evolutionism*—his notion of an automatic advance—his notion that what he himself calls survival value is as much a "*positive value*" as the good or the beautiful: because this means that he fails completely to grasp what I might call the *theme* of history, the nature of culture and its constant struggle with hostile conditions—the struggle, as I have put it, between *objectivism* and *subjectivism*, between the outlook that takes all things as historical in a broad sense and that which takes certain things to be unhistorical—to be above history or independent of history—that which *believes* in ultimate agents and changeless substances (*types of view* which I am calling *subjectivist*).

(Apparent wavering or compromise here between *aesthetic* view of history—*theme*: and *its working out?*—and "interactionist" view. Might have to say that "the nature of culture" is one sort of study and its "struggle" etc., is another—but if only the latter is *historical* study, it would seem that *aesthetic*—or "cultural"—study was still a *necessity*—propaedeutic or accompaniment—for historical study.) *Cf.* philosophy: *what is philosophy* is one question, *what is its history* (what are its vicissitudes) is another—yet, it could be argued, the two questions must be studied together. (Question whether historical study is not *necessary* for aesthetic study, as well as other way round.) *Art* has a history: and so has *aesthetic theory*. But that is not to say that history is any part of the *subject-matter* of aesthetic theory (or that aesthetics is *any sort of historical* study). *Cf.* above, —"external action".

Appendix 2
Correspondence

Extract of a Letter from John Anderson to Janet Baillie 22nd February 1917[1]

...We of the Moral class have been taking advantage of Henry's absence this week not to hand in our essays till Fri. (We haven't got the last one back yet—nor the results of the exam. before Christmas. The papers must have been corrected by this time, but one can hardly ask for the results, though it would remove the agony of suspense.) So to-morrow night will fin me engaged in putting "The Presuppositions of Pluralism" in intelligible form. I have pretty well decided what I am going to say: the difficult will be to spin it out to the usual length.—Alexander's course is fini hed now. I had to miss the last three lectures, but in compensation I was present at a discussion of No. 1, The College, on Sat. morning when Alexander expounded his views to and met criticism from Russell, Scott, Willie and myself.[2] As you may imagine, I didn't put myself forward in that company. But the discussion was very interesting. It was mainly between Alexander and Russell, and I thought Alexander quite maintained his position. In fact, Russell had no sympathisers in the company. Scott, of course, suffers from ignorance of mathematics but besides that, his opinions are more or less fi ed on the model of Caird and Henry Jones. Alexander was showing us a proof of the connectedness of the three characters of time (continuity, irreversibility, i.e., if A is before B, B is not before A, and transitiveness, i.e., if A is before B and B before C, A is before C) with the three dimensions of space. It was rather difficul to follow, but we all made up our minds that we would try to work it out in detail. I think I have discovered that the proof is fallacious. I have shown my argument to the others, but they reserve their judgment. So I am going to write to Alexander for a detailed account of his proof, and at the same time offer my criticism. He is a most genial man, and won't, I am sure, object to this in the least. In fact, he was rather doubtful about the proof himself, and said he would welcome criticism. I was sorry I couldn't make a drawing of him in the act of laughing. But besides the inherent difficult of the task, it was hardly possible in a company of f ve, and memory

[1] University of Sydney Archives, P.A.J.A., Box 46.
[2] Most likely L. J. Russell, J. B. Scott and William Anderson.

is no good in such a case. I may say that, although I am not really much of a draughtsman, I have often amused myself with drawing and sometimes make lucky hits. Alexander is an easy man to draw because he has certain salient features which one can hit off...

Samuel Alexander 1930s

Sketches in Anderson's copy of
the Gifford Lectures 1917-18

Figure 14.

Letter in Defence of Alexander to the *New Age*

[Ed.] This letter appeared in *The New Age* of 3rd November 1921. It is in response to the anonymous and negative review of Alexander's work which had appeared in the previous issue of October 20, 1921. That review had referred to Alexander as "a Jew lecturing to Jews" and as having "semiticised" Spinoza. The review concludes with the suggestion that Alexander had stopped short with Space-Time as the true and irreducible substance but should have gone further to the affirmation of the synthesis of Space and Time in Causality as the one true substance. Anderson's reply led to a period of direct correspondence with Alexander himself.[3]

"Spinoza and Time"

Sir,—The review of Spinoza and Time in your issue of October 20 appears to me to misrepresent Professor Alexander's views on certain important points. Your reviewer argues that Spinoza's system is ruined by Professor Alexander's treatment, which "makes of God merely

---

[3] *The New Age* was very important to Anderson. The full and searchable contents of this journal can be found at *The Modernist Journals Project* web site hosted by Brown University.

the total objective reality". And it appears to be suggested that this is Professor Alexander's "Semitic" view of *Spinoza's* "God". Either suggestion would be a misrepresentation.

Professor Alexander maintains that Spinoza's *Substance*, with the attributes of Extension and Thought, can be interpreted as *Motion* (the "stuff of which all things are made") having Space and Time as attributes, and particular motions as modes. Such philosophical interpretation must be tentative, and may be considered from two points of view. In the firs place, we may conceive Professor Alexander as saying, in elucidation of his own position, "My view of Motion as the stuff of which all things (motions) are made is analogous to Spinoza's view of all finit things as modes of Infinit Substance; and my description of it as Space-Time is analogous to Spinoza's view of the two Infinit Attributes of Substance—Extension and Thought". In the second place, Professor Alexander may be said to maintain that Spinoza's problem of the relation of the Attributes to Substance is solved if we take the attributes as Space and Time; and similarly with the problem of the modes, or of the relation of finite to the infinite Here, then, is a new interpretation of Substance, and a genuine philosophical advance. For, even if Spinoza identifie Substance with God, he was still dealing with the philosophical problem of Substance.

The problem of Deity, for Professor Alexander, is quite a different one, though it is related to the theory of Space-Time. The relation of Time to Space within the whole of Motion he considers analogous to the relation of mind to a body in a person: as he puts it, "Time is the mind of Space". In other words, Time is the active principle, while Space is the passive; things are generated in Space by Time, just as acts are generated in body by mind. In the empirical order mental things (processes) are at a higher level of activity than merely organic processes; and thus mind is spoken of as an "emergent" from life. This marks the difference from the "non-empirical" relation; we cannot call Time an emergent from Space, since there are no activities at a lower level than motions in general. But it is precisely in "emergence" that Professor Alexander find Deity. For men God is the empirical from mind, just as mind is the Deity of purely organic things. Thus, using the analogy given above, we may say that in relation to God (or Spirit) mind is the passive principle, that processes of some special kind (possibly goods or values) are generated in mind by Spirit. Or taking Professor Alexander's other description of the relation—that "Space gives continuity to Time, and Time gives structure to Space", we may say that Spirit is that which gives structure to mind ("psycho-synthesis"?), while mind gives to Spirit continuity, i.e., gives it a place in which it can occur and be determined. The beings in whom such Spirit actually occurs are described in Professor Alexander's terminology as "angels" (who again have their Deity at a higher level)—and I would suggest (though I do not know how far Professor Alexander would agree) that the angelic nature is identical with what we call "genius", and that in its attitude to men it is the comic spirit, which sees how the sentiments which might rise to genius are prevented from doing so by being tied to *desire*. I would also suggest that the sentiment of "ecstacy", which apparently appeals to your reviewer, is not a pure sentiment but is complicated by desire (or is a "compromise-formation"); as is also the sentiment which find Deity as the Substance of the world, instead of as a wonderful emergent from the hearts of men.

It must at least be emphasised that the phrase "of merely empirical importance" as applied to Thought is one which Professor Alexander would not countenance for a moment. He would not say that, because all empirical things arise in Space-Time, this "non-empirical" character is the important thing about them; on the contrary, it is the empirical level to which they rise that constitutes their importance and it is the empirical variety of things that brings beauty into the world. Similarly, in Spinoza, it is the empirical character of the Attribute of Thought that gives value to his conception of God, and Professor Alexander may well believe that he has given a truer interpretation of "the intellectual love of God" as the emergence of Spirit from Mind (or the freeing of Thought from Desire) than is given in the conviction that Thought and Reality are one.

Your reviewer's reference to Causality is similarly open to objection. Motion *is* the synthesis of Space and Time (not their "addition", whatever that may be), and Professor Alexander has endeavoured to show the nature of that synthesis; the way in which Space and Time imply one another, and the fact that empirical knowledge of the one cannot be separated from that of the other. He would certainly say that we do not know anything other than motion, and he takes Causality as a "category", i.e., one of the characters which belong to all motions. Taken by itself, Causality is an abstraction: taken as a character of motions it is not. Taken by themselves Space and Time are abstractions: taken as attributes of Space-Time they are not. And the nature of Space-Time accounts for the mutual implication of division and connection. But where analysis comes in in "the one indivisible causal experience which we live and which we are" must remain a mystery.

Appendix 3
Alexander's Gifford Lectures 1917-18

Course 1 deals with the following main subjects: (i) Space-Time, (ii) The Categories. Course 2 will deal with iii) The order of finit empirical existence, (iv) Deity.

Course I

Lecture I (Friday January 12th)
Introductory: Method and Problem

Notwithstanding the title of these two courses (which will be consecutive) a very large part of them will be occupied, especially in the second course, with the mind; but mind will be introduced in its place in a more comprehensive scheme, which begins with the simplest reality, Space and Time, and ends with the highest quality of existence known to us, Deity. In this introductory lecture I shall explain the reasons for adopting this procedure. But I shall also give a provisional account of the nature of knowing derived directly from our experience of it; partly by way of anticipation, and because we most naturally begin in this way; but partly in order to show that it raises the larger problem.

Philosophy or metaphysics does not differ from the sciences in its method but only in its subject-matter, or rather in its boundaries. Its method is accordingly experiential or empirical, proceeding by description and analysis and using, like the sciences, hypotheses which it submits to verification Its special subject-matter is determined in this way: we distinguish in the world certain pervasive characters of things, such as occupation of space and time, substance, causality, intensity, number, and the like, which everything possesses, from the variable features of things, e.g., materiality, colour, life, consciousness, which are special to certain things. These latter features are empirical; the others are non-empirical, or *a priori*, or "categorial". Philosophy is the empirical or experiential study of the non-empirical and of such subjects (and they are both numerous and important) as arise out of the relation of the empirical to the non-empirical. One of these subjects is that relation between the empirical things called minds and other things, which constitutes knowing them.

For one effect of the empirical method in philosophy is to treat minds as just one group among the whole system of finit existences, the most gifted members known to us in a democracy of finit things. This conflict with a common belief that things are in some way dependent on mind, or that mind has some prerogative position, in consequence of which external things would not be what they are experienced to be apart from mind. But it is enough for my purposes if this empirical view of minds be adopted as a hypothesis of method, leaving the inquiry to show in the event, whether it is successful or not. That is we may put aside all questions as to whether space and time, substance, and the like, and things, are dependent on mind, and consider them, as a botanist considers plants, as they present themselves in experience. Our method then prescribes to us to introduce the study of mind at the end of the scale of finit existences. This will require some patience on the part of my hearers in discussing the simpler and more fundamental and, therefore, abstruser matters which have to come first

Now it is precisely this conception of mind which is derived from an unprejudiced description of the experience of knowing an external object. Direct experience tells us that in such a case there are two distinct existents which are together or compresent with one another, the one the thing known, the other the act of consciousness which knows it. They are, however, experienced differently. The act of mind, the perceiving, imagining, desiring, etc., is lived through, I say "enjoyed"; the object is "contemplated". The one is an experiencing, the other an experienced. Various acts of consciousness are connected together in enjoyment continuously, and the unity of them (the exacter nature of which is postponed) is the mind; just as the perceived table is the unity in which all the ways in which it appears to minds are contained. The mind is thus a thing whose acts have a quality, consciousness; as a plant is a thing whose functions have a quality, life. In knowing an external object we also are aware of our bodily organs, and it becomes a question what is the relation of mental acts to the body. That is open to discussion; I am proceeding on the common view that mind is correlated specially with the nervous system. But what is vital is that, by the deliverance of experience itself, mind is a thing alongside or together with its so-called object. Its relation to its object is thus precisely like that of the table to the floo on which it stands; only that in our case one of the partners is a consciousness, and thus is aware of the other partner. In its own experience, it, as enjoyed, is together with the thing it contemplates. There is nothing in experience to warrant the belief that there is an unexperienced entity mind which is aware both of itself and of objects.

That notion comes from neglecting the difference of the enjoyed and the contemplated.

The acts of mind vary with their objects, and are specifi responses to the objects. But the object is non-mental, and just as much so when it is an image as when it is a percept. The acts of mind are experienced immediately in introspection, which is not an invention of psychology, but is practised by us whenever we say "I see" or "I desire". The mental process is easier to observe and distinguish from the object in complicated acts like willing or thinking or desiring than in simple acts like perceiving or sensing, which is compresent with the green or sweet which is sensed. But in every case the object is distinct from the mind which knows it; an image is as much external and non-mental as the tree which is presented in perception. The various acts of mind do not differ in quality with their object. Their distinctive quality is to be conscious. They differ in what I shall call "direction", and shall leave to be explained in the sequel.

But discussions of the subject show that statements founded on direct experience of the mind itself rarely produce conviction. Moreover, the statement brings us face to face with more fundamental questions. For we experience our minds as standing in spatial and temporal relations with their objects. Further, we are aware that in sensation our mental act is the effect of our object which initiates the sensing act. In willing we in turn are causal in respect of what we will. Further, we experience our own internal causality, and we are aware that our mind is a substantial unity. For both these reasons, therefore, we shall avoid the more tempting procedure of beginning with the mind, and apply ourselves firs to fundamentals common to mind and things.

Lecture II (Monday January 15th)
Physical Space-Time

Space and time for our experience are the media in which bodies move and events occur. They are equivalent to extension and duration (that duration being continuity in succession). They are sometimes regarded as consisting of relations between bodies or events, space as consisting of relations of co-existence, time of relations of succession. But this is a philosophical theory about them, and does not represent our first-han acquaintance with them. Further, they may be considered apart from the bodies which occupy them or the events which occur in them. This is not a process of vicious abstraction, but means only that, even in a material thing, its simpler features of extension and duration may be considered before its less simple features like colour or materiality. Moreover, to experience, not all space and time are fille with *material* bodies and events, and space and time not only may be considered apart but may exist apart from material bodies or events. We are to consider how space and time are related to each other, and we shall fin that neither is a reality without the other, and that instead of two realities—space and time, there is but one reality, which is space-time; and when we have established this indissoluble connection, our theory will be that space-time is a stuff which is the simplest form of reality and that all existents are made out of this stuff, are, as it were, crystals within this matrix.

In dealing with space and time empirically we are not confine to what we learn of them through the senses, but are free to use conceptions like those of points and instants, which are not sensible objects but represent the ideal elements into which space and time can be resolved. For the objects of experience are not exhausted by the objects of the senses. Space and time do, as experienced objects, imply each other mutually. Neither of them taken by itself with its empirical characters can subsist without the other. For time is essentially succession and at the same time continuous. But if time were self-subsistent each instant or other portion of time would, in virtue of the very successiveness of time, cease to be. There would be only a now, and no past or future. But since time in fact is continuous the instant is sustained by something other than time. This which gives sustainment and continuity to a perishing succession is space. In like manner if space were self-subsistent, it would fail to be continuous because it would admit no distinction of parts and, therefore, would be a blank. Time and space, then, each of them for different reasons needs something other than itself to account for the properties which empirically they possess. Time makes space a continuum by securing its divisibility, and space makes time a continuum by securing the connection of its parts. Time is thus intrinsically spatial and space temporal. There are no points or instants but only point-instants. Every point has its date and every instant its place. The parts into which space-time is resolved are thus motions, for any motion through a space is the change of dates of the points within that space. If it were not so inconsistent with ordinary language the infinit whole of space-time might be spoken of as Motion.

The connection of space and time is, however, more intimate than appears from this general statement. It may be shown that each point of space is repeated in time, that is, each point has more than one date; and that each instant is repeated in space, that is, that more than one point occurs at the same instant. This fact underlies the structure and permanence of things. Moreover, besides continuity, time possesses empirically irreversible direction, and also each moment is between two other moments. To these three characters of time correspond the three dimensions of space.

The greater part of these details is necessarily omitted. But in no sense are they a pretence at demonstrating that, for instance, space *must* have three dimensions, but only that the empirical properties of space and time imply each other. Time is not, therefore, in the metaphysical sense, a fourth co-ordinate to the three spatial ones as it may rightly be treated for mathematical purposes, but, though one-dimensional, time has characters which cover those of space.

The simplest basis of reality is thus space-time, in which Space and Time are distinguishable but not self-subsistent elements. Consistently with this we are to regard the history of the world as a perpetual redistribution of motion, or in more exact phrase a perpetual redistribution of the instants of time among the points of space within the one infinit space-time. The world grows and changes not by addition but by internal redistribution, like the movements in a disturbed ant heap.

But not only do we ordinarily think of Space and Time as independent of one another; but also we say that at any one moment the whole of Space is fille with events occurring then, or we think that the whole of Time streams through each point of space. In reality these common ideas are very artificial and require an effort of thought. And if the whole of Space were in reality full of contemporaneous events, history would be a mere now, and there would be no continuity between one now and another, and the world would need to be recreated at each moment, as Descartes held. But, in fact, if we take a "perspective" of the whole of space-time from one instant, we have space completely occupied indeed, but with events of different dates, just as an animal body consists at any one moment of cells of different stages of maturity. But we can readily justify the common notion from the true one. For the total of all these perspectives, which pass or grow one into another, is the whole space-time. Now in this whole system of point-instants we can artific ally select all those points which have the same instant. This artificia "section" gives us the whole of Space with events at the same date. We get then the idea of Space as a framework in which events occur, and correspondingly we can think of a framework of Time occupying a single point. These are the conceptions of Absolute (or Total) Space and Time. They are perfectly legitimate representations of Space and Time taken by themselves. They only become illegitimate if Space is thought to exclude Time or Time Space if, e.g., space is thought to be stationary. But if they are taken to be the elements of space-time with merely provisional omission of the other element, they are intelligible and real.

Lecture III (Friday January 19th)
Mental Space-Time

By mental space and time I do not mean the space and time which belong to our images or thoughts; these, according to our assumption, are nothing but physical space and time, as they are represented in images or thoughts. I mean the space and time in which the mind occurs. If Space and Time are the stuff of which all things are made, it is necessary to show that mind is both spatial and temporal, and, further, that the space and time of mind are not independent but only separable elements in mental space-time and, further, that mental or "enjoyed" space-time is part of the one space-time in which physical things also exist.

Now as to time, it is a commonplace that the mind is in time. Mental life is essentially process. These processes may be maintained in direction, as in contemplating a permanent object like a tree, and they are then called substantive states of mind. Or they may be felt as transitions, as when we are aware of such relations as "but" or "like" or "notwithstanding", and then they are called transitive states of mind. But the substantive states are a department of the transitive ones, and all mental action is transition. Moreover, the time in which mental processes occur is felt to be part of the time to which objects belong. Only we have the vaguest experience of the exact temporal relation of the mental state to its object. We generally think it simultaneous, though measurement shows this to be inaccurate.

But to declare mind spatial seems paradoxical. Yet it is not so, but a plain deliverance of our enjoyment of mind. We feel our consciousness to be voluminous or spread out spatially and we localise it somewhere within our contemplated bodies, and more particularly in our heads. But the place of it, its relation to contemplated space, is of the vaguest kind, just as before with time.

Our localisation of enjoyed space within the space of the body is an incident in the empirical history of our self or person, as the union of body and mind. The experience of the self contains two elements, a subject element which is enjoyed, and an object element, which is contemplated. Even the lower or bodily person contains not only the body but the consciousness of it. The object element is the body, and in the lowest form of experience of the person it occupies the predominant position. In our higher selves we seem to be minds engaged with objects different from the body, such as scenery or mathematics, which occupy our imaginations or thoughts. But examination shows that bodily experiences enter into the personal side of these experiences. This is one way in which we realise the intimate connection of mind and body, and learn that the mind is somewhere where the body is. The other way is the experience that our mental acts are continuous with the external bodily movements by which we express our thoughts or desires or wills.

This is common experience. But later we learn about our brains and of the special concern of special areas in certain processes which are accompanied by consciousness. By the help of this reflect ve experience the vague experience that the mind is somewhere in the body becomes distincter, and we then have an image of a certain contemplated space in which the mind is localised. That is, the enjoyed mind is learnt to be in the same place as the contemplated brain, much as we localise a pain in the toe by identifying their places. In this way we acquire ultimately a map of the mind.

Mind is thus experienced in space as well as in time. But how is the mental space related to the mental time? Has mental space different dates like physical space; or, as might seem from the localisation in brain, are not the past and the future of the mind enjoyed all in the present? To answer this we must examine memory and expectation.

Consider firs contemplated memory, that is, remembered objects. We have to guard against two mistakes. The one is to suppose that what we remember is not present to us directly, but that we have an image of it which in memory is referred to the real object. The fact is that the memory image is the friend or other thing as it presents itself to our minds after we have seen it, at a distance of time. If the friend is seen again we fin that the percept and the memory are different appearances of the same thing—they coalesce. A memory of a thing is an image of the thing along with the experience of its belonging to the past and more particularly to our past. We bring the object up from the past as in desire we bring it up from the future.

The second mistake is to suppose that the memory is present but is somehow referred to the past. This is a misreading of our experience. The memory comes to us as something past, is experienced as past. It is only the act of remembering, linking on the past to our present, which is present.

Lecture IV (Monday January 22nd)
Mental Space-Time *continued*

In the last lecture it was shown that, in remembering objects, the object was presented directly, and was presented to us as past. We have now to examine our memory (or expectation) of ourselves, that is, our enjoyed memory or expectation. I may remember seeing a person and how I then felt, though I never can remember myself without also remembering my object. Once more, as with the memory of objects, it might be thought that when I remember myself, my enjoyment is a present one and is somehow referred to the past. But this is again a misreading. My enjoyment of myself in the past is enjoyed as past; and my expectation of myself in the future is enjoyed as future. They have the character of past and future written on their faces. There is something which is present in the two cases, namely, the present enjoyment of remembering or expecting, whereby my past or future is linked on to the rest of my present enjoyments. But the recalled enjoyment itself is enjoyed not as present but as past. In other words the past is enjoyed as past, just as the past as contemplated is contemplated as past. No doubt this is a difficul saying, but it describes how past or future are enjoyed, and helps us to understand what time is for the person who lives through the time. The objection that the neural process underlying memory takes place in the present is irrelevant. For the neural process is something contemplated by an outsider, but the mental process which accompanies it is enjoyed by me as past or future. A higher intelligence looking on would see that the neural process of my enjoyed past is present along with the neural process of my enjoyed present, but he would also see that the two corresponding enjoyments are not both present in my mind.

When we have satisfie ourselves that we enjoy our past and future as past and future and not as present, we can go back to the relation of enjoyed space to enjoyed time. For now it appears that at any moment my mental space is not occupied only with present mental events, but that part is occupied with present and part with past and future enjoyments. My mental space contains both memory and expectation. Moreover, the memories occupy different places from the present enjoyments. So that we find as a matter of fact, that past and future and present are laid out alongside each other in the map of mental space. Again, as we pass in thought through a train of past and future experiences, the place of them changes in our mental space with the date of the experience.

At the same time we note that many enjoyments may occur at the same time, that is, the present repeats itself in space or is spread out over many mental places; and that a mental place may be repeated in time, for memories of the same kind belong physiologically to the same place in the brain and thus the accompanying enjoyments also do. Subject to certain qualification the mental space and time exhibit, in fact, the same intimacy of connection as we found in physical or contemplated space and time; only, of course, enjoyed space and time are finit and are but parts of the all-embracing Space and Time.

Thus, for instance, the condition of the mind at any one moment is the perspective of the whole mental space-time from the point of view of that moment, and represents a reality, like the perspective of physical space-time. On the other hand the whole mental space may be conceived as occupied with events which have the same date, but such a picture is artificial Thus, as with space and time contemplated, so with space and time enjoyed, it is of the essence of time to be spatial and of space to be temporal, and the one complete reality is space-time and not either Space or Time taken singly. It is useful to contrast this result with the doctrine of M. Bergson, with whom Time has come into its rights, but for whom to represent time as set out in space is to deprive time of its real character. We habitually think of our mental processes as occurring in space, and generally we represent time spatially. This for M. Bergson is to spatialise time. But for us, on the strength of experience, whether it is contemplated or enjoyed experience, time is spatialised intrinsically, and to represent it spatially is not a weakness of our imaginations but accords with its real nature.

Lecture V (Friday February 2nd)
Mathematical Space and Time: Relations In Space And Time

Physical space-time and mental space-time are alike experienced or actual space-time. But what are the Space and Time of mathematics? The question has to be asked, for it is sometimes held that mathematics deals with mere constructions of the mind; and the later developments of mathematics claim to transport us into a neutral region which is neither physical nor mental, and in the end mathematics is identifie with logic and more or less with metaphysics, which then becomes the study, not, as we maintain, of the actual, but of the possible. Part of the present lecture will be a plea that directly or indirectly mathematics deals with actual, empirical, space and time. I shall speak mainly of space.

In the firs place such conceptions as point and instant, continuity, infinit , dimension, which are mathematical, are essentially involved in experienced space and time. They are not fiction or inventions, but represent certain features of space and time in a conceptual form. The only thing fictitiou in points and instants is to suppose that points are not also instants, and that space is an aggregate of points; whereas, being temporal, the points of space are driven by the very nature of time into connection with one another. The highly artificia conceptions of mathematical continuity and infinit are themselves conceptual representations of the given continuity and infinit of space or time.

Next, geometry (and arithmetic too) are empirical sciences. They do not, like metaphysics, ask what space and time are, but what the characters of the figure in space are, or the numbers in the number series. Nor does mathematical space differ from experienced space in being, as is sometimes said, purely conceptual. There are individual circles and parabolas in space, though they are treated, as in every science, as instances of universals. The real difference of geometry from other sciences is that it deals with the empirical forms of what is non-empirical, namely, pure space, without material or other qualities.

But mathematics also generalises. Taking concepts like dimension, given in experienced space, it proceeds, for example, to construct in thought four or more dimensional so-called "spaces", and it may go further and construct relations between entities of which our space is only an instance. But all such constructions arise out of the concepts which enter into actual space.

This leads us to the second subject of this lecture. There are two doctrines of Space and Time; the one on which we have proceeded, that they are or rather space-time is itself an entity; the other that Space and Time are relations between entities. Now relation is a vague word, and if we ask what relations in space and time are, we must answer with W. James that they are themselves spaces and times, e.g., the distance of two points is the line between them. This is implied in Newton's sentence, "Times and spaces are, as it were, the places as well of themselves as of all other things". (Note that the distinction of absolute from relational space or time is quite different from that of absolute and relative space or time.) Now on this view spatial and temporal relations are transactions within space and time between parts of space and time. The hypothesis made here, then, is that space-time is the material (not matter) or stuff or matrix in which things are formed, and that all things are special modification of space-time, eddies in the system of motions, and are, in their ultimate expression, groups of motions. With specifi complexes of motions are correlated *qualities*.

Now "entity" is the generalisation of anything as so described. Consequently it is legitimate for scientifi purposes to treat spatial and temporal and spatial relations as subsisting between such entities. But to do so does not give us the metaphysics of space and time, does not tell us what they are, but substitutes for them what is no doubt an important intellectual construction. It is not ultimate. For the entities between which such relations exist are a mere construction of thought, except for their indirect reference to the space-time in which they are generated; and so also are the relations between them.

At any rate the above hypothesis is the hypothesis which we shall proceed to test.

Lecture VI (Monday February 5th)The Categories
Identity and Diversity. Relation

All things then which are less than space-time itself are differentiations of space-time. But they possess two different sets of characters. The firs belong to all things alike; these are categorial, and are such as being or identity, relation, substance, quantity, causality. The others are empirical, the varying qualities of things; but the variations of categorial characters, such as the special shape or magnitude or number of things, are also empirical.

The categories have no special connection with the mind. The mind has categorial characters, like all other finites and the nature of them may often be seen more easily from the mind. But they are not in any sense due to the mind. They are not imputed to things by the mind; if they are not in things themselves, they are not there at all. Still less are they ways in which the mind regards things. Nor is it enough to note that, alone among characters of things, they belong *both* to minds and things. They do so because they are fundamental characters of any part of space-time as it is experienced. Finites (to disregard infinit things) are identical, causal, universal, etc., because they are bits of space-time, and therefore have all those determinations which are experienced as possessed by any space-time (a phrase I shall use for any portion of space-time). Thus they are not thoughts which are applicable to things, and to pieces of space or time among those things, but things have these characters because of their fundamental spatio-temporal character. space-time, with its categories, is thus the canvas on which the richness of empirical qualities is embroidered. This principle is to be verifie in this and the three following lectures. In investigating the categories we have two consummate guides, firs and above all Plato, and then (with precautions) Kant.

Let us begin with numerical *identity* and *diversity*, or *being* and *bot-being*. Identity is occupation of space-time (that is, of a point-instant or complex of them); diversity the occupation of some other part of space-time. This means that anything is self-identical because it is or occupies a space-time and different from what occupies any other, and this is the most elementary category. The identical is thus "related" to what is different; or identity, in Plato's language, "communicates" with relation. Being and not-being are other terms for the same categories. determinate being or existence is identity as qualifie by diversity, or the union of identity and diversity. But it is clear that identity is not the same thing as diversity, but, on the contrary, the identical is only related to the different.

Two conclusions follow. First, there is no *merely* neutral being, being for thought. All being, even that of universals, as will be explained later, is occupation of space-time. Second, the law of contradiction means that one configuratio of space-time is not the same as a separate one. The other laws of thought are also mere expressions of the fact that anything is a space-time. Hence the impossibility of showing space or time to be self-contradictory seeing that space-time is the standard of what is contradictory.

For convenience *relation* is now taken, out of its natural place. Relation arises from the continuity of space-time. That is, anything is related to something else because any space-time is continuous with other space-times. Hence all the other categories "communicate" with relation (as they do with being). Ultimately all relations are spatio-temporal, and connect their terms so as to make a continuous whole. Empirical relations, e.g., paternity, kingship, are the connections of terms which have qualities, unless they are modification of categorial relations (e.g., greater than, equal, double, etc.). When two terms are related they enter into a total situation and the relation is the spatio-temporal connections which constitute the situation. Thus the relations of king and subject are the acts of the parties to each other, and these in the end are spatio-temporal. Are relations internal or external? They are not internal in the sense in which qualities are; they are not qualities of their terms. But they are not external as separable from their terms. This would deny the continuity of the whole complex of terms as related. For anything as such is related to something else.

But, on the other hand, some relations are intrinsic to their terms and others are extrinsic to them. All relations arising out of the other categories themselves are intrinsic. For example, quantity is a category and everything must be intrinsically greater or less than or equal to anything else. But "qualitied" empirical relations are not necessarily intrinsic; e.g., fatherhood is not intrinsic to man. We have once more the contrast of the fundamental or categorial characters which all things possess and the purely empirical or qualitied ones.

If time allows it will be shown that when relations are treated as ultimately unreal, they are divested of their relational character and that the supposed unreality of spatial or temporal relations comes from separating space and time from one another. For time drives space into relation and space makes time continuous.

Lecture VII (Friday February 9th
Universality and Universals

Everything is at once particular and universal, and it is individual as a particular example of its own universal. Its particularity is its numerical identity, but its universality is its generic identity. Now a thing can be an example of a universal and contain universality because space-time is uniform, or, to put the same thing otherwise, because Space is of constant curvature. Universality means undergoing no distortion through change of place and time.

This may be verifie most easily in the case of manufactured articles like balls, which repeat each other exactly but with most profi from a singular universal. like a man's character, which is the constant plan on which all the particular moments of his history are constructed, that is, it remains within limits unaltered by change of time and place. In true generic universals, dog, c.g., the individuals follow a plan of construction from which they vary only within limits.

Universality as a category is the constancy of a spatiotemporal configuration The categorial universals are the categories. Empirical universals are plans of configuratio of space-time, to which are, of course, correlated qualities, or rather the plans of qualities.

The nature of universals as so described is best understood from the mind. Mental universals are habits or mental dispositions—one species of organic dispositions—and they have for their corresponding objects universals or concepts of external things. The existence of such habits of mind as distinct from imagination of particulars is now well verified Empirical universals then are, in general, habits of Space Time; only whereas in the finit mind these habits are specially localised, the habits of space-time are not localised, but they mean that space-time, in virtue of its constant curvature, can respond with any *sort* of particular when the conditions arise.

We may dismiss the objection that there are universals in Space and Time because Space and Time are universals in respect to particular spaces and times. The point is that there can be universals of finit things because space-time is uniform. But other objections may also be raised, and met, like those urged against the ancient forms (or ideas). At the same time it will be clear that the controversy as to whether universals are separate from particulars or in them disappears for us, because universals and particulars are made of the same stuff, namely, space-time, the particular being the specialised configuration the universal the plan of it, its law of construction. Moreover, the universals being spatio-temporal, that is, plans of movement, are not lifeless or fossilised, but eminently alive.

The relation of the universal to the particulars may be compared to that of the equation of a curve to the various curves which are got by changing the constants in the equation, (e.g., the length of the radius in circles with the same centre).

But the phrase "plan of configurat on" may mislead, for it implies two different meanings. A plan involves parts or elements arranged in a certain way. This does not make a universal a plan, but is what makes one universal different from other universals. But a plan is also the type of several copies. It is in this sense that a universal is a plan. This universality implies repetition or the possibility of it, and repetition is thus vital to universality. This is denied by the conception of what is called the "concrete universal", in which the universal is understood as a system. There are various reasons for the prevalent suspicion of repetition, but none of them have any warrant from the practice of the sciences or from philosophy. We have, in fact, in a scientifi law to distinguish in it what makes it a relation of parts from what makes it a law.

In fact, apart from repetition the universal becomes an individual. Instead of taking the equation of a circle to be the type of all circles, we take it to be the collection of points on the individual circle. But this is an individual circle and not the universal circle. The true universal of the point on the circle is "any point" on the circle. But that is not the circle itself.

Lecture VIII (Monday February 12th)
Substance and Causality

All finites being complexes of space-time, are substances, because any portion of space is temporal or is the theatre of successions; or, what is the same thing, because all succession is spread out in space. This is a fundamental character of any space-time and belongs, therefore, to the finit qualitied things which, in their simplest expression, are configuration of space-time or Motion. Every space persists and every time is extended. This is best seen in complex substances like gold or man, things which possess many qualities united. The qualities are correlated with certain motions, and these motions are contained within a certain voluminous "contour" (the word is borrowed from Mr. C. D. Broad) of space. For example, mental processes are temporal successions within mental space. The simplest substance is such a motion as light, or even uniform motion of a point in a straight line, where the spatial contour within which succession occurs is that of a point. Substantial identity or individuality (in the special sense of that word) is the repetition, within a spatial contour through a lapse of time, of the plan according to which qualitied motions are combined in the thing. What alterations or mutilations of the spatial contour may occur without destroying substantial identity, as in the lopping of a limb, is a matter which is settled by empirical experience.

The qualities of a complex substance—hard, white, sweet, etc.—do not interpenetrate. They are only supposed to do so because they are treated as the work of mind and somehow not in space and time, or otherwise regarded as abstract instead of being correlated with concrete movements. The movement of one quality is in a different place from that of another. They are stippled, as in an engraving, among each other over the space of the substance which seems to contain the qualities uniformly because of the closeness of the stippling. A substance may be described as a spatial volume of a certain contour stippled over with qualities. It will be seen that substance so conceived accounts for the unity of a thing. The interconnection of the qualities of a thing is, however, an intricate matter which follows from the general character of the relations of point-instants.

Causality. No notion has been surrounded with more mystery or controversy, the occasion for which, however, disappears when causality is taken for neither less nor more than it is. Every event is a cause of some other event, because from the empirical continuity of space-time any motion is continued into some other motion. It is indifferent whether we call a cause a substance, like a stone breaking a window, or a motion of the substance, or a substance in respect of some motion. Causation is the relation of continuity between substances in respect of certain motions. In so far as a substance exists it has relation to a different substance, and the relation of continuity between the two is causality. It follows that transeunt and immanent causality are only relatively different. Immanent causality is transeunt causality between two substances contained within a complex substance, and any two substances, like the stone and the window, may be treated as a closed whole and the transeunt causality is then immanent.

Certain propositions are true of causality which fl w from this conception: (1) Mere continuance of the same motion is not causality, nor is the cause of an effect merely the antecedent state of anything.

This splits continuity into adjacent points or instants. (2) Cause is not identical with its effect, but different from it. (3) It is prior to its effect. The supposed co-existence of a cause with its effect is either a misreading of the fact that action and reaction are simultaneous, or of the fact that a cause may continue and so be simultaneous with the proper effect of a previous part of the cause. (4) Hence, except in a logical sense, it is not true that the cause is determined by the effect as much as the effect by the cause. (5) Most important of all is to recognise that causation is a limited relation. The scientifi search for the cause of an event is for an event which is in special intimacy of continuity with it. Hence to call the whole antecedent condition of the universe the cause is to mistake the meaning of causality and also to take the whole of space-time as a cause. Causality, like other categories, applies only to parts of space-time. (6) There is no idea of power or force contained in that of cause.

When cause is understood, with proper regard for what it does not contain and what it does, the objections that have been taken to it on logical and metaphysical grounds will appear to be unsuccessful.

Lecture IX (Friday February 16th)
The One and the Many

It is not possible within my limits to discuss all the categories. I have to omit the important category of *order*, which expresses what was called before the "betweenness" of point-instants; and also the categories of *quantity*, *intensity*, *whole and part*, and *number*, which arise out of the ways in which the space and time are related to one another within a space-time. Nor can I discuss the distinctions of simplicity and complexity amongst the categories themselves. But the last and most complex of them I may observe is *Motion* itself—every finit being a motion. It may reasonably be asked whether a motion is not rather the simplest form of empirical existent. The difficult of deciding such a question (in which I follow Plato) illustrates how flui is the distinction of the *a priori* and the empirical; as is only natural, seeing that they are both determinations of the same stuff.

But there are two claimants to be considered categories which, for different reasons, must be denied their claim. The one is *Change*. Change is not a category, for there may be motions without change; and, secondly, change means the alteration of quality and is empirical. The second claimant is *quality* itself, which is not a category. We can fin no character of all things alike which can be called quality, of which different qualities are modifications in the way in which different quantities are modification of the universal quantity. What we fin is red or blue or sweet. Quality is rather a collective name for such qualities, just as colour is a collective name for red, blue, etc. Quality is, in fact, the distinctively empirical element of things, and in the next lecture we shall examine its relation to the non-empirical. This result verifie our general principle, for there is no determination of space-time which is quality, except the quality of being spatio-temporal.

The rest of this lecture will be occupied with some reflection about the categories in general and about space-time.

The categories have been described by pointing to certain empirical features of space-time. But, being ultimate, they cannot be defined and to some extent the mere description of them involves the use of ideas derived from empirical experience of finit things. This is inevitable. We approach the indefinabl as best we can. Still more palpably do we do this when we speak of space-time as infinit and continuous. Those are ultimate properties we can only accept, and our mathematical or other conceptions of them are in terms of the finite which come out of space-time.

Accordingly the categories which apply to things within space-time do not apply to space-time itself. space-time (and the same thing applies to Space and Time singly) does not exist or come into existence, for that would need a larger space-time; it is not a whole of parts, for a whole is related to another whole and the universe is not a "given whole"; it is not even substance, for a substance is related causally to other substances. These are but metaphorical phrases by which we attempt to describe the indescribable. For this reason space-time has been called by us not substance but the stuff out of which all things are made, as a coat out of cloth. But two mistakes are to be avoided. One is to describe it in negative terms, because it does not admit determination by categories, as something neither substance nor number nor space, etc. But the ultimate is the most positive of things. The second and worse mistake is to invest the universe with characters superior to those which it betrays in its creatures—to call it spaceless or timeless (eternal) in some unique sense. But the universe is itself Space and Time, and is the totality of existence and substances and the like. Space and Time are the infinit elements (attributes, in Spinozistic phrase) of the one space-time.

The world of things is a Many, in contrast to which Space is, in a metaphor, the One. How are the Many related to the One? On one view they are absorbed into it as into some superior ultimate, and are relatively to it unreal and lost in it. On our view the many change and pass, but they are not lost in the ultimate or "absolute", which is space-time, but, such as they are, they are real and retain their reality. A triangle is not unreal because of the surrounding space, nor lost in it; but, on the contrary, is sustained by it. A man is not lost in his society but fulfille by it. In the same way, the many empirical existents (whether finit or, so far as such exist, infinite are not altered by the relations into which they enter as parts of the one space-time, except so far as those relations are extrinsic or purely empirical, and that is nothing but the empirical fact of change and life and death. But even empirical characters are real, though they change. This is the consequence of the truth that things are of the stuff which is the ultimate reality in its simplest and barest expression.

Lecture X (Monday February 19th)
The Clue to Quality: Mind and Brain

Quality is not a category. It has been described hitherto merely as correlated with appropriate movements. We have now to examine this phrase, and this may most easily and clearly be done in the case of mind.

Mind is experienced (enjoyed) as an organisation of processes which possess the distinctive quality of being mind, mentality, or consciousness. But, as we have seen in Lecture II, it is also experienced as being in the same space-time as certain neural processes. Correlation ceases thus to be a satisfactory account of the matter, and we have to say that mental process, and neural process of a certain kind, are identical, or that the neuroses in question carry or possess the quality of mind or consciousness. We think of them separately because we consider the one thing firs in its relation to vital processes which are not conscious, and, secondly, in its distinctive character. The quality mentality is thus not something floate off from its basis, an adjective of it, but is a concrete determination of neural process (and ultimately of spatio-temporal process) of a certain order.

At the same time consciousness is, in relation to life, a new quality. Conscious process is also neural, but is not merely neural; on the contrary it is primarily mental. It belongs to or is identical with a peculiar constellation or complexity of neural conditions, where complexity is taken to include not only intensity but connection of one process with other processes united with it in one structure or organisation. Some neuroses, to say nothing of other vital processes, are not mental. What distinguishes the neuroses which are psychical from those which are not is locality in the nervous system, with all that that locality carries with it. Hence, though mental process is, ideally speaking, expressible without remainder in physiological terms, that conflatio has ceased to be purely physiological. We should fin ourselves directed to the physiological notice and description of it from psychology. In the same way life is not *merely* physico-chemical.

The identity of mental and neural process enables us to reject certain conceptions of the relation of mind and brain. Consciousness is not a mere adjunct to neural process, for this would mean that the neural process would be physiologically the same in the absence of consciousness, which is not true. Nor is mental process merely parallel with neural process. This implies that they are separate, and seems to suppose that mental process is in some way qualifie by its objects, as if green or red were "in" the mind. It is still possible to say that mind and brain interact, provided we do not say that a neural process causes its own mental process or the reverse.

There remains the conception of animism, that the mind is an entity distinct from the body. The metaphysical difficultie cf the conception of something neither enjoyed nor contemplated are passed over. But an examination is made of the arguments which are used to support it. These are such as that our mental process have meaning, or the facts of fusion, e.g., that we may see purple when one eye sees a red disc and the other a blue one. It is urged that in each case the conception is unnecessary.

The identity of a mental and its neural process helps to throw light on two important problems; that of the unity of mind and that of the facts of divided personality and of unconsciousness. The principle is that a mental process, being neural, is part of a larger neural structure, and that mental continuity may be lost without the loss of neural continuity. The unity of mind is, as with other substances, that of its own space-time. But there may be connection between separate mental processes which is not effected at the level of consciousness. Except for the nervous structure this would not be possible. At the same time difficultie are left which cannot at this stage be resolved, as the gaps made by sleep, though we are aware that we are the same self as before we slept. As to the second problem we may urge that mental processes may be replaced by neural ones, and these may lead again upon occasion to mental processes. The unconscious is strictly purely neural and not mental.

Thus the quality of mind means the emergence of a new constellation in what is vital; and we can use this as a clue to understand more easily that emergence of a quality from a form of existence of lower quality which can be traced throughout things. Strictly speaking, mental quality should have come at the end of this series, but the order has been varied for purposes of exposition. This subject will be taken up in the following course. It may be added to avoid misconception, that so far is this identity of mental and neural process from suggesting materialism, that it will as a matter of fact, be seen in the sequel to point in a quite different direction.

Course II

Course 1 deals with the following main subjects: (i) Space-Time, (ii) The Categories. Course 2 will deal with iii) The order of finit empirical existence, (iv) Deity.

The topics of the lectures will be: (iii) The order of qualities (e.g., primary qualities, matter, secondary qualities, life, mind); The features of finit existence arising out of space-time illustrated in the sequel from mind; Mind and Knowing; The nature of Mind and its relation to the bodily organism; The ways in which the mind apprehends space and time, the categories, and the qualities; Things, and their real appearances; Illusion and imagination; Value (a) Truth and Error, (b) Goodness and Evil, (c) Beauty and Ugliness; Freedom.

(iv) Infinit existence: Deity and God; Deity and religious sentiment; Deity and value.

Lecture I (Friday January 11th 1918)
Recapitulation, and a Formula for Space-Time
In the preceding course it was assumed as a hypothesis of method that we might treat minds as one set of things among other things in the universe, and might accordingly disregard the question whether other things depended or not upon mind. Pursuing this empirical method we discovered that Space and Time as empirically known to us are not independent of one another, but are elements in the one space-time. The hypothesis, this time one of substance and not merely of method, was then made that space-time (or motion) was the stuff of which all finit

things were made. They were complexes of space-time. This being so, it was found that the so-called categories were the characters of any bit of space-time and, for this reason, were *a priori* characters of all finite and were their *a priori* characters.

There remained the qualities of things. Quality is not a category, but is the empirical as distinguished from the *a priori* character of things. In order to understand it, we took as our clue the quality of mind or consciousness. We found that when physiological processes in certain parts of the living body, in particular of the nervous system or of the brain, attained a certain kind or degree of complexity, they possessed as a matter of fact the quality of mind. It is proposed to use this clue in order to understand the relations to one another of the qualities in the world, such as materiality, the secondary qualities (colour, etc.), life, and mind, and to show that the combination of body and mind is only the most striking instance of the universal model on which all things in the world (finite and infinites) and the whole world itself, are built.

But, for convenience in the exposition, instead of beginning with matter I shall begin with space-time itself, and indicate a formula of the relation in which Time stands to Space within space-time. But to do so I must complete the description of the clue to be got from mind, by asking how we are aware of the minds of one another. It is not enough to say that your behaviour means for me your mind, of which I am thus directly aware. For it is only my own mind I know at firs hand. The notion of a foreign mind is something extraordinarily new and mysterious. Still less, and for the same reason, can I become aware that you possess a mind by observing that you do actions like mine and concluding to your mind by analogy. There must be some special experience which assures me of your mind, and it is found in the experience of participation with you, so that I am aware of the return which is made to me by your action and not merely of your action (e.g., in the reciprocated pressure of the hands). Instances are rivalry and co-operation, the parental or filia relation, and, later, the experience of intercourse by speech. And, in general, the actions which the partners perform in such a transaction are not similar but different.

Our formula then is that in space-time as a whole or any part of it, Time performs to Space the offic of mind, or, more briefl , that Time is the mind of Space, and that any instant is the mind of its point. The point-instants, which are the "monads", know each other as we know each other. To understand how there can be infinit such minds, like the momentary minds of point-instants, included within the mind of space-time as a whole, we may avail ourselves of the analogy (already used by others, mistakenly as I believe, to explain how God's mind can embrace ours) of divided personalities, which may be included when the individual becomes normal and possesses a single mind. Instants are such isolated minds comprehended within the unity of Time. The mind of Space is the continuum of such "co-conscious" minds.

The difference of space-time from all things with qualities arises from its simplicity or ultimateness. There is no physiological body lower in order than itself of which Time can be the mind. space-time is the firs body-mind, and its mind and its body are co-extensive; but my mind is lodged only in a portion of my body.

Time is thus the animating principle of Space, which keeps the parts of Space in movement. The personificatio of Time as the [mover][a] represents not the real nature of Time, but only the transitoriness of things.

Lecture II (Monday January 14th)
The Order of Qualities

Mind, as we saw, was an "emergent" from life; in a certain portion of a living body a certain constellation of living processes, when it arose, had the quality of mind, and was therefore a mental process. The mental quality is something entirely new, and no one who only knew life could predict that such a constellation of processes would be mind. At the same time mental process, though not merely physiological process, was also physiological process, and could be so expressed without remainder. This conception of emergent qualities which arise in a portion of a body of the next lower quality may be extended over the whole of the order of empirical qualities. They form a hierarchy. A complex of processes on the level L with the distinctive quality l becomes endowed with a quality l/ and the thing which is characterised by this distinctive quality rises to the level L/. The processes with the emergent quality l/ constitute thus the soul or mind of a body which is on the level L with the distinctive quality l. Such language is, strictly speaking, metaphorical. It means actually that the emergent quality performs to its body at a lower level the offic of consciousness to the living body. But the qualities lower than consciousness are not merely lower degrees of consciousness but

---

[a] mower

different from it. Mind and body in us are accordingly only an instance of a universal pattern. This proposition has now to be verifie in detail so far as that is possible.

The qualities materiality, life (as in the plant), mind, colour and other secondary qualities, are but the more obvious and salient members of this hierarchy. There may be, and probably are, other emergents which determine a difference of level; e.g., chemical properties as contrasted with physical ones. But, in particular, there may be levels of quality lower than materiality intervening between it and qualityless space-time. The primary qualities of matter are misnamed qualities, and are nothing but empirical variations of *a priori* characters.

Matter is in this conception a form of existence which at a certain stage of the world's history emerges within space-time from merely spatio-temporal finites But what the history of the process is is just what physics is now engaged in discovering. It is a far cry from space-time to matter, and the interval is probably fille up with other empirical stages of existence. But, whatever view may be taken, materiality when it emerges and however it be define (by inertia or otherwise) is a quality emergent from a simpler determination of space-time if not from space-time itself. It is a complexity of motions with that new quality. Hence it will be seen that space-time, though not matter, is continuous with it, in the same sense as mind is continuous with life. It would seem, too, that the supposed ether which fill Space is a superfluou conception, seeing that Space is absolutely full.

The initial stages of the hierarchy are thus at present the most obscure. When we turn to the secondary qualities of matter we have to recognise (contrary to the current interpretation) that these are emergent qualities of material processes when they are of a certain complexity. Colour resides therefore in the coloured thing. The material processes which go on at the touch of light within the material body possess the emergent quality colour which is thus the soul, or a form of soul, belonging to the coloured thing. (Compare Meredith's conception of colour or Pater's.) The same account implies to the other secondary qualities. They are not the work of the mind, which would imply creation, but apprehended by the mind in things. Nor are they a joint product of the thing and the sense-organ; to raise only the smallest problem, why should they, then, be apprehended as they are in things, and not in the body?

In like manner life is the mind or soul of a material physico-chemical thing, and resides in a portion of it. It is not merely physico-chemical, for it is new, but it is also physico-chemical. Life could not be prophesied from a knowledge of physico-chemical existence, and accordingly there may be facts of life which cannot be fir t approached from the physico-chemical side. But the notion of the necessity of assuming an entelechy or unit of life, different from what is material and discontinuous with it, arises from a false antithesis of the living, or the mental to the mechanical. There is no such thing as mechanism without something corresponding to mind contained within it and animating it, no dead matter. Even bare space-time has its soul which is Time.

It is to be observed that the empirical quality of the lower level is not carried up into the emergent quality of the next level. Life is not material, and consciousness is not alive. The quality l belongs only to the body of the thing with quality l/. What is carried up into the quality of the higher level is only spatio-temporal or categorical characters.

Lecture III (Friday January 18th)
The Empirical Problems, Illustrated From Mind

Philosophy cannot account for the particular qualities of the different grades of existence, but can only note them. But it can account for the relations which subsist between them or within them as being complexes of space-time. Minds are one kind of empirical things which exhibit these relations. Some of these relations are the following:

(1) Every finit as a piece of space-time is compresent with the other finites and connected with them directly or indirectly by causal relations. When the finit is a mind this relation to other finite is that of knowing them, the cognitive relation.

(2) A finit is a substance, or volume of space-time, with internal qualitied processes occupying that volume and having a certain configuration Considered in reference to a percipient mind, the finit is a thing, with place, date, extent, and duration; secondly, has sensible characters; and thirdly, is an object of thought or conception, an instance of a universal. The thing which is mind has corresponding characters, all of them spatio-temporal, with the conscious quality; its processes have place, date, intensity, and pattern, which correspond to the place, date, intensity, and quality of the object known.

(3) A thing is affected differently by other things according to its place, date, and intrinsic receptivity (e.g., a platinum crucible is not affected by

acids which corrode glass; one thing is illuminated from the luminous side of a foreign thing and not from the dark side). Correspondingly the mind's experience of things is selective, and the mind apprehends the appearances of things.

(4) Since finite are connected within space-time any "percipient" finit may be affected by another thing, owing to the combination of that thing with something else, e.g., a stick in water; or the percipient itself may be abnormal. In relation to mind we have then, besides the real appearances or partial aspects of things, their mere appearances and their illusory appearances.

(5) The processes within a substance are in causal relation with one another. In mind this causal interrelation is enjoyed as freedom.

(6) As merely a part subsisting within space-time every finit is accommodated or adapted to the rest. In respect of minds this adaptation to other minds and the world of things is the foundation of values (truth, goodness, and beauty and their correlatives).

It would be pedantic to treat these relations in their simple or abstract character. Merely to describe them is almost impossible, except in terms which imply mind. They are best treated by illustration from mind.

Knowing. When one finit in compresence with another is a mind, the other finit is known by the mind. The mind enjoys itself and the other thing is contemplated by it, unless it is also a mind, in which case the mind has assurance of it. When the object affects the mind by direct causal action the mind has sensing of a sensum. When the mental process is initiated from the mind itself, the object is an image or idea, that is the thing is imagined. In the firs case the mental action is a movement of re-action to the object; in the second it is an anticipatory movement corresponding to the object. In perception the process is part re-action, part anticipatory, and the re-action and the anticipation may change places according to the stage in the perception. In all cases the mental process is a movement of "conation" in response to a non-mental thing, which is now sensed, now imagined or remembered. Mental action is thus on all fours with other organic and material action, except for its greater perfection, e.g., (as compared with a material thing) in making anticipatory movements. This is precisely what was declared in the Introductory lecture to be the verdict of our direct experience of the cognitive relation; but it is now exhibited as a corollary from the merely spatio-temporal character of mind, the spatio-temporal complex which has the quality of -mind or consciousness.

Various conclusions follow:

(1) The distinction of enjoyment and contemplation exists on every level where there is a lower level: e.g., matter "enjoys" itself and "contemplates" primary qualities.

(2) The mind is never an object to itself, but enjoys itself.

(3) The mind is selective, and apprehends the partial aspects of things. But the thing is the continuum of its partial aspects, which, though selected by the mind, are, unless the mind is under illusion, not in the mind but in the thing, but are not the whole of it. Thus the thing is on the same level as its aspects which are the mind's "objects", which thus are partial revelations of the real things. Being a partial occupation of the space-time volume which is the substance of the thing, the partial object is, as it were, fringed with reference to the volume as a whole and means it and its other partial revelations or objects. But it is a mistake to suppose that in apprehending an object, a thing is apprehended also which is of a different order from the objects themselves which are its aspects. Moreover, the selected aspect or object and every complete thing being parts of space-time mean also vaguely or determinately all the rest of space-time, and thus any object is apprehended as a fragment of an infinit whole.

Lecture IV (Monday January 21st)
The Nature of Mental Acts

Mental acts then are responses to things, or to certain partial aspects of things, whether the act is evoked by the present thing, or the act evokes the thing in image and brings us in this fashion into compresence with it. The word acts being understood to include passive and active processes, and conation to have a similar extension of meaning, mental acts are entirely conative, with the reservation of the place to be assigned to feeling, still the most difficul point to determine in the general analysis of mind. Cognition then is conation in so far as conation refers to the object cognised. There is no cognition other than the conation. There are conations on the one side and things cognised on the other (*cognita*). Knowing is only acting, but we call the acting knowing because we are thinking of the thing which is known. Perceiving a thing is not different from the mental act which ends in stretching out the hand to grasp it. We only think so because the response to a thing may be either practical, as in the last case, and alter the object or our relation to it; or it may be theoretical, where the practical action upon the object is suspended and switched off into speech or some other mental action, as in a train of ideas. Knowing is such action suspended in its direct practical effect.

The mental response differs with the object, so that the sensing of green differs from that of red or sweet, and perceiving from imagining. Such differences are not differences of mental quality, for mind has but the one quality of consciousness. They are spatio-temporal differences, differences in the mental movement. Two classes of differences may be distinguished; one the formal ones which distinguish sensation, perception, thinking, and the like; differences in the arrangement of the elementary mental processes; the others are the material differences, according to the quality of the object or its intensity, place, or date. What are the corresponding differences in the mental processes? To the quality of the sensum corresponds in the sensing the (enjoyed) pattern of the physiological (nervous) process, the configuratio of the re-action of the brain to a green or yellow or sweet sensum. It may be called the intrinsic extensity of the sensing to distinguish it from the extrinsic extensity, or extent of the excitement of many such processes together, as in seeing a broad red patch. This pattern, though it proceeds along anatomical lines, is a physiological one, and it is thus the "direction" of the response along these lines which distinguishes sensing of various objective qualities.

The spatio-temporal character of mental processes which corresponds to the degree or amount or intensity of the object, is at present a matter of speculation. Various views have been put forward as to the physiological basis of intensity. In one way or another it is the density of the mental response, perhaps that an intenser stimulus excites more nervous fibre of the same configuratio of response, or possibly produces a denser excitement within a nerve fibre In any case, intensity of sensing is a numerical or spatio-temporal determination.

We may revert for the moment to the cognitive relation in order to consider how in cognition the mental process is related, not to the neural process with which it is identical, but to the bodily or organic (somatic) actions in which it issues, that is to the body as distinguished from the central nervous system. The sensing of red is an enjoyment. It issues in the movement of the eyes towards the object, and this movement is apprehended through a new sensation (*kinaesthetic*). That movement is contemplated just as the colour is. The enjoyment of vision is thus the beginning of the process which ends in these bodily re-actions, afterwards contemplated. Every sensory process is accompanied by these additional sensory experiences of my body, in virtue of which I know that my body is engaged. But a recent theory, highly attractive in its simplicity, regards consciousness not, as here described, as the beginning of a motor or organic process of this sort, but holds that to be conscious of a colour is nothing more than the compresence of two things, one the colour, the other the bodily re-action to it. Consciousness is no longer a special quality of a certain order of re-action. It is found in all compresence, and, as applied to us, means nothing but the object to which we respond. If time allows an attempt will be made to examine this theory.

Lecture V (Friday February lst)
The Ways of Apprehension of Categorial and Empirical Characters

We have still to ask by what different kinds of experiencing the mind apprehends firs of all the categorial characters and primary qualities of things and then the various empirical qualities; as, for instance, it apprehends the secondary qualities by sensations of the special senses, itself in enjoyment, and other minds by assurance of their existence and sympathetic interpretation of their acts.

The space and time of things the mind apprehends by an experience which is simpler and more fundamental than sensation and anterior to it, which may be called Intuition. This follows at once from the interrelation of point-instants in space-time, which has been already compared to the apprehension minds have of each other. Any part of space-time is precisely aware in an extended sense of that term of any other. (The question of illusion is postponed.) Suppose a tract of colour *AB* to excite a tract of the brain *ab*. As merely spatio-temporal the brain centres in *ab* are in a determinate relation to the points of *AB*. But the excitement of *ab* is a conscious excitement. The tract *ab* is thus conscious *of* the tract *AB*. There is thus no need to suppose that the excitement of a brain centre has, in addition, a so-called "local sign", some fresh experience other than colour to indicate the place of the colour which is seen. The locality of the point excited suffices (It is not assumed that *ab* is in any way geometrically like *AB*.) This apprehension of place comes then through sensation of colour or touch (or other sensation) but not *by* sensation.

The same account applies to the time of objects contemplated. But it is true also of all the categorial characters of things which the mind apprehends; their substance, number, causality, etc. These are known intuitively, Moreover, the conscious affection whereby categorial characters are apprehended in things are enjoyed categorial characters in the mind. The mind enjoys its space in seeing an extent of colour; it enjoys its own substantial character in knowing a substance, and it enjoys causality in itself in apprehending causality in the external world (or as between an external thing and itself). This was, in essence, the principle used by Kant in his so-called demonstration of the Principles of the Understanding. It will be illustrated in particular by reference to the difficul case of causality. In observing the motion of the billiard ball on the push of the cue, I enjoy the causality of the mental processes of observing the two motions, although these motions are initiated outside the mind. For causality we have seen (Course I, Lecture VIII) is nothing but the continuity of two motions within one volume of space-time.

Matter, that is the quality of materiality, is apprehended in the experience of resistance, which is not only an organic experience of the strain in our living body, but also of something which resists our body (and is, therefore, a less simple experience than that of movement at our joints). The inertia of material bodies in their action upon one another, as apprehended through sight, is cognised secondarily by reference to the matter revealed in the sense of resistance which itself is mediated through touch. But it is the *materiality* of matter which resistance reveals to us, not its *reality*.

The secondary qualities are apprehended through the special sensations. They have their intrinsic extensity, which is the pattern of the movements underlying them, and is apprehended not as movements, but as colour, etc. From this intrinsic extensity we must distinguish their place, time, extent, duration, which are not sensed at all, but intuited, and are extrinsic to the sensum as sensible. Strictly speaking the sensum has as sensum only the characters of quality and, possibly, intensity. The other characters are intuited, they are apprehended through sensation, but not by it. An important consequence of this is that we do not have a separate visual extension and a separate tactual extension which are co-ordinated by further experience; but we have one extension which is intuited, in one case by the help of sight, in the other by the help of touch, and within this one extent its colour and its touch or pressure are co-ordinated.

Life is apprehended in ourselves by the organic and motor sensations; in other words it is living processes which are the objects of these acts of sensing. Life in us is not enjoyed, but contemplated, and therefore we can transfer the character thus revealed to foreign living things which we apprehend by our special senses only as groups of movement of a certain kind like our own. This process of transference which we saw was not possible in apprehending foreign mind, for mind we only know directly by enjoyment, is possible in life, which is contemplated.

The apprehension of mind in ourselves and others needs no further remark. The order in which all these forms of apprehension are developed in the mind is not necessarily the same as the order in which the qualities apprehended are developed in the world's history. Thus life is later than matter and its secondary qualities. But organic sensations are more primitive in the mind than the special sensations. Experience of the bodily life of the self is of more fundamental importance for the self than experience of external things.

Lecture VI (Monday February 4th)
Appearances and Illusions

A thing is the synthesis of its appearances. But the synthesis is in no sense the work of the mind. The appearances are selected by the mind, but are already synthesised within the volume of space-time of the thing. But repeated experience of things enables us to distinguish its appearances into three sorts, its real appearances, its mere appearances, and illusions or illusory experiences. The two latter sorts are rejected from the spatio-temporal contour of the thing, the one set or mere appearances because they are appearances not of the thing by itself but belong to the thing in conjunction with some other thing; the illusions because in them the mind intrudes its defects or prejudices and imports into the object an element which does not belong to it. The varying appearances of things, even the real appearances, are so often taken to mean that secondary qualities are the work of the mind that it is important to discuss all the classes of appearances, though it is often debateable to which class an appearance belongs. But one thing is clear that secondary qualities are no more the work of the mind than primary ones. For there is the same variability in these, and the spatial and temporal characters of things appear sometimes as real, sometimes as mere appearances, sometimes as illusions.

The real appearances of a thing belong to the thing and their variation is due to the selectiveness of the mind. Thus the heat of a fir varies in intensity with the distance of the observer, according to a certain law; when he is further off he selects a smaller part of the total intensity of the heat in the thing. What the qualities of the thing really are is determined by thought on the basis of this experience, and by the help of measuring instruments, the use of which implies thinking and not mere sensation.

Mere appearances are illustrated by the stick which looks bent in water, or the change of pitch in the engine-whistle as it approaches or recedes. Such appearances belong really not to the thing itself, but to the thing along with its surroundings.

The objects of intuition, the primary qualities of things, are subject to similar variations. Real intuitive appearances are such as perspectives; as, for example, the elliptic appearance of the penny seen obliquely. It may be shown that these objects are selected from the reality under the conditions in which it is apprehended, namely, through colour-vision. An instance of mere appearances in primary qualities is the displacement of the position of an object when seen in a mirror. The appearance belongs to the thing taken together with the mirror, and again under the conditions of vision.

These conditions explain how intuitional appearance is possible. We have intuitions not by, but only through, sensations. But the senses are fitte to apprehend not place or extent, but their proper objects, colour, etc. Were the parts of space-time conscious we should have perfect knowledge of every part of space and time. In the extended and metaphorical sense of knowledge this is what the point-instant has. The monad or point-instant is your natural mathematician. What the mathematician discovers by reflectio it knows intuitively. But intuition in us is evoked only through sense, and it suffers by the disabilities of sensation. Touch is less exposed to error than the other senses, but it, too, leads us astray as to primary qualities. Our senses thus cheat us twice over, once as to sensible experience and indirectly as to intuitional experience.

Illusory appearances on the other hand imply the intervention of the mind. (E.g., the stick bent in water is not an illusion unless the stick is itself believed to be bent.) It is misperception due to what may loosely be called imagination. Correspondingly, all imagination is to some extent illusory. But the illusory appearance is not mental. On the contrary, it is contemplated and claims to be real. Moreover, not only is it objective but all its parts are appearances of the real world. When I see the grey paper green on a red ground I am merely referring the real element red to its wrong place. The world of illusion is the same world as the world of true perception but seen squintingly, so that a part of it which does not belong to the thing seen is referred to that thing. This wrong reference, not the object itself misplaced, is the work of the mind For the element wrongly referred is that which corresponds to the disturbing mental condition.

Illusion, therefore, is related not only to imagination pure and simple, but to art, and leads us on to values. The illusory appearance is an undesigned work of art, and art in its turn involves illusion. Constructive imagination is another illustration of how the mind's own action imports into the object contemplated an arrangement and meaning corresponding to the mental process itself.

Lecture VII (Friday February 8th)
Values: Truth and Error

The characters of objects described hitherto belong to them as distinct from the minds which know them. But objects acquire qualities from their relation to the mind in so far as it possesses these objects. These are the tertiary qualities or values: truth, goodness, beauty, with their corresponding opposites. They arise from the spatio-temporal fact that minds are adapted to reality and are not isolated. In this adaptation minds come primarily into relations of competition with one another—through their objects, for minds only exist so far as they have objects. From this competition arises a collective or standard mind; that is certain minds are in agreement or communion with one another and exclude the rest. This is expressed in judgments of value. In relation to the mind which has or possesses them, objects have the added qualities of truth or error, etc., and the mind is in the condition of appreciation. Thus a pure red has its intrinsic secondary quality of redness independently of the mind, and causes a certain pleasure. But in its relation to the mind, it pleases after a different fashion, and is beautiful to the standard mind and ugly to the others.

The tertiary qualities are thus superadded to the intrinsic qualities of things, and belong to an amalgamation of the thing and the apprehending mind. They are thus human creations.

But they are not the less real. The thing is real, the mind is real, and the combination of mind and thing in which the mind possesses the thing and the thing is possessed by mind is real. But the truth or beauty of the object exists only in the combination. What idealism asserts of every

object, that it exists only in relation to the mind, is true of the tertiary
qualities, but untrue of the secondary ones. When colour is alleged to
be the work of the mind, we have the paradox that the mind sees a set
of vibrations not as vibrations, but as colour. But in seeing the colour
as beautiful, the colour is seen as colour and the beauty is super-added
from its relation to the mind, in virtue of which it pleases after a certain
fashion (or aesthetically).

But though values are human, they are not exceptional. There are
sub-human "values" arising out of adaptation. This is the meaning of
Darwinism, which gives the natural history of values in the living world.
That valuation in this extended sense goes downwards through the whole
scale is at present only a hypothesis.

Truth and Error. The distinction of the different values arises from
the character of the relation of mind and object in the reality which is
made up of both. In truth the mind follows reality. Truth consists of
propositions or facts in the real world as possessed by minds which
know them. Accordingly the reality is neither true nor false, but is
reality, that is, it occupies space-time in some configuratio or other.
But truth and error are determined primarily by the reality, that is by
objects themselves, and the mind follows in their wake. In goodness, we
shall see, the good objects follow in the wake of the minds which will
them.

Accordingly when we ask what truth is we cannot say it is the
correspondence of our beliefs to reality, for reality is only known to us
by beliefs, or what is the same thing all our beliefs claim to be reality.
Truth consists in the coherence of propositions; and this coherence is
determined by the objects themselves. Error is an incoherent belief, in
the sense that the erroneous proposition is incompatible with reality, and
shows itself to be so when tested by experiment. Thus it is an error that
fishe can live out of water, because when taken out of water a fis dies.
Truth is thus coherence amongst our judgments as entertained by us and
error incoherence, But reality is never incoherent (for incoherence is not
the same thing as the real opposition of forces, as when a block is pulled
two different ways), and therefore strictly speaking not coherent either.

Error is the reality as it is possessed by a mind which is not
standardised. It implies the intrusion of the personal peculiarities
of the mind into its judgments. But while error, like truth, is a creation
of mind, its object is still reality which is the same reality as is cognised

in truth but is misplaced in its connections. The mind in error sees the same reality as the true mind, but squints at it.

For simplicity it has been assumed that propositions are concerned with external reality or are contemplated. But there are also enjoyed propositions (propositions concerned with mind), and these in like manner may be true or false.

Lecture VIII (Monday February 11th)
Values: Goodness and Beauty

The moral values of *goodness and evil* are more obviously dependent on mind. For whereas the coherence among minds which is truth follows and is determined by the coherence amongst the objects of knowledge, it is primarily the coherence amongst wills which determines what objects are good. The objects of will (I omit for shortness willed enjoyments) are likewise propositions or connections of fact, e.g., so much wine is drunk, this life is destroyed. But what makes such facts good or bad is their accordance or discordance with the wills of persons. Accordingly, we attach moral goodness to the characters of agents, and we call external facts good in so far as they constitute the satisfactions of persons. Such goods are the moral institutions. The test of goodness is the coherence among the agents who maintain these institutions by their wills. The system of goods or the good is thus that into which human beings in society settle down in the attempt to adapt themselves to one another, always in relation to the external world which is the condition and the object of their willing. Goodness represents thus the solution of a problem in human nature in society. Moral laws are the principles of conciliation of such adapted condition. Evil accordingly is the will (or its object) which is incompatible with that solution. But, as with error, moral evil deals with precisely the same human nature and external world as goodness but misplaces the elements. It is moral error.

How closely truth and goodness run parallel is best understood by bearing in mind that speculation is only a form of practice, in which the practical issue is suspended.

It follows from the above (1) that both truth and goodness belong to mind or things only as partners in a union of the two; (2) that there are no degrees of truth or goodness, but only degrees in their perfection, that is the range of elements they harmonise.

In the aesthetic values of beauty and ugliness, the connection of mind and its object is closer than in either of the two other kinds of value.

In the latter, the mind and its object are relatively detached from each other. But in beauty they are organic to each other and part of the object is supplied from the mind itself. Hence, in comparison with a perception the aesthetic object contains illusion. For while the elements the mind supplies in a correct perception are actually in the thing perceived, the statue we see animated with life is not really alive. This applies to all expressiveness in art (which means not the importation of human sentiment but the expressiveness appropriate to the thing itself); and it is true of natural beauty as well. On the other hand, in comparison with illusion the aesthetic object is not illusory but a new reality and is real in the aesthetic combination of things and mind.

Beauty means in the object coherence amongst its various elements, some perceived and some imported by imagination. But it pleases the mind in a certain fashion, which also means coherence, not merely amongst the acts of perceiving and imagining in the individual (compare Kant's account of aesthetic judgment) but what is more important, coherence amongst the persons who appreciate beauty and are standard individuals. They agree in judging they see the block of marble to be alive, etc. Hence the disinterestedness of the aesthetic pleasure.

The relations of the values to one another is intricate. Each from its own point of view includes the other two, which for it are technical. Thus beauty requires knowledge and moral devotion to the work of production or appreciation. From the practical point of view all values are included amongst moral values. But for philosophy it is truth which is pre-eminent. For truth is the possession by minds of reality, and the values are new realities arising from the combination of mind and its objects and take their place in the whole system of realities.

Time does not permit the discussion of the last of the empirical problems, which arise from the spatio-temporal nature of things, that of freedom. But it is not difficul to see that the sense of freedom is the enjoyment of causal determination, or freedom is such determination as it is enjoyed and not contemplated. Consequently, it arises wherever the distinction of enjoyment and contemplation exists and that is on every level of existence (except the purely spatio-temporal one). Man is not alone in being free, but only in the reflect ve consciousness of it. Freedom is "spread through the world".

Thus all the main features of mind (even the existence of value) are seen to be special cases of universal features of things. There is only one pattern on which things are built and the mind is the conspicuous instance of it in the case where the spatio-temporal complex has the quality of consciousness. On this it is that the affinit which man in certain moods feels with all things is grounded.

Lecture IX (Friday February 15th)
Deity and God

For religion God must be define as the object of worship; for philosophy as the being which possesses deity (or the beings so qualified if there should prove to be many such). Without the experience given in the religious sentiment itself, or suggested in philosophy from the data of experience, God is a meaningless conception. We know what religious sentiment is, and God is that upon which it is directed. Is there any specifi quality deity which accords with the rest of our philosophical experience? If so, we can then ask what is the being which possesses it, and whether this being coincides with the object of worship?

We have been dealing hitherto with the hierarchy of the empirical qualities of finites They are evolved in time and by time, and each new quality arises from a level of existence distinguished by the preceding quality. Mind is the last quality we know in the series. But mind is itself the birth of time and time which is real and infinit does not stop with mind.

The next higher empirical quality in the order, a quality which the world is engaged in evolving, is deity. The universe as containing Time for one of its elements and having produced mind is pregnant with the next higher quality. What that quality is we cannot know, we should firs have to become divine. It may be represented by analogy as the "colour" or the "mind" of the whole universe. This conception of deity is perfectly general. On any level of existence of the world deity is the quality looming in front. To the material thing with secondary qualities, it is what turned out to be life, to the merely living thing it is what turned out to be mind. Though we cannot know by acquaintance what deity is, it is at least not spirit or mind. That would be like saying that mind was only life or life only physico-chemical process.

Such being deity, God is the universe as possessing deity. Of such a being, the world is the body and deity the mind. We can best represent his nature by thinking firs of a finit deity and then making the necessary corrections in the picture. All the empirical finite within space-time are thus for deity what organic sensa are for mind. A portion of the conscious finite (not necessarily human minds) becomes so complex as to have the quality of deity, just as our mind is a portion of the physiological processes which is set apart for possessing consciousness. Moreover as our brains or minds represent physiologically the whole of our body so God's deity represents the whole infinit world of space-time with all its qualities as far as mind, and is thus lodged in an infinit part of God's body. Thus God is infinit both in body and in deity, though his deity is only a part of the universe. It is this which distinguishes him from empirical finites

But the God so described as possessing deity is an ideal and this is the paradox of the conception of God. For when the quality of deity is actually attained in the empirical development of the world in Time, instead of the one infinit being we should have many finit beings with the divine quality, or finit gods (these, are the angels), beyond whom a new empirical quality would loom, which would be for them deity (that is would be for them what deity is for us). God as the world possessing deity is thus never actual, though his body which is space-time is actual. But God exists in so far as the world tends towards the birth of deity, or is in travail with deity.

Both theism and pantheism are implied in this conception, but in different senses. God's deity transcends all finite in the universe, and though contained with them in the universe is above and beyond them. Since it is deity or divinity which distinguishes him, the conception is so far theistic and predominantly so. But God's body is the whole universe of space-time and what it contains, as animated by his deity, and so far as his body is concerned the conception is one of pantheism. As deity he transcends and is outside the region of all finites as body he is immanent because he is identical with space-time with all the empirical qualities emergent within it.

The question may be asked why not identify God with space-time itself? The answer is twofold. It would neglect the empirical qualities. The universe may be expressed without remainder in terms of space and time, but it is not merely spatio-temporal. It is matter, and life, and mind, and goes on to deity. Secondly, space-time could not be or at least is not the object of worship. But the religious sentiment is a fact of experience which philosophy cannot neglect any more than other facts. We have to ask how far the metaphysical conception of a world big with deity satisfie that sentiment.

Lecture X (Monday February 18th)
Deity, Religious Sentiment, and Values

The religious sentiment, whatever the sources from which it is fed, is a feeling as distinctive and as natural as appetite or love, and directed like them upon its appropriate object, something beyond and higher than ourselves. In its highest form, its object is the universe as animated by deity and it is our outgoing towards this object. Our religious consciousness is our response to the world as a whole with this higher quality of deity. But while the other passions both arise in us periodically of themselves and are stimulated by the sight of their objects, God so far as he exists is a perpetual presence and the religious feeling is evoked in us in times of sensitiveness by the play of the world upon us. Hence religion appears, as described by W. James after its extreme or less normal manifestations, as an uprush of feeling from the depths of our personality; and it is most easily understood by comparison with such simple feelings as we, or some of us, experience from the varying weather or the electrical state of the atmosphere. Thus the religious object is no mere imagination but a reality—the world tending to deity—which actually operates upon our body and mind and evokes religious sentiment, which sentiment issues as other passions do in its appropriate external gestures, those of prayer and praise.

The philosophical conception of God agrees with the characters demanded of God by the religious sentiment. These are (1) that God is a being greater than man, (2) is of a quality wholly different from man, a belief concealed under the imaginative and inadequate conceptions of his omnipotence, omniscience, providence, as if he were merely a superior man; (3) the most important of all, his responsiveness to man, and in two senses: that God supports man's weakness and sustains man by his love, as a father; secondly, that we trust and obey him because he is worthy of our trust, rendering to him a dignifie obedience. For God's deity is the outcome of a process in which we are participants, our efforts in part determine what his deity shall be, and we matter to him as he matters to us.

But God's deity is an empirical character as much as consciousness or life and is lodged in only a portion of the universe, though an infinit portion. Hence God is in no sense timeless or out of Space. Nor is he in the strict sense a creator of the universe. God's body is the universe itself, and is creative since all things arise within it through the operation of time. But God is the universe as possessing deity; and deity, which is his distinctive character, is itself created and the outcome of Time. His deity is the realisation of the "prophetic soul" of the world.

More difficul is the relation of deity to the values. Religion has been described as the conservation of value. But in fact religion is a distinctive feeling, though some persons may lack it, as some are colour-blind; and it is altogether different from any appreciation of value. Its relation to the values and, in particular, to goodness is of the closest, and God is most readily and fruitfully approached through morality. For deity is an emergent from mind, and the sense of it invests the moral values with its own colour, so that goodness becomes obedience to God, and evil sinfulness. But it is a new empirical quality distinct from value, no mere enlargement and refinemen of goodness and the sense of it no mere enthusiasm for such an ideal of conduct; and, in like manner, no mere enlargement of what is beautiful or sublime or true.

On the other hand, while deity is something distinct from value, it is true that all value is conserved in God. Deity is on the side of goodness, truth, and beauty. For these are the manifestations of mind which prevail against the unvalues (evil, error, and ugliness), and the new quality of deity is determined along that line. Thus deity is on the side of value, just as life belongs to the bodily parts which remain and function while the other parts die. But God's body contains all things, and is unlike in this respect the finit living body. The bodily excrement is still contained within the universal body. Thus deity is neither good nor evil but divine. But God contains in his body all evil as well as good, and the evil is material within God's body which is used up for creating deity, as grass grows from ingredients in the soil which are no longer alive. Evil is therefore real, but though turned to the purposes of deity is not as such on the line on which the new quality of deity is created.

Our apprehension of another person's mind is one of assurance or faith. Our apprehension of deity is also one of faith. But the faith is not based on the same experience, and it has wider and deeper foundations. For the quality of deity is nothing more than a further instance of the nisus of the world towards fresh qualities, and deity is rooted in the whole of reality, not merely like the mind of another person rooted in a finit body. And as we believe in another's mind through intercourse with it, so we believe in God through the intercourse we have with him in religion. This sentiment is confirme speculatively by the recognition of God as the infinit universe possessing deity.

Appendix 4
Lectures on Logic 1948

I

General Line which this course will follow: Defence of the four forms—A, E, I, O. (Every proposition has two terms, subject and predicate; two possible qualities—affirmat ve and negative copula; two possible quantities—universal and particular.) Defence of view that these cover all issues—these must be the ways in which issues can be put (though some statements may present more than one issue, still it is only issues in these forms that can be presented). Consideration of this view will involve the raising of important questions on logic as the theory of reality.

The two questions dominating the theory of the (four) forms are: (i) contradiction; (ii) implication. (Necessity of seeing, with regard to any significan assertion, what it denies and how it can be denied, what it implies and how it can be proved or inferred. Any significan assertion—any possible form—must be capable of taking its place in an argument.) According to the traditional view (the doctrine of the four forms) the proposition is analysable into subject, predicate, copula (affirmat ve or negative) and sign of quantity (universal or particular). This analysis (this formal presentation) of the proposition is based on the fact that the proposition must be an issue—something about which people can disagree, something which can be taken to be true or taken to be false. And the firs point to be made is that even disagreement implies a measure of agreement—that in order to disagree people must be disagreeing about the same thing: they must have what we may call a point of reference—and that gives us the notion of the subject of a proposition—a place to which one can go in order to see whether the proposition is true or false; and it is in terms of that that I say that the subject of the proposition has the function of location or placing. And it should be understood that in any given dispute it is not necessary that the disputants should be able to go there and then to the subject—there might be physical or social conditions preventing their doing so— but the subject must be something to which someone can go at some time, or else the dispute would not be about anything at all—there would not be a real issue but, at most, a form of words—or perhaps we could simply say of noises, because when we speak of a noise as a word it is because it directs attention to a specifi thing.

And then in order that there may be an issue (a disagreement) there must also be a point of disagreement, there must be something in respect of which people are disputing about the subject, and that gives us the notion of the predicate, of that which in relation to the subject or point of reference is in dispute; and further we can express this dispute by saying that it is a question of asserting or denying the predicate of the subject, of the predicate's being applicable or not applicable to the subject—and so we arrive at the next two points: the function of the predicate is description or characterisation, and the function of the copula as distinguishing positive (or affirmat ve) and negative characterisation. And thus we have our issue so far specifie as whether X is or is not Y (X being the subject and Y being the predicate). It would not greatly matter, as regards the function of the two terms, whether we say that X locates Y and Y describes or characterises X or that X locates the situation or fact which Y describes. In any case we have the two distinct terms with their two distinct functions, and it is a criticism of certain types of theory of the proposition that they confuse or ignore this distinction.

The important point about the copula is that it is always part of the verb "to be", and the point about this is that the sole function of the copula is to mark the distinction between assertion and denial—in other words, that it is part of the form of the proposition: and if the verb in an ordinary sentence is not part of the verb "to be", then it combines two meanings, one of which is the simple copula and the other of which is part of one of the terms—part of the material of the assertion. Thus if it is said that X sits in a chair, then logically we render that as X is sitting in a chair, in this way making it quite clear what the issue is—what it is that is being asserted (and could be denied) about X. (We have dealt above with the question of quality.)

Now we approach the question of quantity in this way (still on the basis of the treatment of the proposition as an issue) that, while in a given proposition there are the two distinct terms with their two distinct functions, there is no division of terms into the two classes of subjects and predicates, but any term can have either function—anything that can locate can describe and vice versa (anything that can locate can be located and vice versa; anything that can describe can be described and vice versa). And you can see, in terms of the language of agreement and disagreement, that, though we can call the predicate the point of disagreement, there must be a certain agreement in the case if there is to be a dispute, that just as the disputants must be talking about the same subject so it must be the same thing that is being asserted and denied about the subject—that, while there is dispute about whether the predicate is there or not, there must be agreement about what it is that is the subject of dispute. That means that every point of disagreement can be a point of agreement, i.e., every predicate can be a subject.

But likewise every subject can be a predicate: though the function of the subject is location or placing, the subject in a proposition is not a mere place (something which could be designated simply by an expression like "here") but is something concrete or positive, in other words is of a certain character, in other words, could be used as predicate or description. And that means that both terms in a proposition are general or descriptive terms—that while in the formula X is Y we have indicated one place where Y is to be found, viz., X, and have not indicated any place where X is to be found (any subject of which X is a predicate), we take X as well as Y as capable of being located, and in so far as it is a general description (in so far as it has meaning) we have to take it as capable of occupying various places, or having various instances, and in fact I would argue that any term always does have various instances—a point I shall consider with reference to the singular proposition. But firs of all we have to take every term as potentially plural, and that is why we always use plurals in our propositions—instead of using a simple location formula "Where X is, Y is" we write "All X are Y" (XaY).

This consideration of potential or implicit plurality arising from the consideration of all terms as descriptive has led us to the consideration of quantity as well as quality of propositions. But now, coming back to the treatment of a proposition as an issue, if we take X is Y as Where X is, Y is and that as XaY and take X is not Y as Where X is, Y is not, and that as XeY, we see that the two universal propositions A and E do not defin a single issue—that while they cannot both be true, they can both be false (that the one is not the simple denial of the other); and that in order to get that simple denial of the universal proposition (something whose falsity or truth is equivalent to the truth or falsity of the universal) we have to introduce the particular propositions I and O—so that E and I state one issue, and A and O state another issue (viz., in the latter case, it is true and it is false that wherever X is, Y is: XaY or XoY)—and these two issues are confused with one another if we simply set E against A.

Now these four forms have been arrived at by a quite general argument—an argument concerning the form which a proposition must take if it is to be an issue—and thus, as far as the argument is sound, it establishes that these are the four forms of what can be true or false—what can be asserted or denied, and what can function in an argument, i.e., can imply or be implied.

II

General argument offered for the four forms (from the nature of an issue). If this argument is sound, all alternative forms (in speech or recognised by certain logicians) must be reduced to the four forms in order that the issue they raise may be made definite The fina point—by which we added the distinction of quantity (universal and particular) to the distinction of quality (affirmat ve and negative) and the distinction of the two terms (subject and predicate)—was that any term can both locate and characterise, is not a mere thing or a mere character but is a sort of thing. The question arises of the relation of the view that all terms have generality (and may be used as predicates) to the question of singulars.

A singular proposition is taken to be one in which the subject is a particular thing or "individual" (represented by a proper name), and the question is how this can have generality—and how the logician is to be justifie in his treatment of singulars as universals (e.g., "Socrates is a man" as an A proposition). Now it seems fairly easy to take X is Y (as the traditional logician does) as an A proposition—viz., by saying that X is a class with only one member and that the whole of the class (even if there is only one) is Y or, what is equivalent, that no member of the class is Y. It is still easier on my location formula; just as "All men are mortal" is treated as meaning "Where there is a man, there is a mortal" or "Where humanity is, mortality is", so "Socrates is a man" can be taken as "Where Socrates is, humanity is" (where in each case meaning wherever).

It would seem that, on the above views, we should treat the singular negative proposition in the same manner, viz., as a universal proposition: e.g., "Socrates is not covetous" could be explained as meaning "Where Socrates is, covetousness is not" (or where Socrates is present, covetousness is absent) and that would be an E proposition. But our singulars seem thus to give us only universal propositions (A and E) and make no provision for particulars (I and O); and this would mean, in terms of our previous argument, that you could not state a clear and single issue by means of singulars—or that a singular had no definit contradictory, which would mean that it was not a real issue. Thus "Socrates is not a man", interpreted in the same manner as the other examples, would be an E proposition and would not be the contradictory but the contrary of "Socrates is a man", which would mean that while both propositions could not be true they could both be false. But that is not something we should ordinarily admit; rather we should think that "Socrates is a man" and "Socrates is not a man" indicate a clear and single issue, that, while one of them must be false, also one of them must be true.

To clear up this question of opposition among singulars, we have to go into the question of the singular term; and the possibility of a more exact quantificatio is already suggested by the use of the formula "Where X is, Y is", because it would be understood in that connection that X might be in many different places, that there might be many different "instances of X"; but, however many there were, they would all by Y. Now what could we mean by saying that there could be many instances of Socrates? The whole point of our use of the name seems to be that there is only one Socrates; for while there might be (and were) a number of people called Socrates, that is no more logically significan than that there are many different sorts of thing called "bill" (e.g., an account, a bird's beak, an old-fashioned weapon), for that merely means that a number of different terms have the same sound (and the same spelling) used to signify them. When we ask in what sense there can be many instances of Socrates, we mean instances of the Socrates who was the teacher or inspirer of Plato and was condemned to death in 399B.C.

Now one thing that would naturally be meant by "an instance of Socrates" (cf. an instance of man or humanity) is a subject of which Socrates is a predicate. And logicians (like Mill) who believe in the singular or "individual" argue that an individual (that which would be designated by a proper name) cannot be used as a predicate but only as a subject. But, if there were any term which could not be used as a predicate, we could not understand or attach any significanc to it. If the term Socrates had no generality but were a mere label, we could not, as the phrase goes, recognise Socrates; we do so only because we know him as a being of a certain kind, as having "the Socratic character". And if to recognise Socrates is to recognise the Socratic character then clearly we have something that can be a predicate (cf. That is Socrates), that can and does characterise. (We say, then, "This is an occurrence of the Socratic character".)

The next point is that there are a multitude of occurrences of this Socratic character—not in the sense that there are other people resembling Socrates but in the sense that the description applies to Socrates at various stages of his life, so that recognising Socrates is recognising the recurrence of a certain character, just as recognising a human being (saying "This is a man" or "This is human") is recognising the recurrence of the human character, though not necessarily in what we call "the same man". On that understanding the term Socrates has both intension and extension (or connotation and denotation), i.e., it has both predicates and subjects, and so the question of quantity (or the distinction between universal and particular) is one that could arise, and is often raised in a popular way, viz., by the use of adverbs, by an apparent modificatio of the copula, though in strict form it would be the variation in quantity—i.e., the distinction is popularly made by the use of the adverbs "always" and "sometimes", so that the contradictory of "Socrates is always a man" would not be "Socrates is never a man" but "Socrates is sometimes not a man". The strict logical form of the contradictories will still be A and O (SaH and SoH: All Socratic are human and Some Socratic are not human—where "Socratic" = beings[1] of the Socratic character), and that relation of contradiction would be quite distinct from the relation of contrareity between the two universal propositions (A and E; always and never). (People might say that humanity could not be a variable, and particularly an alternating, character—like sleeping and waking; that any being was either always a man or never a man. However, that does not affect the formal point (that "always-never" represents contrareity, not contradiction); and we can see that there are characters which Socrates sometimes has and sometimes has not, so that we can get actual cases of the falsity of both universals; it is still true that in cases like the one mentioned (as in any other case) the two universals are contraries and

---

[1] [JA] It could possibly be held that the most natural thing to mean by "Socratic" is Socratic activities or activities of the Socratic character. There is certainly a whole class of such activities (things Socrates has done)—and different members of this class could be concurrent—Socrates could be doing A and doing B at the same time, without either A characterising B nor B characterising A. That is to say that, if we take the history of Socrates as supplying us with different instances of the term "Socratic", we do not have to take one such instance as comprising "all that Socrates is doing at a given time".

not contradictories—even if in empirical fact there are not beings who are "occasionally human and occasionally not": these are, of course, in some metaphorical senses of "human".)

One reason why we do not put such statements in strict form, why we make an exception of the singulars even at the risk of confusion about opposition or the singleness of issues, is the real difference between the members of the class Socrates (or beings of the Socratic character)—viz., the former form one continuous series or history ("the life of Socrates") whereas the latter form a great number of distinct series or lives; and it may be argued that, while it is logically important to recognise the similarity between two such classes of occurrence (Socratic and human), it is equally so to recognise the difference between them—recognise, it may be said, that what we fin in the class men is a plurality of individuals like Socrates. However, it must be answered that however important historical continuity may be (such continuity as we fin in the life of Socrates) it is logically impossible to recognise a pure individual, to know anything except as a certain kind or sort of thing, and so, with reference to what we call an individual, we do not get away from plurality or from distinctions of quantity (universal and particular) and we do not get away from "convertibility", the capacity of any term to be a subject of predicates and a predicate of subjects.

(I do not intend to give many references; I'll criticise the views of "certain logicians" regarding the import of the proposition, etc., but I won't give precise quotations. I'll develop, in relation to such views, what seems to me the true theory of the proposition—of the four fundamental forms, A, E, I, O. Anyone who likes can read logical works in conjunction with the course; e.g., Keynes, Formal Logic, on the place of existence in the significanc of the proposition. Some reference may be made to Bosanquet, *Logic*.[2] But it will be mainly a direct argument on the leading questions of propositional theory.)

III

"This is Socrates". Some logicians deny that this is predication, say that it is the is of identity (and is distinct from other is-es). (We should have to say "This is identical with Socrates", i.e., to return to ordinary predication, in order to make our meaning clear.) The point being that, even if you believe in the ambiguity of "is" (the ambiguous

---

[2] Bernard Bosanquet, *Logic: or the Morphology of Knowledge*. Oxford: Clarendon Press, 1911. Two Volumes.

copula), you still have to use it (to use "is") unambiguously in order to assert anything about it (the ambiguous copula). (It is) the only way we can regard the copula as part of the form instead of part of the material—viz., unambiguously (as unambiguous). (The points of distinction of "one" copula from "another" can only be material.) This non-ambiguity is inseparable from the theory of the proposition as a yes-or-no question—this theory showing how the functions of subject and predicate are to be distinguished. And this sort of consideration would apply to any other sense of "is" (other, that is, than "yes or no")—you would have to get what was not formal into the terms and have an unambiguous copula.

Here we may consider the question of "existence"—which is one sense of "is". The four forms are often reduced to assertions of existence and non-existence—particular propositions being assertions of existence and universal propositions assertions of non-existence.

XaY—$X\overline{Y}$ don't exist
XeY—XY don't exist
XiY—XY exist
XoY—$X\overline{Y}$ exist

And this is connected with the doctrine of the import of the proposition held by Keynes, viz., that particular propositions assert the existence of their subject, whereas universal propositions don't assert the existence of their subject: so that if one has a non-existent (term?) X, one can say both $X\overline{Y}$ do not exist and XY do not exist: so that where you have a non-existent term X, the two universal propositions, XaY and XeY (and equally XaZ and XeZ—the pair of universals with subject X and any term as predicate) would both be true.

Now that is opposed to the view I take of the logical term and of the import of the proposition: I would argue that in asserting any X-Y proposition we assume the existence of X, Y, and their opposites: we assume the validity of the ordinary operations of obversion, conversion and subalternation, the last not being valid on the Keynes' view, for if we say A ∴ I (XaY ∴ XiY) we assert in the conclusion the existence of X which was not asserted in the premise. And the point seems to me to be a quite simple one, viz., that the universal proposition on the other view (other than mine) would be quite unintelligible—that if there is no point of reference, no place to which we could go to consider the truth or falsity of the assertion, then the assertion can convey nothing to us—we could not say anything about its truth or falsity—in other words, it is not really an assertion but just a group of words or symbols. Every term (and its opposite) exists: each refers to a set of places, distinguished from another set of places: each is a means of indication and a means of distinction.

We sometimes express a doubt as to whether something (e.g., God) exists or not. In that case we have some implicit definitio of the term (e.g., "infinit mind"—of God) and the issue is whether some minds are infinit (where the subject is a real point of reference). When people disagree about whether XiY or XeY, those who believe XiY will (or, at least, may) make assertions of the form XYaZ; but those who believe XeY will say that XYaZ gives us no point of reference (and so is not really a proposition) and will take the argument back to the point of reference X (or Y). There would be no need for this reference back if the person who believes GaZ could take us to G (or XY): could point it out. Of course, a person may put up XiY as a supposition but, if the proposition is never established, it is not established that XYaZ has any meaning (is a proposition).

Coming back to the existence-nonexistence interpretation—we see firs of all that the same relations of contradiction are supposed to hold, i.e., that we have the same mechanism of assertion and denial as before; and thus the question is still whether something can or cannot be said about a certain subject, and that brings us back to our original copula, with the reduction of the number of predicates of our assertions to one—the question whether XY (are or are not) existent. But it only leads to confusion to put the issue in this way, because what we are being asked to do here (what we are said to do in making an assertion) is to distinguish between the existent and the non-existent—a thing we cannot do because there are not any non-existent to distinguish from the existent—because we cannot say that there are two classes of things, those that exist and those that do not exist—i.e., having brought these forms back to the predicative form, we have that objection to make to the constant predicate. But we can equally object to the subject by saying that the expression XY is meaningless except by reference to the ordinary predicative proposition—that its meaning is that of a conjunction, an addition of characters—it means things which are X and which also are Y—so that the general objection to the theory we are criticising is that it not only leads to confusion regarding logical assertions and logical relations, but it depends for its intelligibility on that very formulation of the proposition which it is trying to supersede.

Finally, the notion of existence does not really provide us with a predicate (with a difference or distinguishing mark); it is just a particular way of expressing the copula, so that when we say XY exist we are saying that there are XY or Some X are Y (or XiY), where the force of the original "exists" remains in the "are" of the fina form. There is nothing else that we can mean by existence.

This argument has been along the lines on which we supported the notion (theory?) of the four forms, especially on the notion of contradiction, but also there is the important question of implication. If we took existence-nonexistence assertions and tried to make an argument with them, we should get, e.g., XY exist, XZ do not exist, ∴ Y$\bar{Z}$ exist. This is a sort of argument whose validity we should never see in this form: if we were going to see the validity or invalidity of arguments, we should have to use the ordinary predicative form—XiY, XeZ ∴YoZ. And if we liked we could translate it into the other (existence) form, but there would be no point in doing so. You could work out a set of rules for existence-nonexistence arguments, knowing the character of valid syllogism; but they would be rules of an apparently arbitrary character—it would be only by referring back to the AEIO forms that we should see the force of the argument, see the connection between premises and conclusion. (E.g., Barbara: YaZ, XaY ∴ XaZ ⟶ Y$\bar{Z}$ do not exist, X$\bar{Y}$ do not exist ∴ X$\bar{Z}$ do not exist. The rule would be the elimination of opposites—in the premises—but we could not see why without going back to the original <ordinary predicative> form.)

IV (29th April 1948) (First version)[3]

Comparable to existence-nonexistence view of the proposition, you have the consistency-inconsistency view of argument. *Cf.* the antilogism: substitution for syllogism of the statement of three propositions (the two premises and the contradictory of the conclusion of any valid syllogism) which cannot all be true. But in order to see that the three propositions cannot be true at the same time you have to argue in the syllogistic way: it is only from (the validity of) some syllogistic argument that you can see the inconsistency.

---

[3]Two versions of Lecture 4 are included in Anderson's handwritten notes, the firs includes reference to student notes by "P.F.", perhaps Paul Foulkes, the second by "A.J.A.", Sandy Anderson.

Example to be worked from the four rules of syllogism. The conclusion and one premise of a valid syllogism never imply the other premise: i.e., if p, q ∴ r is a valid syllogism, p, r ∴ q is an invalid syllogism. (Worked in notes at end of this course. See Addendum I.)

Importance, in argument as in statement, of recognising relations that are not symmetrical.   (Consistency and inconsistency are both symmetrical relations.)   Locke's terminology (agreement and disagreement among ideas) exemplifie the weakness in question: the A proposition is not covered by the notion of agreement ("A" is a non-symmetrical relation). *Cf.* my review of *Studies in the History of Ideas* Volume III (Columbia University)[4]—contribution of Ernest Nagel, overlooking non-symmetricality in argument.   Same sort of thing in Idealist logicians—Bosanquet on proposition as "connection of contents"—connection a symmetrical expression: does not cover the A proposition: obscures (just as "existence-nonexistence" theory does) the important distinction between the functions of subject and predicate (a distinction required for any proposition):   particularly, subject's function of location (subject as place) is ignored in speaking of "connection of contents" (connection of conceptions or notions). *Cf.* my "Hypotheticals"—X is Y is different proposition from Y is X, etc.[5]

class view of propositions: treating proposition as stating relation between two classes. (Here again we have attempts to distinguish kinds of assertion or of copula: the "is" of membership of a class, as in "Socrates is a man", and the "is"—or "are"—of inclusion, as in "All men are mortal"; etc.)

Taking the possible relations between two given classes to be those illustrated by the f ve diagrams we can see, first that a single proposition

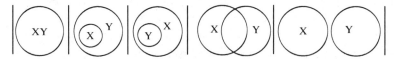

Figure 15.

does not assert one of these relations, except in the case of E which quite unambiguously indicates the relation of exclusion—but in other cases this is not so: e.g., XaY leaves it uncertain whether X and Y are coextensive or Y includes X. You may know that mortals includes

[4]"Studies in the History of Ideas, Volume III", A.J.P.P. XV (4) December 1937).
[5]"Hypotheticals", A.J.P. XXX (1) May 1952, pp 1-16. Reprinted in *Studies.*

men, but that knowledge is not conveyed simply by saying "All men are mortals"; you require for that class relation XaY and YoX, just as you require for co-extension the two propositions XaY and YaX: and with that ambiguity you cannot take XaY itself as asserting a class relation. Similarly, if you took XoY, that leaves open the three possibilities that X includes Y, that X and Y intersect and that X and Y are exclusive; and finall XiY leaves open all four possibilities other than exclusion. In view of these uncertainties, then, you cannot take a proposition as asserting a class relation, but, on the other hand, you can with a group of such propositions ("predicative propositions")unambiguously indicate any of the class relations—co-extension by XaY, YaX; inclusion of X in Y by XaY, YoX, and inclusion of Y in X by XoY, YaX; intersection by XoY, YoX and either of the I propositions (needs three); exclusion by a single proposition (either XeY or YeX). Thus using the regular A,E,I,O forms we can without ambiguity and particularly without introducing ambiguity into the copula (without having kinds of truth) represent each of the f ve possible class relations between two terms.

Then (as in the case of the existence theory) we can criticise the class relation theory by reference to contradiction. The contradictory of a class relation is not itself a class relation. You can take the E proposition to represent the class relation of exclusion, but if you deny the E proposition you are not asserting another possible class relation; you are only saying it can be one of the other four possible class relations, and that would not be intelligible if to assert a proposition were the same as to assert a class relation. (Not having a certain class relation is not having a certain class relation: you would be driven, as in the case of existence, to attach expressions like exclusion to the terms and to state the issue as whether X is exclusive of Y or X is not exclusive of Y, i.e., to come back to predicative form—and even then you would have to go back to A, I, E, O (to E, in particular) to know what the predicate meant.)

Similarly with implication or argument. If you wanted to see what followed from a number of assertions of class relation, your conclusion would not in general be a class relation (special cases where it could be: e.g., X includes Y, X excludes Z $\therefore$ Y excludes Z), and to see what conclusion followed you would have to express the argument syllogistically (as could also be done in the special cases referred to). Suppose X and Y intersect: then, with the additional datum Z includes X, to fin the relation between Y and Z—the data are compatible with

Z intersecting with Y and also with Z including Y; and to show clearly what was the relation between Y and Z, you would have to take XaZ and combine it in different syllogisms with XiY and XoY (the other two propositions ZoX and YoX being of no use for the argument): and your two conclusions would be ZiY (or YiZ) and ZoY—from which you could then say that the class relation between Y and Z is either intersection or inclusion of Y in Z (according as YoZ or YaZ).

Now while the above indicates that a general theory of the proposition as a class relation is untenable, we may consider a special theory that arose out of the attempt to deal with one of the difficulties viz., the difficult , given XaY, as to whether the relation is co-extension or inclusion of X in Y. That is the theory of the "quantificatio of the predicate", according to which "All X are Y" is an incomplete statement, requiring to be made more precise by saying either "All X are all Y" or "All X are some Y"—these representing co-extension and inclusion (of X in Y) respectively.

As before, we can object to the attempt to represent each of these two relations by a single proposition when (each of them) can be represented quite clearly by two propositions in the ordinary form. We can point out that to try to get all assertions into such quantifie forms, to maintain that every proposition when clearly and fully asserted has the predicate quantifie as well as the subject, ignores the fact that very often we do not know what the quantificatio of the predicate should be; we should be quite definitel prepared to assert All X are Y, but we do not know whether YaX or not, and this quantificatio theory prevents us from stating our knowledge that wherever there is an X there is a Y, though that is part of what would be known even if we were able to go on to quantify. And the whole theory (Hamilton's) illustrates a common tendency but one leading to confusion, viz., when we get further knowledge of any given subject-matter, to try to pack the additional knowledge into the formula we used for our previous knowledge and thus render our original formula ambiguous (varying in meaning according to what additional knowledge we get—besides having the meaning of the original knowledge when we do not get the additional knowledge we should like to have, do not fin out which of the alternative possibilities is fulfilled) Our knowledge (of the complications of a situation) is always incomplete in some respect, and nothing but confusion can result from the attempt to have a single formula covering all its aspects. A comparable case (to that of XaY, with no committal on the YaX-YoX issue) is that of the particular proposition; some people try to convey by the formula XiY (especially, by the way they emphasise "Some"—or even by taking it to be what "some" as such conveys) that some X are not Y; at any rate, when they happen to have the additional information XoY (when they know that both XiY and XoY), they regard either of these two propositions (perhaps especially XiY) as conveying both. This, as before, introduces confusion into the use of the assertion Some X are Y in cases where we do not have the additional information, where we know that there are other X than those we are acquainted with (which could all be Y) but do not know whether these other X are Y or not.

In these cases again—All X are all Y, and All X are some Y—we have a symmetrical relation; it would not matter in what order we put these quantifie terms—in fact, you could say that here you have an attempt to treat the proposition as an equation (All X = all Y), and that view could never be applied to propositions in general; it fails at the outset for the same sort of reason as we noticed in previous cases, viz., that the contradictory of an equation is not an equation, that if it is intelligible to say "All X = all Y" it must be intelligible to say "All X do not equal all Y" (All X is not equal to all Y) and hence it is necessary to understand the assertion otherwise than as an equation or assertion of equality.

(As against "quantificatio of the predicate" in general, we may say that the attachment of a sign of quantity to a term shows that it is the subject. If we attach a sign of quantity to both terms, this shows that we are trying to combine in one assertion two (or more?) propositions—and we do not have the meaning of the whole assertion till we have separated the distinct propositions and have only one quantifie term (only one subject) in each, i.e., till we have separated X-Y propositions from Y-X propositions. (Hamilton, avoiding this, has some formulae—e.g., Some X are not some Y—to which he cannot give a consistent explanation. But no theory, other than that of the four forms, can be presented consistently—it being based on the view of the proposition as an issue, this entailing both the distinction between subject and predicate and the attaching of the sign of quantity to the subject, as well as the other points involved in the theory of the four forms. Note the special importance, in the discussion of all the theories, of the question

"How is this contradicted or denied?" It must be equally clear—equally propositional—to say not-p and to say p (p is false and p is true.)

Addendum to Lecture 4[6]

I.

From one premise and the conclusion of a valid syllogism (as premises) the other premise cannot be inferred (as a conclusion): i.e., if p, q ∴ r is a valid syllogism (no presumption as to whether p is major or minor), then p, r ∴ q is an invalid syllogism (N.B. It is a syllogism, for, from the original syllogism, p and r have a common term, and each of the terms which are not common (to p and r) appears in q.)[7]

p, q ∴ r is a valid syllogism:

(1) If p is negative, r is negative (Rule IV)
∴ p, r ∴ q is invalid (Rule III)

(2) If p is affirmat ve and does not distribute the term common to it and r, r does not distribute that term (Rule II)
∴ p, r ∴ q is invalid (Rule I)

(3) If p is affirmat ve and does distribute the term common to it and r, it does not distribute the term common to it and q; therefore q does distribute that term (Rule I)
∴ p, r ∴ q is invalid (Rule II).

This emphasises the order in syllogistic argument and in the propositions themselves which occur in the syllogism—as against the view that syllogism is part of the "logic of consistency" (consistency being a reversible relation—not having order.)

If p, q ∴ r meant "r is consistent with p and q", then we could equally say p, r ∴ q ("q is consistent with p and r": i.e., p, q and r are consistent with one another).

Similarly, if each proposition in an affirmat ve syllogism was a statement of consistency, the syllogism would be expressible as "A is consistent with B and B with C ∴ A with C"; and then we could equally argue "A is consistent with B and A with C (= C with A); ∴ C with B (= B with C)". But the syllogism is not so expressible—"the syllogism of consistency" would be III and invalid (undistributed middle).

"Consistency" theorists rely on the antilogism (take syllogism as part of the logic of consistency and inconsistency): thus "p, q and r cannot

---

[6] The following points I. and II. were added to the end of the lecture notes as addenda to Lecture 4, possibly in 1952.
[7] [JA] With no presumption as to order of terms in each proposition: if p is an X-Y proposition, q is a Y-Z proposition, r is an X-Z proposition, then p, r ∴ q is X-Y, X-Z ∴ Y-Z (i.e., a syllogism).

all be true" (these three propositions are inconsistent) involves no order among p, q and r. But why is this (inconsistency) so? How do we make it out? Because of syllogism—of form and order.

II. Other examples of working with rules.

A. Two valid syllogisms have a common premise and the other premises are contradictories.

(1) The two syllogisms have the same terms, and the same middle term.

(2) One of the contradictories is negative ∴ the common premise is affirmat ve (Rule III)

(3) One of the contradictories does not distribute the middle term ∴ commone premise does (Rule I). Hence common premise is of form MaX (where M is the middle term).

(4) The syllogism with the negative contradictory has a negative conclusion (Rule IV). Therefore, X is the subject of this conclusion (which is XoY)—(Rule II)

(5) Therefore, the negative contradictory distributes Y (Rule II). Therefore, the affirmat ve contradictory does not distribute Y. Therefore, the affirmat ve conclusion is I (XiY or YiX)—(Rule II).

Hence the two conclusions are in subcontrary relation. (Note, what is utilised above: if one of two contradictories does not distribute a term, the other does; if one of two contradictories does distribute a term, the other does not. (XaY, XoY; Xey, XiY.)

B. Two valid syllogisms have a common premise and the conclusions are contradictories.

(1) The two syllogisms have the same terms (the same middle, the same minor and the same major).

(2) One of the conclusions is affirmat ve, therefore both premises in this syllogism are affirmat ve (and thus the common premise is affirmat ve)—(Rule IV).

(3) The term common to the common premise and the conclusion is distributed in one of the conclusions (note above) therefore it is distributed in the common premise (Rule II). From (2) and (3), common premise is of form XaM (where M is middle term).

(4) Therefore, the other premise in the affirmat ve syllogism distributes M (Rule I), i.e., the other premise is MaY.

(5) Therefore, Y is undistributed in the conclusion of the affirmat ve syllogism (see note on contradictories).

(6) Therefore, the other premise in the negative syllogism distributes Y (Rule II) and (as in (4)) is also distributes M (Rule I). That is, the other premise is the negative syllogism is MeY or YcM.

Thus the premises other than the common premise are in contrary relation. It would be possible to get from these premises contrary conclusions; but, sticking to the requirement of contradictory conclusions, we fin that the syllogism with the particular conclusion has always either a weakened conclusion or a strengthened premise.

IV 30th April 1948 (Second version)

Proposition considered as class relation or relation between classes. Different doctrines will be discussed—e.g., doctrine of different is-es: e.g., the "is" of class membership (Socrates is a man) and the "is" of inclusion (All men are mortal). As against these views, we always have to return to the unambiguous copula. Those who try to avoid the predicative form don't manage it.

Locke, with his theory of agreement and disagreement, can account for the I proposition, but not for the A which is not symmetrical. You get people who cannot see the non-symmetry of the proposition and who try to make logic a question of consistency (a symmetrical relation). So with regard to the syllogism, you have the attempt to represent it by means of the antilogism (three propositions which cannot all be true—are inconsistent). But you have to understand the syllogism in order to see what that the three propositions (the premises, and the contradictory of the conclusion, of any valid syllogism) cannot all be true. Another theory (connected with symmetry) is that of Bosanquet—the treatment of the proposition as a connection of concepts (contents) (a symmetrical expression): but this does not do justice to non-symmetry (e.g., of the A) or to the character of the proposition as an issue (distinction of functions of subject and predicate).

Proposition as class relation. Quite clearly the E proposition does inform us of the class relation between the subject and the predicate, viz., exclusion, and the assertion of exclusion in turn informs us of the E proposition. But that is the only case in which a single proposition and a statement of class relation are interchangeable. If you take the other possible relations between any two given terms (X and Y) you will fin that a single X-Y proposition does not inform us which of these relations holds—that XaY leaves it an open question whether X and Y are coextensive or Y includes X; and similarly XoY leaves it uncertain whether X includes Y, the two intersect or they are exclusive; and finall XiY gives you four possibilities—anything except exclusion. We can see then that the proposition, apart from the E, does not tell us unambiguously what the class relation is. At the same time, we can state all these class relations quite unambiguously by using a number of A, E, I, O propositions—co-extension, the two A's; inclusion of Y in X, XoY and YaX—and correspondingly for inclusion of X in Y; intersection, three propositions (the two O's and either of the two I's). That means that we do not have to go beyond the predicative proposition to represent class relations—that we can do it clearly with the A, E, I, O forms.

Then we can attack the class relation view by the same methods as before—with reference to contradiction and implication. The contradictory of the assertion of a class relation is not itself the assertion of a class relation. If we take the E (either XeY or YeX) as representing exclusion (of X and Y), then to deny exclusion is to assert the possibility of four different kinds of class relation, and if we take it that an assertion is not intelligible unless it has an intelligible contradictory, then that means that in treating a class relation assertion as an issue, we are recognising types of assertion other than class relation assertions—seeing, therefore, that it is impossible to identify the proposition as such with a class relation.

Secondly, with reference to inference or implication, inferences from a class relation or a number of class relations are not in general class relations. Some arguments, of course, could be put in that way (you could say A excludes B and B includes C $\therefore$ A excludes C) but others could not—if the data were that X and Y intersect and Z includes X, then you would have two different possible class relations between Y and Z: viz., Z intersects with Y, and Z includes Y. And the precise conclusion that can be drawn from the data has to be shown by syllogism, i.e., we have to combine with our three intersection propositions the propositions XaZ and ZoX; actually, ZoX and YoX are of no use in the argument, but, taking the other three propositions XiY (or YiX), XoY and XaZ, we infer from XiY and XaZ that YiZ (or ZiY) and from XaZ and XoY that ZoY: and having those two syllogistic conclusions we can then see that Z either includes Y or intersects with it.

Thus consideration of both contradiction and implication (in regard to "class relation" assertions) forces us back on the AEIO propositions;

all the possible class relations can be presented unambiguously by using a number of propositions of the AEIO forms, so that there is not the slightest need to introduce a special class of propositions which assert class relations, just as there is not any possibility of identifying assertions in general with class relations.

Having rejected that general view, we can consider a particular variety of it, or a theory of a similar type at least, viz., the theory of quantificatio of the predicate (Hamilton). This theory may be said to take its departure from the uncertainty which arises in the case of the A proposition (XaY), viz., whether YaX or YoX, and the uncertainty is taken to be resolved by replacing A propositions by two kinds of propositions—those in which the predicate has the sign of universal quantity attached to it and those in which it has the sign of particular quantity (All X are all Y: All X are some Y). Now it can easily be shown that this way of stating issues cannot be carried out consistently—that we cannot cover all types of possible assertion by unambiguous formulae of this type. But limiting ourselves for the moment to the treatment of A, we can say that this sort of form cannot be treated as the true form or real meaning of every assertion we make, because when we say XaY, or Wherever X is, Y is, it is quite possible for us not to know whether YaX or not, and so the quantificatio formula involves an attempt to make us go beyond the information we have, while, if we do get that additional information, it will include the information we began with, viz., where X is, Y is, together with Where Y is, X is, or not as the case may be.

A point to be noticed with regard to these two quantifying statements is that again we have the proposition represented as symmetrical, in fact as an equation—"All X = all Y", which could equally be expressed as "All Y = all X" (there is no question of an order)—and similarly with "All X = some Y", where you could equally say "Some Y = all X". And considering the view that all intelligible propositions are equations (what we might call the equational view of the proposition), that can be met as before by saying that the contradictory of an equation is not an equation, that All X does not equal all Y is not an equation and yet must be a clear and definit type of assertion. (In "Relational Arguments" an equation, a statement of equality, is taken to be a statement of the co-extension of two classes—i.e., two propositions—and the real argument, ordinarily presented in terms of equality, is taken to be a number of syllogisms).

V

Now one point made in connection with other theories I was rejecting was that they could not deal with implication. So with quantificatio view. If we say "All A are all B", how can we draw inferences, and, in particular, what can we do when told "This is A"? According to the regular syllogistic formula (form?), we should have to say (to draw the conclusion) "This is all B". But people would not want to draw this conclusion, which would depend on using the firs "all" distributively (=any, etc.) whereas the second all was being used collectively. But if you take the conclusion that people would draw, viz., "This is B" (without the all), then that brings us back to the superfluousnes of the all attached to the predicate in the major premise—to the fact that our argument is a syllogism in the ordinary form, having AaB as one premise, and even if it is also true that BaA, that fact is quite irrelevant to the argument. Summing up, then, in order to bring out implication, you would have to take the sign of quantity distributively; and that would be a general objection to the quantificatio theory which says that it takes the signs of quantity collectively: which does so, at any rate, whatever it says. All A are all B (which means the equation All A = all B: i.e., which has not really an order of terms) could also be expressed in the form "The collection of A's is the same as the collection of B's", and similarly All A are some B as "The collection of A's is the same as a part of the collection of B's"—and, apart from the difficult of "is the same as" (i.e., of what is copula and what is part of a term), we have the above-mentioned difficultie about the inferences we actually draw—which can be got over only by recognising that the "equation" means two distinct propositions (AaB, BaA), one of which we use as a premise in some of our inferences and the other in others. But unless we decisively recognise the two propositions (with only one quantificatio in each) we shall have a confused view of our inferences and may land in fallacy (that is, may confuse between the "consequences" of AaB and the "consequences" of BaA). As before, all our information is contained in the group of A, E, I or O propositions we have in each case, and it is only by recognising this (by distinguishing the A's, E's, I's and O's involved) that we avoid confusion.

Latta, in criticism of Hamilton's eight forms of proposition, says that Hamilton could not distinguish Some A are not some B from All A are all B. (Incidentally, would Hamilton not have to admit a form Some A are not some A?) The argument is: Some A (call them M) are not some B (call them P)—but there are the rest of A (call them N) and the rest of B (call them Q). That is, Some A (M but not N) are not some B (P but not Q). That is, M are not P but M are Q; and N are not not P (i.e., N are P). That is, the whole of A (M and N) are the whole of B (Q and P). Thus "Some A are not some B" means that "All A are all B" (the two collectives are identical). So Latta shows that at least some of the eight "distinct" quantifie forms are not distinct.

Latta's demonstration depends on taking "some" to mean "some only", "some but not all" ("some X" as a part, less than the whole of the collection X). Cf. 37, footnote, on meaning of "some"—it means not none and doesn't mean not all: if we know XoY (not all X are Y), that is still a quite different proposition from XiY, i.e., from it is not the case that no X are Y).

Distribution

A common way of expressing the distinction between distribution and non-distribution is to say that a term is distributed in a proposition when the proposition refers to the term in the whole of its extension (or refers to the whole of the class characterised by the term) and a term is undistributed in a proposition when the proposition does not refer to it in the whole of its extension (or where what we are saying cannot be said about any part of the class we like to take). But this sort of position leads to the view, not that the statement does not apply to the whole class but that we do not know that it applies to the whole class—that that ignorance is what is meant by saying that the term is undistributed—which in turn leads on to the quantificatio view we have just been considering ("we do not know that All X are Y applies to all Y but it may do so, viz., when YaX is true")—which would be similar to "we do not know that Some X are Y applies to all X but it may do so, viz., when XaY is true": i.e., when we say XiY, we might really mean XaY, only we do not know it; or, when our statement is made quite precise, we have to say either XaY or XiY, XoY—and then you have the same problem with the predicate (i.e., whether YaX or YiX, YoX).

Now, even if it is the case that XaY, XiY never means that; it never does apply to the whole of X; and if you take the predicate in XaY, the position is the same, that even if it is also true that YaX (a statement that "applies to the whole of Y"), XaY never means YaX and can never be said to apply to the whole of Y.

Perhaps a better way of putting it is that a proposition in which X is distributed applies to any X we like to take and a proposition in which X is undistributed does not apply to any X we like to take, so that to say, e.g., that mortal is undistributed in All men are mortal is to say that the statement does not apply to any mortal we like to take—if it did, we could say that All men are Socrates or All men are horses—which is not what we mean. But the point is made still more precise by saying that the question is whether we are entitled to substitute for the given term any part of its extension or, more accurately, anything that belongs to its extension, the term being distributed if we are so entitled and not distributed if we are not. But that substitution is really syllogism: take XaY, and then Z which are X (i.e., ZaX); to say that we are entitled to substitute Z for X in XaY is to say that we are entitled to draw the conclusion ZaY—is to say that the syllogism XaY, ZaX ∴ ZaY is valid. That validity is the meaning of X's being distributed in the proposition XaY. And similarly to say that X is undistributed in XiY is to say that, taking ZaX, you are not entitled to substitute Z for X in the original proposition (getting ZiY)—in other words, the syllogism XiY, ZaX ∴ ZiY is invalid: that is what is meant by saying that X in XiY is undistributed. Or take the case of Y in XaY: given that W belongs to the extension of Y (i.e., WaY), then you cannot (are not entitled to) substitute W for Y, getting XaW; in other words, the syllogism WaY, XaY ∴ XaW is invalid and that is what is meant by saying that Y is undistributed in XaY.

That creates a difficulty—apparen circularity—in the theory of syllogistic rules. If we were asked why those two syllogisms were invalid, we should say—because they have undistributed middle; thus it would appear that we were explaining the invalidity in terms of absence of distribution and the absence of distribution in terms of invalidity. Now the solution seems to be that non-distribution is not an explanation of invalidity—that we must distinguish distribution from non-distribution by distinguishing a valid from an invalid argument—and thus that we must be able to recognise valid and invalid arguments directly, to recognise implication and non-implication in different cases. And if this were not so we should have no reason for submitting to the traditional rules, and if someone said "You are committing undistributed middle", we could say "Yes, that is the way I like to argue"—the rules would have no force at all if they were laid down by authority, they would have force only if we could see validity and invalidity directly. But once, as a result of this direct observation, we have established the notions of distribution and non-distribution and classifie valid and invalid syllogisms, we can see that the rules (here, in particular, the firs two rules) are criteria of validity (in fact, that is what they mean: cf. "In a valid syllogism, if M is undistributed in one premise, it is distributed in the other" as strict formulation of the firs rule, and so on) and thereafter we can apply those rules in a quite mechanical way without having to go back to the beginning and think the whole thing out. Having got rules we can proceed, but it is still the case that to explain what distribution and non-distribution mean, we must do so by reference to the validity and the invalidity of certain syllogisms.

Connection of "quantification with individualism: term as individual or collection of individuals. Thus if we say "All X are Y", we are saying here are X's, these are all the X's, and if every one of them is Y, then we are identifying them with Y's, and if these are all the Y's, then X's being Y's is true of all Y as well as of all X (i.e., the X's are the Y's). It is this view of the proposition as an identificatio or set of identification that leads to difficult about whether Y is distributed or not in XaY (so X in XiY, etc.) The point would be that in place of any predicative relation we should here simply have identity or a number of identities—the X's are the same as the Y's, or this X is the same as this Y—and we should not be concerned with being X or being Y, we should not connect "All men are mortal" with the notion of being a man and that of being mortal, but just with the fact that the set of things we label men can also be labelled mortal, and that there can be not other mortals. But in that case there would be no explaining why they were so labelled—how the same individual thing could have different labels (man and mortal) or how different things could have the same label (man): these could be explained only if we recognised the character of being a man and the character of being mortal, if we recognised the generality of terms, the fact that they can all be predicates, and the general distinction between subject and predicate in the proposition. Failing that, we could never say this X is this Y—we could only say this is this; and in fact we could not even say that, for taking "this" to mean the thing indicated, we cannot indicate or mark off anything except as a thing of some general character. Terms ("things") not prior to propositions. (Now if Y is a general term, then in applying it to the X's we are not identifying individuals with one another, and there is no question of Y being distributed in XaY.)

VI

I pointed out the confusion in the Hamiltonian view, when the question of implication is raised, between distributive and collective uses of "all" (and "some"). In fact, the whole equational theory (All X = all Y; All X = some Y) takes the collective or quantitative view—regards the whole or part of a class as a collection or amount, and the proposition as stating the equality (or identity) of two amounts. But the members of a class are not in general collected at all; they are not heaped together; and it is possible for us to consider them as a group (and use quantity or spatial extension—*cf.* Euler's circles—as illustration) simply because we fin each of them to be of a certain character: i.e., because we take them distributively and use the ordinary predicative proposition. Thus the whole doctrine of quantificatio of the predicate errs in substituting collective for distributive use (of "all" and "some") and even then requires distributive use in order to be intelligible (and to allow for inference).

(I shall be discussing modality in preference to relational statements and arguments. The latter are supposed to present a "difficulty for a predicative logic. What is meant by a "difficulty" *Cf.* Hume—you cannot call "a difficulty what purports to be a demonstration of the untenability of your position. Either it is a refutation of your view or it contains some confusion (fallacy or ambiguity) and is not really a difficult . If it is a refutation, there must be something wrong with the argument by which your view was established. If you can still see nothing wrong with that argument, and yet cannot see the confusion in the opposing argument, you can set the latter aside for future consideration. (You know that there are certain types of confusion—e.g., between words and what they mean—that regularly affect theory, that permit Sophistry or "material fallacy"—*cf.* the *Euthydemus*.) (Cf. "the contradiction" presented by Russell in the theory of classes; it turns on the distinction between "the class as one" and "the class as many"; it is solved by pointing out, against Russell, that there is no such thing as "the class as one", that "class" means "extension", the various things of which a given term (X) can be predicated, and to make a collection of members of the class X is a quite different thing from talking about the class, i.e., the various members.) *Cf.* mathematical logicians looking for "paradoxes". There can be no contradiction in things and the existence of a paradox merely means that there is some confusion in ouir thinking (or our terminology). We know that, even if we have not yet found out what the confusion is. So, if we accept the argument for a predicative logic with the four forms, we may not see, at a given time, just how relational statements fi into that scheme, but that is no reason for believing that they do not fi in—and no reason to expect to be handed a solution, instead of thinking the matter out in terms of previous discussions.)

"Modality"[8]

(Modal assertions—assertions of possibility, existence and necessity: what may be, what is, and what must be.) We have here again an attempt to qualify the copula: i.e., when you say "X must be Y" or "X may be Y", you are saying "X is necessarily Y" or "X is possibly Y", where "necessarily" and "possibly" are supposed to go with the copula and not with the predicate (to indicate kinds of assertions and not kinds of things), i.e., where Y is in the one case predicated of X in the necessary manner and in the other case in the possible manner—and there would be the third case of actuality (or existence): Y predicated of X in the actual manner(!).

But again we should be confronted with problems (insoluble) regarding these different types of statement, and especially as to the way of contradicting or denying them: because, on the face of it, "X is not necessarily Y" is not an assertion of necessity (an assertion "in the necessary manner" or "in the fiel of necessity"), i.e., the copula of this negative statement (whatever it may be taken to be) has not the meaning of necessary being: and so by the simple statement of an issue we have introduced another form of copula—and the issue can only be a confused one. (Question of interpretation as "X's being Y has necessity" or "lacks necessity" —→ X's being Y is necessary: X's being Y is not necessary. (*Cf.* discussion of "existence" theory). As before, we are brought back to the old copula—the unambiguous copula—with a highly peculiar predicate: in fact, a meaningless predicate, since it is a mixture of the formal and the material.)

Even if it were said that the contradictory of a statement of necessity is a statement of possibility, and vice versa, (that the contradictory of "X is necessarily Y" is "X is possibly not Y", and the contradictory of "X is possibly Y" is "X is necessarily not Y"), we could know that only by considering an issue which could be raised and settled in an

---

[8][JA] Much of the ensuing discussion utilised in "Empiricism and Logic", a new paper written for *Studies*.

unambiguous way, only by returning to the unambiguous copula and treating the supposed modification of the copula as modification of the terms or of the form (particularly, of the quantity) of the (categorical) proposition. (The difference of quality is of course the difference between the affirmat ve and the negative copula—amounting to the function of the copula in umambiguously indicating an issue, with the two ways of settling it: more exactly, function of copula is no more than that of indicating an issue—with the two ways, etc.—a question whether something is so or not, without any suggestion of what that something is, that is not trenching in any way on the work of the terms.)

The main way of treating the matter, then, is by reference to quantity, i.e., taking an assertion of necessity as a universal assertion, an assertion of possibility as a particular, both being in fact assertions of actuality (all assertions being assertions of actuality). "X is necessarily Y" now appears as XaY and "X is possibly Y" as XiY; and correspondingly with the contradictions of these. The alternative to that (in terms of predicative logic and unambiguous copula—and leaving certain special cases out of account for the moment) is to treat necessity as a character of certain things or situations and possibility as a character of other things or situations (to treat them as predicates—which means they would also be subjects): which is clearly untenable. We cannot look at any actual situation and see in it a quality of being necessary or a quality of being possible; there are not a class of necessary things and a class of unnecessary things, a class of possible things and a class of impossible things, any more than there are a class of existing things and a class of non-existing things.

The different kinds of modal assertions, if they could be admitted at all, would have to hold in different universes and that would make it impossible for us to know two such contrasted types of assertions and to relate them in any way, and impossible to treat them as issues. (We could not know, e.g., that "X is necessarily Y" and "X is possibly not Y" are contradictories, are opposed "solutions" of a single issue.) And it is along the same lines that we can object to the doctrine of "universes of discourse" or field within which propositions hold, viz., that we have to be able to contradict them (i.e., we have to know what their contradictory is), and when the issue is plainly stated, what was taken as the "field is seen to be part of the terms. Suppose we say that in the fiel or class of men fair hair goes with blue eyes: i.e., in the fiel of discourse

men "All blue-eyed are fair-haired". To treat that as a definit issue
we have to add men to the terms and say "All blue-eyed men are fair-
haired men" (or simply, "All blue-eyed men are fair-haired"). (Theory
of "opposites within a field   and "virtual contrapositives"—cf. "The
Problem of Causality".[9])

The above view of modality does not cover the whole ground. While,
in the main, it is merely a question of universality and particularity, there
are complications connected with the question of our knowledge. When
we say something is necessarily so (or must be so), we may mean that
we know it or are certain of it; more particularly, when we say something
is possibly so (or may be so), we commonly mean that we do not know
that it is not so. This, then, is not a question of the distinction quantity
(universal or particular): it is a question of a proposition having different
terms (from the one said to be necessarily or possibly so), a proposition
about us or our beliefs. Thus if we said "Plato may have written the
Menexenus", our meaning would be "I do not know that Plato did not
write the Menexenus".

Sometimes the question of necessity or possibility is the more precise
one of proof or absence of proof. We say—All men are mortal and
Socrates is a man, so Socrates must be mortal; where what we are saying
is not merely that Socrates is mortal but that the proposition "Socrates is
mortal" is proved: i.e., is implied by propositions we believe to be true.
Here the "must be" has the same force as therefore, it has the significanc
of being inferred as a conclusion (and, of course, it is relative to the
given premises—"on these data X must be Y"—or, on these data, X is
Y is necessarily so).

As "must be" amounts to "is proved to be", in this usage, we have the
corresponding use of "may be" as equivalent to "is not proved not to be"
(proved—necessary; not disproved—possible). If we said—Socrates is
mortal and Socrates is a man, but all men may not be mortal (or it is
possible that not all men are mortal), then our meaning would be that the
proposition "Some men are not mortal" is not disproved (= "All men are
mortal" is not proved by the given premises") by the given information
(again, relative to data: "on these data, X may be Y"—or "X is Y is
possibly so"; in this case, "Some men are not mortal" is possibly so). Or,
as necessary (or must be) corresponds to therefore, possible (or may be)
corresponds to not therefore not. We may also have a more general use of

---

[9] "The Problem of Causality", *A.J.P.P.* XVI (2) August 1938: 127-42. Reprinted in *Studies* pp.126-36. Reference to virtual contrapositives *Studies* page 130.

possible; as contrasted with the non-implication of a conclusion (say, All men are mortal) by a given set of data, we might have its non-implication (our inability to prove it) by any information we posssessed. Then we should say "Possibly some men are not mortal", meaning simply that we are not able to prove that all men are mortal. (This comes closer to the firs use of possibly—in relation to our beliefs: where "p is possibly true", or "p is possible", means "I do not know that p is not true".)

These more complicated cases, while they may be awkward to put into logical form, still do not take us beyond the predicative logic with its A, E, I, O forms. But perhaps the more common cases are those of the use of "necessary" for a universal proposition (asserting that actually all X are Y) and of "possible" for a particular proposition (asserting that actually some X are Y); this "actuality" not being a form of modality contrasted with possibility and necessity but just being (a way of expressing) the common copula—the unambiguous are (or is) of predication.

VII

I connected the question of modality with the question of "universes of discourse" (cf. "mythology"—centaurs, etc.) and suggested that, if we reject (any) doctrine of kinds or regions of truth, we have to take the "field as part of the terms: i.e., the logical form of "In the fiel X, AaB" is AXaBX (or simply AXaB). The alternative is to take the fiel or "universe" of discourse as involving a qualificatio of the copula (kind of truth): thus to say "In the fiel men all fair-haired are blue-eyed" is to say "All fair-haired are humanly (or humanly speaking) blue-eyed" (i.e., if we are excluding the incorporation of the fiel in the terms (which brings us back to an ordinary proposition, with no question of a field) the only remaining possibility is its incorporation in the copula—cf. Pragmatists and Protagoras): and it would be shown as in other cases, by reference to contradiction and implication, that it was impossible to keep this qualificatio in the copula—that it was necessary to put in the terms and retain unambigious (true or false; so or not) copula: i.e., maintain the distinction between absolute truthy and absolute falsity as what is involved in any issue whatever. (No kinds or degrees of truth—no relative truth.)

Connection of universes of discourse with "virtual contrapositives" (based on "virtual opposites" or "opposites within a field") See "The

Problem of Causality": question of "negative instances" in the solution of a causal problem.[10]

(1) Negative instances verify propositions in the same way as positive instances do, when it is a question of true opposites. Thus the proposition AaB is verifie in the same way by cases of "joint absence" (things which are neither A nor B) as by cases of "joint presence" (things which are both A and B). Take X as a case of joint presence: then you have verificatio of AaB in the syllogism AaB, XaA $\therefore$ XaB—and taking Y as a case of joint absence, you have verificatio of AaB in the syllogism AaB, YeB $\therefore$ YeA. Now, if you take the obverses of the two propositions with Y as subject, you have verificatio of AaB in the form of verificatio of the equivalent proposition $\bar{B}a\bar{A}$, in the same type of syllogism as the firs here: viz., $\bar{B}a\bar{A}$, Ya$\bar{B}$ $\therefore$ Ya$\bar{A}$. The two propositions AaB and $\bar{B}a\bar{A}$ are equivalent (they are contrapositives of one another) and anything that verifie one verifie the other.

(2) But the position is different if (as I argue is regularly the case in questions of causal relation) the question is of positive and negative instances, or cases of joint presence and cases of joint absence, in a special field in that case, you no longer have contrapositives or equivalents and so you no longer have two propositions any verificatio of one of which is a verificatio of the other—you have instead "virtual contrapositives", containing "virtual opposites" or "opposites within a field" A good deal of confusion is caused in argument by neglect of the distinction between a real opposite and a virtual opposite: especially with complex terms—the opposite of the term XY being frequently taken to by $\bar{X}\bar{Y}$. (*Cf.* the perhaps humorously intended "inversion" of "All truthful men are mortal" to give "Some truthful men are immortal": (a) untruthful men is not the opposite of truthful men, though it could be called "the opposite within the fiel of men"; (b) immortal is not the opposite of mortal, though it could be taken, by those who believe in the existence of immortals, as the opposite of mortal within the fiel rational beings: the real opposite of mortal is non-mortal, which includes both immortals if there are any and inanimate things which are not "liable to death" because they are not alive. In general, the opposite of a term X is anything that is not X, i.e., is non-X: the opposite of "truthful men" is "things which are not truthful men" and includes (i) men who are not truthful, (ii) all the things that are not men at all.

---

[10]*Ibid.*, pp. 129ff.

The position is that we can get what may be called a virtual contrapositive (contrapositive within a field by a perfectly valid process if certain assumptions are made, and particularly if we have the information that the opposites do exist within a field If we have not that information, then we can come to quite false conclusions from true premises by proceeding as if we had, i.e., by using the "virtual contrapositive".

Calling the fiel X and starting with AaB ("In the fiel X, all A are B")we should have, according to the "universe of discourse" theory, the contrapositive $\bar{B}a\bar{A}$ ("In the fiel of X, all $\bar{B}$ are $\bar{A}$"). But this assumes what is not given, that there are any $\bar{B}$ (or any $\bar{A}$) in the fiel X at all. If we state the issue fully by adding X to the terms, we have AXaBX and, as its "contrapositive", $\bar{B}Xa\bar{A}X$. Arguing from this conclusion: by conversion we get $\bar{A}i\bar{B}X$; then, dropping X from the predicate, $\bar{A}Xi\bar{B}$; then, dropping $\bar{A}$ from the subject, $Xi\bar{B}$ (= XoB). This second dropping of part of a term is justifie if there are X which are $\bar{A}$; in that case, according to the argument, there will be X which are $\bar{B}$. But it is perfectly possible on the intial datum (AXaBX or AXaB) that there should be X which are not A and yet no X which are not B. (It is even possible that no X are either $\bar{A}$ or $\bar{B}$—it is possible, when we say AXaBX, that XaA and XaB.) Thus, in the example previously given, "All truthful men are mortal", it is the case that there are men who are not truthful, but these men are also mortal. But if we had allowed the "contraposition" of "All truthful men are mortal men" to "All non-mortal men are non-truthful men" (expansion of "In the fiel men, all truthful are mortal" with the inference from it of "In the fiel men, all non-mortal are non-truthful"), we could, as above, by perfectly valid argument have gone on to the false conclusion "Some men are not mortal".

The fallacy involved in this drawing of a false conclusion from a true datum is to be found in the firs stage of the argument, the part that passes for contraposition. In fact we could not have validly made the passage to this "virtual contrapositive" unless we firs (or independently) knew that some men are not mortal, unless that had been an additional datum. But, when we do know that XoB, we can quite validly pass from AXaBX to $\bar{B}Xa\bar{A}X$ (as stated in "The Problem of Causality".)

Given AXaBX and XoB (the existence of the opposite of B within the fiel X) we can infer $\bar{B}Xa\bar{A}X$ as follows (besides being able to infer XoA (the existence of the opposite of A within the fiel X)—

(1) AXaBX ∴ AXaB (dropping X from predicate)

(2) AXaB ∴ AXe$\overline{\text{B}}$ (obverse)

(3) AXc$\overline{\text{B}}$ ∴ AXe$\overline{\text{B}}$X (if Xi$\overline{\text{B}}$). (The crucial step: the inference may be said to be made from the two data AXe$\overline{\text{B}}$ and Xi$\overline{\text{B}}$)[11]

(4) AXe$\overline{\text{B}}$X ∴ $\overline{\text{B}}$XeAX (converse)

(5) $\overline{\text{B}}$XeAX ∴ $\overline{\text{B}}$XeA (A special type of inference: roughly expressed as—since $\overline{\text{B}}$XaX, all that prevents them from being AX must be that they are not A)

(6) $\overline{\text{B}}$XeA ∴ $\overline{\text{B}}$Xa$\overline{\text{A}}$ (obverse)

(7) $\overline{\text{B}}$Xa$\overline{\text{A}}$ ∴ $\overline{\text{B}}$Xa$\overline{\text{A}}$X (adding part of the subject—i.e., one character in a given conjunctive term—to predicate: as we can always do in an affirmat ve proposition.)

By these seven steps we have arrived at the "virtual contrapositive" and we can reverse the process (get from $\overline{\text{B}}$Xa$\overline{\text{A}}$X to AXaBX) if we have a corresponding datum: in this case XiA (i.e., if there are X which have the opposite character from the one attached to X in the predicate of the proposition being argued from). So we can say broadly that "virtual contraposition" is possible if the terms A, B, and their opposites all exist within the fiel X.

(Nothing further in detail about adding and dropping constituents to and from terms; "added determinants" etc. (added determinants is a question of conjunction; there are different rules for passing back and forward between a simple term and a disjunctive term of which it is a constituent); except that (a) to add a determinant we must have the additional information that it exists within the field (b) we can always, under that condition, add a determinant to a distributed term (but additional conditions required in the case of an undistributed term) and that we can always subtract a determinant from an undistributed term but not validly from a distributed term.

Examples. XaY: given XiA, we can infer AXaAY (or simply AXaY).[12] But from AXaY we cannot infer XaY (i.e., we can drop determinant A from undistributed AY in AXaAY and get AXaY, but we cannot drop determinant A from distributed AX so as to get XaY). Or if XiA, then if XaY, AXaY; but if AXaY, it is possible that XoY.)

---

[11][JA] Marginal note: *No*: see concluding note in addenda below (Addendum III, Ed.)

[12][JA] Correct view, I think, (see Addendum III below), is that XaY implies AXaAY (and similarly AXaY) provided the latter is a proposition (i.e., provided that XiA). But while XiA is thus a condition of the soundness of the inference, it is not a second premise.

General question of complex terms (terms made up "constituent terms")leads to question of arguments (non-syllogistic) involving such terms. Two main types—"conjunctive arguments" and "disjunctive arguments". Connected also with conditionals (hypotheticals, etc.).

(1) Conjunctive. AaX, AaY ∴ AaXY (Conclusion is new because neither premise tells us that there is such a combination as XY). This can also be called combination of predicates or intensive combination. XY is a "conjunctive term".

(2) Disjunctive. AaX, BaX ∴ (A or B)aX. This can be called combination of subjects or extensive combination. A or B is a "disjunctive term". (Neither premise says that A and B resemble one another—which is conveyed in the conclusion).

These are only examples. In conjunctive argument at least it is not necessary that all premises should be A (cf. AiX, AaY ∴ AiXY).

These two (combination of characters and combination of classes) are what Russell calls respectively logical product and logical sum. The logical product of X and Y is XY; the logical sum of X and Y is X or Y; these are different terms, and it is possible that one should exist and the other not (e.g., there is a logical sum of men and women, it is possible to speak of the two classes together—in this case, together making up a larger class—but there is not a logical product of them—there is no being who is at once a man and a woman.)

Important to have a consistent logical usage; in ordinary speech we use "and" for both sum and product; we say "men and women" and we also say that someone is "short and stout". Better to use "or" for sum and "and" only for product. (Generally we omit it from product and say XY: e.g., "rational animal"—as in algebraic "products".)

Addendum to Lecture 7[13]

Added Determinants

The question whether we should say that XaY and XiA together imply AXaY, or that XaY implies AXaY, provided that AXaY is a proposition (i.e., provided that XiA).

If we took the former view, then, when XiA is false, it is still significant thus, two significan propositions (two propositions) imply something that is not significan (not a proposition). It seems to me that we could not say that two things which are concrete issues imply

---

[13] The following note was added to the end of the lecture notes as addendum to Lecture 7, possibly in 1952.

something that is not an issue at all. Hence, I think we are forced back on the second view that when XaY and AXaY are both propositions, the firs implies the second, and that XiA, while it is a condition of the validity of this argument, is not a premise of it. (Of course, we can consider formal possibilities of argument, when we do not know whether XiA or not—whether "AX" is a real term or not. But we cannot say that two arguments of the same form are one valid and the other invalid—or have one of them a real conclusion and the other not; so we have to drop the firs proposed theory—of inference from two premises.)

Also, it is a mere evasion to go from XiA (AX is a real term) to AXaX, and turn the argument into a syllogism (XaY, AXaX ∴ AXaY), since AXaX is not a proposition (is not an issue) and so cannot be a premise in a syllogism.

The question of "unreal terms" having opposite characters (of the compatibility of "contraries" when the subject "does not exist") is also relevant here. Using the same form here (i.e., as in the first discarded alternative), we have:

(1) All squares are non-round, Some squares are circular, therefore All square circles (or circular squares) are non-round.

(2) All circles are round, Some circles are squares (or Some squares are circles), therefore All square circles are round.

Taking the obverse of the firs conclusion, we have A and E propositions with the same subject and the same predicate, but regarded as not incompatible because the subject does not exist. But we could not advance both (1) and (2) as arguments, because the premises of the two can be represented by the three propositions "No squares are round", "All circles are round", "Some squares are circles"—and as these propositions cannot all be true (though they are all equally significant) it is idle to talk of the results we arrive at by a pair of arguments containing all three (or equivalents of all three) as premises.

VIII

I distinguished between conjunctive terms and disjunctive terms, between XY (intensive combination) and X or Y (extensive combination). It is important to note distinction between the two, because these combinations of two given terms may not exist. As above, extensive combination exists and intensive combination does not exist in the case of men and women. In the case of animals and non-men, the intensive combination exists but the extensive does not (since its opposite does not). Note that the opposite of a conjunctive term is a disjunctive term, and the opposite of a disjunctive term is a conjunctive term. XY has as its opposites $\bar{X}$ or $\bar{Y}$ ("either not X or not Y") = not both X and Y); X or Y has as its opposite $\bar{X}\bar{Y}$ ("both not X and not Y" = neither X nor Y = not either X or Y).

It is easy enough to see that certain conjunctions are not real (that XY is not a real term when XeY): for, although both X and Y exist, thety do not exist in combination; and if we were given the term XY or, better, the proposition XYaZ, there would be no point of reference, nowhere we could go to see whether the "proposition" was true or not. In fact, XYaZ is not a proposition: there is only a combination of words, which some people might (wrongly) think conveyed a proposition (or a combination of expectations which people might wrongly think could be fulfilled. On the other hand, it is harder to accept the view that certain disjunctions are not real terms, because it would seem natural, if we could talk of a class X and of a class Y, that we could talk about these two classes in combination. But this view must be rejected if we adhere to the position that any real term has a real opposite (that any proposition has an obverse, that every term distinguishes as well as characterises); for then, if the conjunction XY does not exist, the disjunction $\bar{X}$ or $\bar{Y}$ docs not exist or is not a real term—even though $\bar{X}$ is a real term and $\bar{Y}$ is a real term.

This can be approached in another way (though still on the understanding that any real term has a real opposite). If two classes X and Y both exclude a third class Z, then X and Y are each $\bar{Z}$, and we could have the proposition (X or Y)a$\bar{Z}$ (anything that is either X or Y is non-Z) or the negative proposition (X or Y)eZ. But if X and Y do not both exclude a third class, i.e., if together they include everything (if each is coextensive with the opposite of the other or if each includes the opposite of the other), then in order to treat their disjunction as a term and especially as a term with intension (it has been assumed (argued) that every term has intension), in order to say (X or Y)aW—implying XaW and YaW—we should have to say that everything is W; that nothing is non-W: that W has not a real opposite).

For instance, if we took non-men and mortals, in saying "(non-men or mortals)aW", we should be saying that everything is W, that W has no real opposite—just as "non-men or mortals" has no real opposite,

X *coextensive* with
opposite of Y etc.

X *including* opposite of Y
Y *including* opposite of X

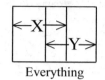

$\overleftarrow{\text{Everything}}\!\!\rightarrow$ Everything

Figure 16.

for its opposite would be "non-mortal men" and these do not exist. We recognise X or Y as a term, then, only when $\overline{XY}$ is a term (i.e., only when $X\overline{\mathrm{i}}\overline{Y}$).

In connection with disjunction, there is the question of the meaning of "or".

(1) Exhaustive. (X or Y)aZ means that Z occurs throughout the whole range of the two classes, X and Y; Wa(X or Y) means that throughout the class W, one or other of the predicates X and Y occurs, that these predicates "exhaust" the class W (or that there are no W which are neither X nor Y). This is expressed by saying that the alternatives in a disjunction are exhaustive (that disjunction is a sum or extensive combination).

(2) Exclusive. The view I should reject (a view held by Bosanquet and other Idealists) is that the alternatives are also exclusive—exclude one another—cannot both occur together; that when we say Wa(X or Y), we mean not only that any W has one or other of the characters X and Y but that no W has both of these characters (i.e., that any W has one and only one of the characters X and Y). More generally that when we use the term X or Y we imply that XeY (that X and Y are exclusive classes)—thus, that when we say (X or Y)aZ, we imply that X and Y are separate species of Z. (On this question, *cf.*, Bosanquet's controversy with G. R. T. Ross—Bosanquet's reply in the appendix to the chapter on Disjunction in his Logic.)[14]

No doubt people frequently take alternatives as exclusive, and there might be a technical use of "or" according to which it means exclusiveness as well as exhaustiveness. On the other hand, this usage may involve mere confusion on the part of those who adopt

---

[14]Bosanquet, *op. cit.* Appendix to Chapter VIII, "On Some Recent Discussions of Disjunction", Volume 1, pp. 355-362.

it—confusion because it simply happens in some cases that alternatives are exclusive, and this exclusiveness is then read into cases where it is not so (in accordance with the tendency previously mentioned, a tendency which is the main basis of fallacy, to treat all relations as symmetrical, in this case, to go from "If not X, Y" to "If Y, not X". Cf. Freudian view of the tendency of "the unconscious" to reversal of relations; and cf. the Freudians' own tendency to treat any pair of connected or "associated" things as mutually implicatory). Bosanquet would argue, of course, that all relations are symmetrical (i.e., when properly understood). But Ross shows clearly that certain arguments which we accept as valid would not be valid if we interpreted "or" to signify exclusive alternatives; and that indicates that there is a regular use of "or" (of disjunction) according to which exclusiveness is not necessarily involved. (Cf. provision that was at one time in force in Sydney: "All matriculants in Arts must have passed in either Latin or Greek". This was not taken to mean that matriculants were forbidden to take both Latin and Greek; in fact, most of those who took Greek took Latin as well. It was merely understood that one at least of the two must have been taken; that no one who had neither Latin nor Greek could matriculate in Arts.)

This leads to a point which settles the matter as regards usage—that either...or must be taken as the opposite of neither...nor, that "either" means "not neither" (that in no relevant case can both of the alternatives be dropped); and it is quite a different thing to say "not both" (that in no relevant case can both alternatives be adopted).

X or Y is the opposite of both $\bar{X}$ and $\bar{Y}$

$\bar{X}$ or $\bar{Y}$ is the opposite of both X and Y

Idealists include ($\bar{X}$ or $\bar{Y}$) in the meaning of (X or Y), when they are manifestly quite different things—vary quite independently from case to case. In other words, "either" means "not neither" and that is all that it means.[15]

We could have things divided (using "division" in a popular way) into X, Y and $\bar{X}\bar{Y}$ (things which are neither X nor Y) whether X and Y excluded one another or not.

---

[15] [JA] Cf. the meaning of "some". "Some" means "not none" and that is all it means. (XiY leaves XaY or XoY as open question.) Here also there are cases where we do not know (which doesn't hinder us from being quite sure of XiY); but, even in the cases where we do know, XiY never means XoY, any more than it ever means XaY. Only confusion can result from not keeping distinct issues (here the E-I issue and the A-O issue) distinct. (Cf. also XaY leaving open the YaX-YoX question: and the confusion involved in sometimes treating XaY as meaning co-extension and sometimes as meaning the inclusion of X in Y. In all these cases (disjunction, particular propositions, the "is" of inclusion and the "is" of identity), (a) we don't have to have the additional information, and (b) if we do have it, we should state it separately. (A general type of error—packing all additional information into initial formula.)

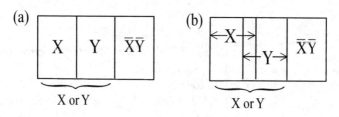

Figure 17.

X or Y excludes $\overline{XY}$ (and includes everything else) whether XeY or XiY.

If we adopt the Bosanquet view, we make it impossible for ourselves to deal with (or present logically) a situation in which one of two conditions must be fulfilled and both are fulfille in some cases—or where we know that one must be fulfille but do not know whether both can be fulfille or not. Whereas, if we adopt the anti-Bosanquet view, not only is it, as has been shown, in accordance with ordinary language, but it is perfectly simple to deal with the special case (which Bosanquet thinks is the universal situation) where two given alternatives are exclusive, as well as exhaustive—where we can say "not both" as well as "not neither"—viz., by making two disjunctive assertions; by saying Wa(X or Y) and Wa($\overline{X}$ or $\overline{Y}$)—which would together indicate that W has one and only one of the characters X and Y; or that one and only one of the conditions X and Y is fulfille in any given case within the fiel W.

(Wa($\overline{X}$ or $\overline{Y}$) = no W is both X and Y, i.e., no W is neither $\overline{X}$ nor $\overline{Y}$

Either X or Y = not neither X nor Y, i.e., not both $\overline{X}$ and $\overline{Y}$.)

Thus, without getting any new and confusing use of the expression "or" (taking the ordinary use in which it does not by itself imply exhaustive alternatives), we are able by means of this ordinary "or" to cover cases where two possibilities are exhaustive and exclusive, as well as to cover cases where they are exhaustive but not exclusive (and cases where we know they are exhaustive but do not know whether they are exclusive); by using two different propositions where we have the two independent pieces of information—"not neither" and "not both".

IX

Hypotheticals (using the expression "if...then".)

There are a number of different uses of the "if...then" form. In the firs place, it is used merely to indicate universality, e.g., "if anything is human, it is mortal"; the logical form of that is simply "All men are mortal"—what is called the categorical proposition (i.e., of A, E, I or O form) as contrasted with the hypothetical proposition (though I have argued, of course, that all assertions, when we get them to their fina and exact form, will be A, E, I or O). We could say of course that a hypothetical way of expressing the matter hints at or suggests something more than just the universal proposition, viz., the possibility of firs figur syllogisms of which the A proposition in question is the major premise: i.e., it says or conveys that all men are mortal and that if you had a minor of the form X is a man, you could get the conclusion X is mortal. However, you do not have such a syllogism (no matter how you may speculate about possibilities) until X has been specified and in fact all you are really given is the proposition (i.e., a "categorical" proposition).

Secondly, the hypothetical form can signify implication: i.e., if p, q can be regarded as an alternative way of saying p ∴ q; or at least the difference between the two formulations will be expressed not in terms of the objective situation but in terms of the attitude of some particular persons to the situation, so that "p ∴ q" will be taken to represent the position of a person who asserts p and therefore infers q, while "if p, q" may be taken as indicating that any person who did assert p would be justifie in deducing q from it, but not that there actually is any such person. However, this distinction by reference to the attitudes of persons is not a distinction for logic—not, at any rate, as far as logic is concerned with p, q and their relations. Logic in both cases will be concerned with the relationship p implies q, and whether a particular person believes p or merely considers the possibility of someone's believing or asserting it will not affect that logical relation.

There are still special cases in this connection—we sometimes say "if p, q" without believing that p by itself implies q. Thus instead of saying "if anything is a man, it is mortal" we sometimes say "If Socrates is a man, Socrates is mortal", though we do not believe (or would be mistaken if we did) that the single proposition Socrates is a man implies the other proposition Socrates is mortal. Actually, we have an argument of which a premise has been omitted because it is taken for granted as obvious, but in a full statement of the argument we shall have to make explicit what had been taken for granted—we should have to say that if Socrates is a man, then, seeing that all men are mortal, Socrates is mortal—which is only a way of stating the syllogism "All men are mortal, Socrates is a man, therefore Socrates is mortal". There are a variety of things that are taken for granted, assumed (believed) to be true: cf. the question of "the consequences of p"—what would be true if p were true—where we take as such consequences what are consequences not of p alone but of p together with various true propositions (propositions we believe to be true). Thus we should say "if p, then q, r, s, t, etc.", where a great many additional premises would be required to make clear from what q, r, s, t, etc., do follow. Since it is a question of causality as well as of properties, we often should have a great deal of work to show what are the other premises involved in the implication of "what follows from p"; but it is still a question of implication, and the implication "depends on" (requires for its full statement) the additional premises. Of course, absence of full statement, omission of things "taken for granted", very often occurs over fallacies—allows things to pass as "consequences of p" which are not so at all.

There is a third case—the only one in which there is much point in using the hypothetical form, though even then the exact or complete form would be categorical—a third case where we are dealing not with a relation between terms or between propositions but with a relation between "possibilities".

If you take the hypothetical "if p, q", which could be expressed more fully "if p if true, q is true", then that is taking p and q as propositions (the sort of thing that can be true), and what is said is equivalent to saying "if q is false, p is false"; which is a quite general rule in implication, viz., if proposition (1) implies proposition (2), then the contradictory of (2) implies the contradictory of (1). However, we fin these two equivalent contentions "if p, q" and "if not-q, not-p" expressed (replaced?) by two equivalent propositions (contrapositions, in fact) PaQ and $\overline{Q}a\overline{P}$, where P is translated as "cases in which p is true" and $\overline{P}$ as "cases in which p is false". Now to say that p may be true or false is to indicate that it is a proposition, but if it is a proposition it will in fact be simply true or false—it will not be true in some cases and false in other cases—such a question of alternative cases simply does not arise. The distinction of cases, then, indicates that "p" is not strictly a proposition but what Russell calls a "propositional function", i.e., a formula containing a variable and capable of being made into a proposition by giving a specifi value to the variable: so that "X is a man" would be such a propositional function on the understanding that X is a variable which can have a multiplicity of values. Particular terms can replace X in this formula so as to give a proposition (e.g., Socrates is a man), and some of the propositions so obtained will be true and some of them false.

Another way of putting it is to say that a propositional function stands for (is what is common to) a class of propositions—e.g., the various propositions which end in "is a man"—for, of course, instead of putting in an indeterminate "X", we might as well leave a gap, it being understood, of course, that there might be a special way of fillin up the gap, that it would have to be such as would make a proposition, and in this case would have to be what we call "an individual".

Now the question is not just (in the hypothetical) of a relation between such functions or between possibilities but of the relation between possibilities within a certain region or field though this fiel goes unstated in the simply hypothetical form "if p, q". In other words, we are not just leaving the gap in the functions to be fille in by anything at all, because that would simply take us back to the firs case, the A proposition; but we are leaving the gap to be fille by things of a certain kind, things belonging to a certain genus or field within which various possibilities exist. Now, when we get the full statement of the field we come back to an A proposition, though a more complicated one than the original form. But we can leave the fiel unstated and go on talking and arguing in the hypothetical form with fair accuracy, though with some risk of uncertainty and fallacy, because what is left unstated may actually be different in different cases, and this may not be noticed. There is the question whether "hypotheticals" are not (the?) cases of double distribution: because p and q in proper form have to have quantity. Thus "if AaB, CiD" = All X of which All A are B are X of which some C are D" (where X is the field) When hypotheticals do not have quantity, it is just a question of bad statement of a categorical: e.g., "if anyone is a man," etc.

Let us say that the functions or possibilities are related in the fiel F: then "if p, q" when fully stated would be "All F such that p are (F) such that q". For example, we make such assertions as "If the barometer is falling, bad weather is coming, and if the barometer is rising, good weather is coming" (Quantities? All barometers within some region?): now these possibilities of the rising and falling of the barometer, and of the occurrence of good or bad weather, might be said to occur within the fiel of atmospheric conditions. (Question whether good and bad weather are themselves atmospheric conditions—though movements in the barometer are not.) And it could be contended that, if you did not have some such background for a hypothetical statement, then there could be no connection between the antecedent and the consequent, and in the examples we have considered there would seem to be a magical rather than a scientifi connection between the barometer and the weather [what is required for scientifi connection is some continuity (continuous processes from one to another) between the conditions said to be related: would this be provided in the cases referred to by taking the fiel to be that of atmospheric pressures?] so the assertion of the existence of the fiel might be taken as another way of asserting that we could fin the connection step by step between the state of the barometer and the state or tendency of the weather. (*Cf.* "Hypotheticals", for discussion of these problems—with the suggestion that the doctrine of "material implication" provides no continuity and may thus be said to give a magical conception of implication.)[16]

So then, "if the barometer is falling, bad weather is coming" will be fully stated as "All atmospheric conditions such that the barometer is falling are atmospheric conditions such that bad weather is coming"—full statement brings us back to an A proposition, though a rather complicated one; but statement and argument in the hypothetical form being unobjectionable even if we do not mention the field so long as there is not doubt or confusion as to what the fiel is. Sometimes, as here, hard to formulate it. Question is whether there is any opposition between "pressures" as fiel and "regions" as field—whethe the fiel is not "pressure-regions": so that "All pressure-regions in which all barometers are falling are pressure-regions in which all ('approaching') weather is bad". Hypothetical, then, may be an approach to form: where we get rough connections, where our notions of some of the factors are vague. And science would seek to get from the rough to the precise—from the hypothetical to the categorical.

---

[16]"Hypotheticals", op. cit., *Studies* p. 145.

X

Connection between the hypothetical and the disjunctive: if p, q = not-p or q; p or q = if not-p, q. If you recognise that equivalence, you can transform a hypothetical argument into a disjunctive, and vice versa.

Mixed hypothetical syllogism: if p, q; p, ∴ q

Equals:

Disjunctive syllogism:

not-p or q; p, ∴ q

Cf.: p or q; not-p, ∴ q

If you took the firs premise in the mixed hypothetical as a relation between propositions, the argument would contain a redundancy, i.e., if p, q would be logically the same as p ∴ q—you would just have twice over the relationship that p implies q, the only difference being in the attitude of the person who is considering this implication, where in the one case he asserts p and concludes q, whereas in the other case he merely considers the possibility of asserting p and concluding q; but logic being indifferent to whether a particular person makes a particular assertion or not—being concerned merely with the relationship between the propositions themselves. And when in actual fact a mixed hypothetical syllogism is employed, the p and q of the second premise and conclusion are not the same as the p and q of the firs premise. Take a rough example: if it is raining, I shall take my umbrella; it is raining ∴ I shall take my umbrella. The point here is that the second premise and conclusion refer to some particular case which is not referred to in the firs premise—the firs premise is concerned merely with a general relation between possibilities, the second says that one possibility is fulfille in that case also. (One opposing view to this is that the firs premise contains particular cases too—if it is raining today, I shall take my umbrella today; it is raining today ∴ I shall take my umbrella today—That view has already been criticised as involving redundancy). And the full statement would be, taking A as the field A(p)aA(q) (All A such that p are A such that q), This A is A(p) ∴ This A is A(q). (Here we do not have mere repetition, saying twice over that q follows from p.) The fiel may be left unstated, with, nevertheless, retention of the distinction between general relation and special case: All occasions on which condition p is fulfille are occasions on which condition q is fulfilled

In this sort of argument, the mixed hypothetical, we have two valid forms, named in each case after the function of the second premise in relation to the first (1) affirmin the antecedent, (2) denying the consequent. In "if p, q", p is called the antecedent and q the consequent.) (1) If p, q; p ∴ q. (2) If p, q; not-q ∴ not-p—which is transformed into affirmin the antecedent in accordance with the equivalence recognised in hypothetical arguments between if p, q and if not-q, not-p: an equivalence which corresponds to the relation of contraposition, except that, in so far as we are considering relationships within a given field what we have here is a virtual contrapositive and not a true contrapositive (i.e., not PaQ and Q̄aP̄, but APaAQ and AQ̄aAP̄); and confusion is caused in such (hypothetical) arguments if we have assumed without examination that the opposite possibilities all do exist within the given field just as confusion is caused in virtual contraposition if we have not taken a similar precaution.

However, omitting the fiel for the sake of brevity, you could also represent this denial of the consequent as follows (in categorical form): if p, q; not-q ∴ not-p ⟶ PaQ, XeQ ∴ XeP. (All cases of fulfillmen of p are cases of fulfillmen of q; X is not a case of fulfillmen of q ∴ etc.)

Then again we have two invalid arguments in the mixed hypothetical form: affirmin the consequent and denying the antecedent. (The "syllogisms" are said to commit the fallacy of affirmin the consequent and the fallacy of denying the antecedent respectively.) The arguments are—if p, q; q ∴ p (categorical parallel—PaQ, XaQ ∴ XaP—undistributed middle); if p, q; not-p ∴ not-q (categorical parallel PaQ, XeP ∴ XeQ—illicit major).

Disjunctive syllogism. Only one valid form, corresponding to the two valid hypothetical forms, and only one invalid form, corresponding to the two invalid hypothetical forms—viz., (1) Valid—denying an alternative (p or q; not-p ∴ q—or p or q; not-q ∴ p (same form, since no logical distinction between p or q and q or p—alternatives have no logical order); the second premise denies one of the alternatives in the firs premise; hence the conclusion affirm the other of the alternatives in the firs premise; and (2) Invalid—affirmin an alternative (p or q; p ∴ not-q—as before, same form as p or q; q ∴ not-p); the second premise affirm one of the alternatives in the firs premise; hence (fallaciously) the conclusion denies the other of the alternatives in the firs premise.

This is regarded as not true by those who hold that alternatives are both exclusive and exhaustive (i.e., they maintain that affirmin an alternative is not a fallacy) but in doing so they assume that p or q = not-p or not-q

p or q =   If not-p, q   =not-p or not-q
                  If p, not-q
                  (exhaustive and exclusive)

Bosanquet argues that if we had exact knowledge we could reverse the hypothetical (have if p,q and if q,p), that all "real" relations are (general and) symmetrical. But even when we solve a problem (find give a genus (field and a property that varies within it—that is possessed as a property by one species of the genus—another property necessary and sufficien for the occurrence of the firs property in the genus: i.e., a difference), the original statement of the problem (XiY, XoY) is no less true, no less a statement of real facts, than the solution (DXaY, $\overline{D}$XeY) (or DXaY, YXaD—to bring out the symmetry or reversibility.) That is, "real facts" (true propositions) can be particular propositions just as they can be universal propositions.

General Considerations. The question for those who maintain that the hypothetical is a particular kind of proposition—that if p, q is something that cannot be put, without loss of meaning, into the AEIO forms—is (just as in the case, e.g., of modal propositions, assertions of necessity and possibility as contrasted with assertions of actuality) how we are going to contradict such an assertion—because clearly if p, q and if p, not-q are not contradictions (it is possible that, given p is true, we cannot determine whether q is true or false—that p implies neither q nor not-q, so that the two above propositions are both false (if p, q and if p, not-q). And that amounts to saying that the hypothetical corresponds to a universal proposition and to get a particular proposition we should have to go beyond the hypothetical form: but now, if we try to do that, we fin ourselves driven back to the categorical form—we fin that these contradictions can only understood as I or O propositions. For example, we might try to do it adverbially—we might try to represent the falsity of if p, q by if p, sometimes not-q—but to get any sense of what these occasions of truth and falsity might be, we should have to refer back to the field or, even without specifying the field we should have to say something like "All cases in which p is fulfille are cases in which q is fulfilled" and so have the contradictory as "Some cases in which p is fulfille are cases in which q is not fulfilled (i.e., we have gone back to categorical forms A, O, etc.—here, PaQ, PiQ̄)—and the same would apply if we used the expression "may be"; if we said "If p is fulfilled q is fulfilled and contradicted that by saying "If p is fulfilled q may not be fulfilled (Some cases of the p kind are not cases of the q kind).

Here we are understanding that p and q are possibilities or propositional functions, that they are not themselves propositions; but if we were concerned with propositions (i.e., if p and q were propositions) we could certainly set against one another the two assertions "if p is true, q is true" and "if p is true, q is false"—in other words, the assertion p implies q and the assertion p does not imply q (assertions which, granting some difficult about their quantity, are categorical). And that raises the general question whether we can treat an implication as an assertion—a relation between propositions as a proposition—and it would certainly seem that we can, that we can be right or wrong about an implication just as we can be right or wrong about a predication (or a simple proposition). In fact, it might be said that this is in accordance with the view that the proposition is, so to speak, the logical unit (or that, whatever we assert, we assert a situation)—that just as a term can be taken as an implicit proposition, as definin (conveying?) place and character without formally distinguishing them, so an argument can be taken as a proposition, as an assertion of implication that may be true or false even though it has as constituents a number of propositions which are true or false (whose truth or falsity is a different question from the truth or falsity of the implication.)

(Any knowledge is knowledge of a situation (just as any occurrence is occurrence of a situation); and to assert a situation is the same thing as to assert a proposition. The constituents of a situation are situations; and what a situation is a constiuent of is always a situation. We can still distinguish an argument from a single statement, just as we distinguish a statement from a term.)

See again "Hypotheticals"[17] for question of contradicting a hypothetical: where it is contended that no consistent usage can be arrived at except by going back to "categoricals". The main point is the equivalence of the "hypothetical" if p, q to the "disjunctive" not-p or q and the contradiction of the latter by p and not-q. But, while no one can pretend that this is in hypothetical form—i.e., can pretend that a whole section of logic is concerned with "hypotheticals"—it is, in terms of the

---

[17] Ibid., pp. 146–47.

assumptions regularly made in dealing with "the logic of conditionals" fundamentally ambiguous or definitel misleading: i.e., no consistent view of the conjunction of "functions"—suggestion always of some "particular case", not just of something corresponding to I and O which is needed for straight contradiction.

Index